T0046361

KREISKY, ISRAEL, AND JEWISH IDENTITY

DANIEL ASCHHEIM

STUDIES IN CENTRAL EUROPEAN HISTORY CULTURE & LITERATURE
Series Edited by Günter Bischof

UNIVERSITY OF NEW ORLEANS PRESS

Kreisky, Israel, and Jewish Identity.
ISBN: 978-1-60801-242-8

Top cover image: "Israelische Außenministerin [sic] Golda Meir zu Gesprächen im Bundeskanzleramt bei Bundeskanzler Bruno Kreisky." October 2, 1973. Courtesy of Votava / Imagno / picturedesk.com. Available from: tinyurl.com/picturedesk

Lower cover image: "1973: Golda Meir and Chancellor Bruno Kreisky in Vienna." October 2, 1973. Repository: Archives. University of Wisconsin-Milwaukee Libraries. Available from: https://collections.lib.uwm.edu/digital/collection/pgm/id/73/

Book and cover design by Alex Dimeff.

Library of Congress Cataloging-in-Publication Data

Names: Aschheim, Daniel, 1988- author. | Bischof, Günter, 1953- writer of
    preface.
Title: Kreisky, Israel, and Jewish identity / Daniel Aschheim.
Description: New Orleans : University of New Orleans Press, [2022] |
    Series: Studies in Central European history, culture & literature |
    Includes bibliographical references.
Identifiers: LCCN 2022016233 (print) | LCCN 2022016234 (ebook) | ISBN
    9781608012428 (paperback) | ISBN 9781608012879 (ebook)
Subjects: LCSH: Kreisky, Bruno. | Statesmen--Austria--Biography. |
    Jews--Austria--Identity. | Jewish politicians--Austria--Biography. |
    Socialists--Austria--Biography. | Holocaust, Jewish
    (1939-1945)--Influence. | Arab-Israeli conflict--1973-1993--Influence. |
    Austria--Politics and government--1945- | Austria--Biography.
Classification: LCC DB98.K7 A83 2022 (print) | LCC DB98.K7 (ebook) | DDC
    943.605092 [B]--dc23/eng/20220425
LC record available at https://lccn.loc.gov/2022016233
LC ebook record available at https://lccn.loc.gov/2022016234

Printed on acid-free paper
First edition

UNIVERSITY OF NEW ORLEANS PRESS
2000 Lakeshore Drive
New Orleans, Louisiana 70119
unopress.org

KREISKY, ISRAEL,
AND JEWISH IDENTITY

For my amazing wife, Elisa,
and the sunshine of our life—Ella

CONTENTS

ACKNOWLEDGMENTS

This book and the research behind it would not have been possible without the exceptional support of Dr. Günter Bischof and Dr. Tobias Ebbrecht-Hartmann.

Their attentiveness, responsiveness, enthusiasm, knowledge, and attention to detail supported my research from my master's paper to this book. I am grateful for their great aid along the way. I would also like to thank Elisheva Moatti for assisting in all administration matters and being there for me. Furthermore, I would like to mention and thank the editors of this book, Lauren Garcia and Christian Stenico.

Finally, I would like to sincerely thank my wife, Elisa, who pushed me and gave me the motivation to write during challenging times; my parents, Steve and Hannah, who supported, advised, and helped throughout the process; and my daughter, Ella, who came into this world during unprecedented times and brought light to it.

PREFACE
BY GÜNTER BISCHOF

Bruno Kreisky, Austria's longest-serving chancellor (1970–83) after World War II, was an exceedingly complex figure. Being elected four times in a land with a long antisemitic tradition surprised him and many other people. He made his career initially in the Austrian Foreign Service, where he was posted to the embassy in Stockholm, responsible for the entire Scandinavian region, an institution with a long tradition of conservative aristocratic members but few Jews. In 1951, the newly elected president Theodor Körner (SPÖ) appointed young Kreisky as an advisor to his cabinet. He made a name for himself as a shrewd foreign policy analyst and, in 1953, the party made sure he was appointed state secretary in the Foreign Ministry, headed by conservative ÖVP leaders Karl Gruber and soon Leopold Figl. In the ÖVP/SPÖ grand coalition governments, so typical of the postwar period, the Socialists wanted to have a voice in the making of Austrian foreign policy. At a time when four powers still occupied the country, foreign policy and the attainment of a state (peace) treaty ending the occupation were still at the top of the Austrian political agenda. The state treaty was finally signed by the Soviet Union, the United States, Great Britain, and France, along with Figl, and this milestone undoubtedly reflected well on Bruno Kreisky's career. Austria now became a neutral country in the Cold War.

In 1959 he became foreign minister in an independent ministry now no longer under the purview of the Federal Chancellery. Kreisky made a name for himself, defining an independent "active neutrality policy" in an era of severe East-West conflict. Given his success as a foreign minister, Kreisky was elected as leader of the Socialist Party in 1966. From 1966 to 1970, ÖVP-Chancellor Josef Klaus directed the first non-"grand coalition" government in postwar Austria. Kreisky was elected leader of the SPÖ, and he began to modernize his party; in the 1970 elections, the SPÖ came out the strongest party with forty-eight-point-four percent of the vote; Kreisky became the chancellor of a minority Socialist government. In 1971 he gained the absolute majority with fifty percent and formed an SPÖ cabinet. In this cabinet, he included four ministers with a Nazi past. This led to a conflict with the "Nazi hunter" Simon Wiesenthal, who publicly criticized Kreisky's cabinet choices. As Daniel Aschheim lays out in this book, this ironically led to Kreisky as a Jew defending someone with a Nazi past against accusations by a fellow Jew. After the 1975 elections, when the SPÖ gained fifty-point-four percent of the vote, Kreisky worked closely with the leader of the FPÖ, Friedrich Peter (with five-point-four percent of the vote). Wiesenthal again reminded Kreisky that Peter had served in an infamous SS unit in World War II and should not be graced with any leadership position in Austrian politics; moreover, the majority of FPÖ voters were former Nazis. As Aschheim points out, the conflict between these two prominent Austrian Jews was a prime example of Kreisky's ambiguous relationship with his Jewish identity.[1]

---

1   We have a number of biographical studies of Bruno Kreisky. Kreisky and his team of advisers wrote three volumes of memoirs; this rich source makes studying Kreisky's biography a very attractive subject for historians. For biographical studies, see Elisabeth Röhrlich, *Kreiskys Aussenpolitik: Zwischen österreichischer Identität und internationalem Programm* (Göttingen: V&R unipress, 2009); Wolfgang Petrisch, *Bruno Kreisky: Die Biographie* (St. Pölten: Residenz Verlag, 2011), now in its 6th edition; Petrisch, *Bruno Kreisky: Ein biographischer Essay* (Vienna: Kremayr & Scheriau, 2000); Heinz Fischer, *Die Kreisky Jahre, 1967–1983* (Vienna: Löcker Verlag, 1993); Günter Bischof, and Anton Pelinka, eds., *The Kreisky Era in Austria*, Contemporary Austrian Studies 2 (New Brunswick, NJ: Transaction Publishers, 1994); H. Pierre Secher, *Bruno Kreisky: Chancellor of Austria. A Political Biography* (Pittsburg: Dorrance Publishing, 1993); Werner Gatty et al., eds., *Die Ära Kreisky: Österreich im Wandel 1970 bis 1983* (Innsbruck: StudienVerlag, 1997); critical from an ÖVP perspective is Robert Kriechbaumer, *Die Ära Kreisky: Österreich 1970–1983* (Vienna: Böhlau Verlag,

While Kreisky's fraught relationship with Israel in the context of otherwise excellent Austrian relations with Israel has been the subject of early studies like Helga Embacher's and Margit Reiter's, his advocacy of the postwar Austrian "victim's doctrine" has puzzled scholars greatly, Aschheim among them.[2] After all, it was highly puzzling for a Jew who had lost more than twenty family members in the Holocaust to embrace a doctrine that stated that Austria had been the "first victim of Hitlerite aggression." However, Kreisky surely would never have made a career in the Austrian foreign service and postwar Austrian politics had he not supported this notion of Austrian victimhood in World War II. Only late in Kreisky's life, when Kurt Waldheim was elected president of Austria in 1986, did this "victim's doctrine," which had often been ridiculed abroad, fall into disrepair. Subsequently, historians began to study Austrian World War II perpetrators, and Kreisky's successor, Socialist chancellor Franz Vranitzky talked of Austrian "co-responsibility" for war crimes committed by Austrian perpetrators. While Austria may have been wiped off the map by the Third Reich's invasion of 1938 and the "Anschluss," many Austrians supported the Nazis and their war of aggression and extermination. Starting in the 1990s, the prevailing doctrine became that both Austrian "victims and perpetrators" characterized the role of the non-existing country and its population during World War II.[3]

2004); the three volumes of biography (the third volume published posthumously by Kreisky's team of advisers) were published in English in a one-volume edition, see Matthew Paul Berg, ed., *The Struggle for a Democratic Austria: Bruno Kreisky on Peace and Social Justice* (New York: Berghahn, 2000); Röhrlich analyzes the memoir project extensively, see *Kreiskys Aussenpolitik*, 373–88; for a cameo portrait on the "dialectical chancellor" see Oliver Rathkolb, *Die paradoxe Republik: Österreich 1945 bis 2005* (Vienna: Zsolnay, 2005), 184–96.

2   Helga Embacher, and Margit Reiter, *Gratwanderungen: die Beziehungen zwischen Österreich und Israel im Schatten der Vergangenheit* (Vienna: Picus, 1998); Röhrlich devotes a subchapter to his ambiguous relationship with his "Jewish heritage," see *Kreiskys Aussenpolitik*, 343–63.

3   Cornelius Lehnguth, *Waldheim und die Folgen: Der parteipolitische Umgang mit dem Nationalsozialismus in Österreich*, Studien zur historischen Sozialwissenschaft 35 (Frankfurt am Main: Campus, 2013).

As chancellor of Austria, Kreisky's principal political interest remained his foreign policy, which he tended to dominate during his thirteen years in office. A particular passion of his foreign policy agenda became the Near East. He wanted to mediate peace between Arabs and Jews. He felt that no permanent peace could be constructed unless the Palestinians were included in the peace process and eventually would gain statehood (with their territories on the West Bank and Gaza). Only what today is called a "two-state solution" would bring permanent peace. In his second volume of memoirs, he explains his motives behind his Near Eastern policies:

1) As a Socialist, he could not tolerate people being violently expelled from their homeland. As Kreisky himself had been driven out of Austria by the Nazis in 1938 and had become a refugee in his wartime Swedish exile, this was a very personal matter to him;

2) Israel would become a permanent "crusader state" unless it decided to pursue a peaceful "good neighborly" policy;

3) The West could not permanently ignore the interests of the Arab world, given its dependency on Arab oil.[4]

Kreisky traveled to Egypt as early as 1964 and met with President Nasser. Once he became chancellor, he was also elected Vice President of the Socialist International (his friend Willy Brandt, the former chancellor of Germany, was elected President). He used this platform to conduct three "study missions" to the Near East (1974, 1975, 1976), visiting most Arab countries and talking to their leaders. On the first such mission in 1974, he also visited Israel and spoke to Prime Minister Golda Meir. On this mission, he also visited Egypt and spoke to President Sadat, who recommended he meet Yasser Arafat, the leader of the PLO. Kreisky

---

4 Bruno Kreisky, *Im Strom der Politik: Der Memoiren zweiter Teil* (Vienna: Kremayr & Scheriau, 1988), 307; Petritsch, *Bruno Kreisky*, 217.

met him and eventually became close to him. The study missions resulted in reports that recommended including the Palestinians in the peace process. The only solution would be the "creation of a Palestinian state."[5]

In many respects, the culmination of Kreisky's Near Eastern policy came with the "Marchegg incident" that is also at the heart of Aschheim's study. In this terrorist attack in the Marchegg railroad station on the Austrian-Slovakian border, two Syrian terrorists took four hostages (three Russian Jewish emigrants and one local policeman). They demanded the closing of a transit camp in Schönau for Jewish emigrants leaving the Soviet Union for a new life in Israel. Aschheim adds to the explanation of Kreisky's response to the attack by using new documents from the Israeli ambassador in Vienna and other files from the Israeli national archives. No historian had gotten access to these files hitherto. Kreisky responded to the hostage situation by giving in to the terrorists' demands to close the Schönau transit camp. Kreisky insisted in his memoirs that his main objective was to "save lives," which he did. The terrorists released the hostages and received a plane to fly home. Kreisky later said he had wanted to close Schönau in any case because the Jewish Agency had treated it like extraterritorial terrain in Austria. However, Kreisky opened a new camp in Wöllersdorf for Soviet Jewish emigrants, putting the Austrian Red Cross in control and giving Jewish emigrants the option to go to other countries besides Israel. One week after the "Marchegg incident," the Yom Kippur War erupted in Israel and overshadowed all events at the time.[6]

---

5   Kreisky, *Im Strom der Politik*, 319, 326–41 (quote 337); Petritsch, *Bruno Kreisky*, 224–33; Röhrlich, Kreisky's Aussenpolitik, 313–319; Hans Thalberg, "Die Nahostpolitik," in Erich Bielka, Peter Jankowitch, and Hans Thalberg, eds., *Die Ära Kreisky: Schwerpunkt der österreichischen Aussenpolitik* (Vienna: Europaverlag, 1983); Bruno Kreisky, *Das Nahostproblem: Reden, Kommentare, Interviews* (Vienna: Europaverlag, 1985).
6   Kreisky, *Im Strom der Politik*, 32–33; Petritsch, *Bruno Kreisky*, 217–21; Röhrlich, *Kreisky's Aussenpolitik*, 302–307; Embacher and Reiter, *Gratwanderungen*, 146–55.

Kreisky was roundly criticized abroad and at home for "giving in to terrorist demands" and for his alleged "Jewish self-hatred." President Nixon asked Kreisky to reverse his decision on Schönau, and Prime Minister Golda Meir even came to Vienna to talk Kreisky out of closing Schönau. Kreisky did not budge in a frosty meeting (where Meir created the myth that she was not even served a glass of water), signaling what may be the lowest point in Austrian-Israeli postwar relations.[7] Kreisky's domestic opposition in the ÖVP charged that his controversial Near Eastern policy attracted terrorist attacks like Marchegg into Austria. Doing business with the "terrorist" Arafat, being the first country to recognize the PLO as the legitimate representation of the Palestinian people, and inviting Arafat to come to Vienna, may have been the most controversial parts of Kreisky's bold Near Eastern policies. The ÖVP has been claiming ever since that Kreisky's Near Eastern policies damaged neutral Austria's good image in the world.[8]

Most surprisingly, American authors covering the history of the Israeli-Palestinian conflicts have entirely ignored Kreisky's role as Near Eastern peacemaker and promoter of Arafat and the Palestinian cause. James L. Gelvin fails to mention Kreisky promoting a "two-state solution" long before the Oslo Accords of 1993–1995.[9] Similarly, William Quandt ignores Kreisky in his history of the Near Eastern peace process. Quandt's history focuses on the role of the United States in this process, so maybe silencing Kreisky's role is acceptable.[10] Similarly, Abraham Ben-Zvi ignores Kreisky's role in Near Eastern policies in his history of US-Israeli relations, even though Kreisky was a trusted go-between and consultant for Presidents Nixon and Ford.[11] Maybe

---

7   Röhrlich, *Kreiskys Aussenpolitik*, 305–307.

8   Kriechbaumer, *Die Ära Kreisky*, 268–83, 285–419.

9   James L. Gelvin, *The Israel-Palestine Conflict: A History,* 4th ed. (Cambridge: Cambridge University Press, 2021).

10   William B. Quandt, *Peace Process: American Diplomacy and the Arab-Israeli Conflict since 1967* (Washington: Brookings Institution, 1993).

11   Abram Ben-Zvi, *The United States and Israel: The Limits of the Special Relationship* (New York: Columbia University Press, 1993).

one could even argue that without Kreisky's role as a mediator in the Near East in the 1970s, the Oslo process would not have been possible twenty years later. President Carter acknowledged Kreisky's role in the Near Eastern peace process, which Carter furthered with the "Camp David agreement" between Egypt's Sadat and Israel's Begin. Sadly, instead of a peaceful solution, we have had two Palestinian "intifadas" and four eruptions of Israeli-Palestinian violence, Hamas extremists firing rockets on Israel and Israel retaliating disproportionally. As Steve Coll argued in his recent editorial in the *New Yorker* about "Hamas's forever war against Israel's existence": "It was, as usual. Always clear who the losers would be: Gaza's two million people, who were trapped in a humanitarian crisis even before the bombs fell." Meanwhile, Israel's "rejection of reconciliation with Palestinians" will "fail to deliver security," as Bruno Kreisky, who always tried to prevent such violence, knew fifty years ago already.[12]

Larose, LA, June 2021

---

12 Steve Coll, "Ceasefire and Impasse," in *The New Yorker*, May 31, 2021, 13–14.

CHAPTER 1 : INTRODUCTION

INTRODUCTION

The personal and professional life of Bruno Kreisky (1911–1990), Austria's long-serving Socialist chancellor from August 1970 to May 1983, has been the focus of many books and articles. However, his ambiguous and complex relationship to his Jewishness, the State of Israel and Zionism, and connections to his overall political project and global aspirations remain only partially researched. This book aims to remedy this situation through systematic research and sustained original interviews. The interviews include Israeli and Austrian politicians, Foreign Ministry officials and diplomats, journalists, academics, activists, Kreisky's acquaintances and friends, and members of the Austrian Jewish community.

The book revolves around understanding and illuminating the myriad ways Kreisky's Jewishness was—or was not—a formative factor in his treatment of "Jewish" questions within Austrian politics, Austrian-Israeli relations, and his active engagement in Middle Eastern affairs. As a politician and a statesman, Kreisky was involved in numerous geopolitical events of importance. However, the episodes highlighted in this book best exemplify the dynamics and obscurities of Kreisky's personality and political actions when it comes to how his Jewishness influenced his decisions. These episodes and themes include:

- Jewishness in Historical Context

- Kreisky and the Austrian "Victim's Doctrine"

- The Kreisky-Peter-Wiesenthal Affair

- Kreisky and the Waldheim Affair

- Kreisky and the 1973 Marchegg Incident

- Kreisky, Zionism, Israel, and the Palestinian Arab World

This book will render these events part of a much more comprehensive analysis of Kreisky, his politics, Jewishness, and Middle Eastern policy. In this context, the episodes will illustrate critical points concerning his general policy-making decisions and how facets of his identity entered into these questions. Moreover, the book will also establish that regardless of one's opinion of Kreisky, this determined statesman put Austria at the center of international politics.

Through the lens of Kreisky's Jewishness and its influence, this book will present the paradoxes, tensions, weaknesses, and achievements of Bruno Kreisky—Austrian patriot, committed Socialist, and acculturated Jew. The first and only Jewish leader of Austria, the man whom many loved and many loved to hate—is among the most influential and controversial political leaders since World War II. The focus here will be upon how Kreisky's policies reflected his biography and attitudes (e.g., his entanglements with Judaism, Socialism, and the Middle Eastern conflict). In addition, this book will examine how Bruno Kreisky's vague and intricate relationship to his Jewishness affected his positions toward Israel, Zionism, the Arab World, Austria's past, and his political project and global aspirations. This examination will contribute to scholarship in various areas: international relations; how personality influences policy; political biography; and the intersections between Jewish, Israeli, and European politics and history.

As a field, history has focused on narrative descriptions of the past, and interpretation has been the principal basis for organizing and explaining data (Mitchell and Egudo 2003). The research in this book is based on qualitative research, using the historical-narrative approach. Historical narratives construct a story about reality rather than directly representing it (ibid.). This approach describes and analyzes past events, problems, issues, and facts, using data gathered from written and oral histories. "Narrative" might be the term assigned to any text or discourse, or it might be the text used in a mode of inquiry in qualitative research (Chase 2005), with a specific focus on the stories told by individuals (Polkinghorne 1988). In "narrative analysis," researchers collect descriptions of events (ibid.) and then configure them into a story using a plotline (Mitchell and Egudo 2003, 8). This approach describes "what was" to recreate the past. The methodology in this book instead follows the approach taken by Clandinin and Connelly (2000) as the methods of conducting a narrative study do not follow a lock-step approach but represent an informal collection of topics (Creswell 1998).

This narrative-based historical research on Bruno Kreisky relies on interviews with individuals who had significant stories or experiences to contribute. Their accounts provide a multifaceted picture of the man in question and the life he led. Information about the context of these narratives was collected, and the participants' stories were, in turn, dissected. The narrative-inquiry approach is not limited to interviews but also uses field texts, such as autobiographies, journals, notes, letters, conversations, family stories, photos, and artifacts, among other related items, for analysis and research (Clandinin and Connelly 2000). The information gathered in these interviews and field texts concentrates on studying a single person, collecting data to construct a narrative about the individual's experience and the meanings they attributed to them.

Conducted according to Uwe Flick's (2002) episodic-interview model, the interviewees for this book were not requested to produce one long narrative but, instead, several shorter narratives through a periodical invitation to present their accounts. These episodic interviews sought to exploit the advantages of the narrative interview and semi-structured interview since episodical narratives act as an approach to the experiences relevant to the subject. Simultaneously, the interviewer can direct the discussion with key questions concerning the situations discussed. Per Aarikka-Stenroos (2010), in episodic interviews, both data types (i.e., "narrative" and "answer") are used (Flick 2002).

Most interviews were conducted privately face to face, some in the interviewees' homes or offices, and some in public spaces. Others were conducted via phone or Zoom. The duration of the interviews ranged from thirty minutes to six hours (two hours being the average) without a set time limit. The aim was to allow the interviewees to express their stories in a relaxed manner. Open questions were used to motivate the interviewees to provide the most accurate accounts.

The initial focus in examining the influence of Kreisky's Jewishness on his decision-making was on Kreisky's attributes and complexities, bearing in mind not to enter the field of psychological research. The first step of this analysis focused on Kreisky's writings and autobiography, including his speeches, correspondence, and published interviews. The next step involved reviewing academic texts on Kreisky and accounts by different people in his orbit, thereby drawing a more comprehensive picture of his personality. These sources were carefully and critically evaluated to ensure being as objective as possible, especially since personal attitudes and emotional and political biases influenced many of them.

Another central source was Hebrew documents located at the Israel State Archives. These included protocols, correspondences, letters, and various publications from the Israeli prime minister's office (e.g., texts by Golda Meir, Menachem Begin, and

Yitzhak Rabin) concerning Israel's relations with Austria during the Kreisky era. Many confidential telegrams and communications between the Israeli embassy in Vienna and the Ministry of Foreign Affairs, dealing with Kreisky and Austrian matters, are also explored and cited extensively in this volume. The vast majority of these documents have not been previously researched or published. They constitute a rich and valuable Israeli "inside" view of Austrian-Israeli relations and, in particular, encounters and conflicts with Kreisky. Additionally, these documents act as a documentary check on the oral interviews conducted for this book, which are, by nature, subjective and based on subsequent recollection.

However, the interviews are instrumental in painting a more comprehensive picture of Kreisky than the more reductive portrayals that are often characteristic of the existing literature. Those who favor Kreisky tend to glorify him and ignore his weaknesses, while his critics present him in entirely negative terms. Too often, these are stereotypical perceptions, verging on "pop psychology." This book does not purport to be a psycho-historical study but is a straight reportage regarding those interviewed. An effort was made to balance the negative picture typical of the Israeli mainstream through conducting multiple interviews. Because existing sources—like the ones included in the literature review section—have focused mainly on Kreisky's unpopular aspects, this book paid particular attention to providing sources and narratives that present Kreisky's complicated nature and the positive aspects of his personality and actions.

Narrative interviews may enhance the internal validity because the method prevents respondents' experiences from becoming fragmented. Compared with more structured interviews that require each respondent to answer a standardized set of questions, they may allow for more accurate and trustworthy accounts (Elliott 2005). This approach can then help reveal a more multifaceted portrayal of the subject—in this case, Kreisky. The need for a balanced, comprehensive view thus explains the full range

of interviews conducted. Given these procedures, narrative research, while challenging, also holds the promise of attaining a
certain depth.

One limitation of oral-history interviews as sources is that
they are inevitably biased in some way or another. Therefore, one
has to be critical and careful when drawing conclusions from
them. As Leon Edel comments in his book *Writing Lives* (1987),
multiple issues arise in collecting, analyzing, and telling individual stories. Active collaboration with the participant is necessary,
and researchers need to be mindful of their own personal and political background, which shapes how they "restory" the account.
Stefinee Pinnegar and J. Gary Daynes also speak on these problematic aspects of storytelling in their essay "Locating Narrative
Inquiry Historically: Thematics in the Turn to Narrative" (2007).
They refer to questions of historical-narrative building and ask:
Who owns the story? Who can tell it? Who can change it? Whose
version is convincing? What happens when narratives compete?
As a community, what do stories do among us? Challenges might
emerge in data gathering and reporting due to interview conventions, sensitivity, and ethics. As Aarikka-Stenroos (2010) puts
it, participants are more used to structured interviews. Because
interviewers in oral-history interviews do not ask questions directly, the interviewee has more freedom to decide what and how
to talk about the topic, making the situation challenging to all
parties. The researcher must be a patient and active listener when
collecting the narratives. At the same time, one also needs to gen-
tly guide the narrator to stay within the research area.

These guidelines and limitations were considered when com-
piling the interviews in this book. The interviewed individuals
include:

Erwin Lanc: Austrian politician and Kreisky's minister
of transport (1973–77), interior minister (1977–83), and
foreign minister (1983–84)

Georg Lennkh: member of Kreisky's cabinet and his personal advisor on foreign relations; served as the head of special missions to the Middle East and North Africa (1978–82)

Wolfgang Petritsch: Kreisky's longtime secretary and an Austrian diplomat

Thomas Nowotny: Kreisky's personal secretary and an Austrian diplomat

Margit Schmidt: Kreisky's personal assistant for twenty-five years; currently serves as the head of the Bruno Kreisky Forum

Barbara Taufar: journalist and diplomat that served as Kreisky's representative in Israel during the 1970s and was considered "Kreisky's man in Israel"

Hannah Liko: Austria's current ambassador to Israel (appointed in 2019)

Ariel Muzicant: Austrian Israeli businessman who served as the president of the Israelitische Kultusgemeinde Wien (Jewish Community of Vienna)

Ilan Knapp: founder and head of the Jüdisches Berufliches Bildungszentrum (Jewish Vocational Training Center) in Vienna, the head of the Austrian Institute for Research on Vocational Training, and a member of the Austrian Expert Board for Integration

Oliver Rathkolb: Austrian historian and a professor of contemporary history at the University of Vienna who worked with Kreisky on his three-volume memoirs, as well as edited books about Kreisky; considered the top academic expert on Kreisky

Elisabeth Röhrlich: associate professor of history at the University of Vienna

Yissakhar Ben-Yaacov: Israel's ambassador to Austria (1979–83)

Talya Lador-Fresher: Israel's ambassador to Austria (2015–19)

Naomi Ben-Ami: Israeli government official and the former head of Lishkat Hakesher (liaison bureau), also known as Nativ

Uri Avnery: Israeli writer; founder of the Gush Shalom peace movement; and the mediator who introduced Issam Sartawi and Yasser Arafat to Kreisky

Yehezkel Beinisch: top Israeli lawyer who was responsible for Kreisky's transactions in Israel; personally took care of Kreisky's Israeli brother, Paul

Menachem Oberbaum: former Israeli *Maariv* correspondent to Vienna and current director of Shaare Zedek's Center for Integrative Complementary Medicine

Eldad Beck: Israeli journalist and author

Shaul Shay: military historian and former deputy head of the Israeli National Security Council

Tom Segev: Israeli historian, author, and journalist

Hagai Zoref: former head of the Documents and Commemoration Department at the Israel State Archives

Martin Šmok: Czech researcher, writer, and filmmaker

Fred Lazin: American professor of political science and a Soviet Jewry expert

Another valuable resource was the interviews journalist and diplomat Barbara Taufar conducted with dominant Israeli political figures that had been in direct contact with Kreisky. Among others, these interviews included:

Shimon Peres: leading Israeli politician who served as the president of Israel (2007–14) and as the prime minister of Israel (1984–86 & 1995–96)

Yossi Sarid: Israeli politician who served as minister of education (1999–2000) and minister of the environment (1992–96)

Micha Harish: an Israeli politician who served as minister of industry and trade (1992–96)

Yona Klimowitzky: Israeli prime minister and leader of the opposition Menachem Begin's close secretary (1973–83)

Elazar Granot: Israeli politician and writer who served as member of the Knesset for Alignment and Mapam

Dedi Zucker: Israeli peace activist and politician who served as a member of the Knesset for Ratz, Meretz

These interviews, which took place in 1997, were found at the Bruno Kreisky Archives in Vienna and contain acutely relevant information on Kreisky's personality, his Jewishness, his relations with Israel, his politics, and his policies in the Middle East. Some of the interviews were critical of Kreisky, while some defended his policies, yet all provide an exceedingly helpful point of reference for understanding Kreisky's public and private persona more intimately.

This book will demonstrate a way of reconstructing a multi-faceted personality through a multi-perspective approach based on a relatively new research methodology: the "entangled-history" perspective. The basic assumptions of this method are that neither nations, empires, nor civilizations can be the exclusive and exhaustive units and categories of historiography. Instead, as entities, they were formed through interaction and global circulation in which they related to one another. By questioning the absolute centrality of national borders and inquiring about processes of non-state-based exchanges, entangled history examines dependencies, interferences, interdependencies, and—as the name suggests—entanglements while emphasizing the multidirectional character of transfers (Bauck and Maier 2015).

To fully understand the connections and actions taken during the various events discussed in this book, it was not enough to research the behavior of the involved sides' political leaderships. It was equally important to investigate the connections between all parties involved, including the public opinion in Israel and Austria, the media coverage, and the narratives presented at the time by all involved parties. The concept of entanglement endeavors to better understand the dynamic interconnectedness of media across semiotic, technological, institutional, and political boundaries in history (Cronqvist and Hilgert 2017).

Consequently, this book presents a transnational perspective. It focuses on the interconnectedness of Israeli and Austrian societies (both the general population and the Jewish community) and their entangled histories and memories. Whereas some understand transnational history as an umbrella term, others see a plurality of different approaches or grant other labels a position of primacy. Unfortunately, historians still do not agree on a precise definition of transnational history (Patel 2010). This book uses the relatively loose definition by Akira Iriye and Pierre-Yves Saunier, the editors of *The Palgrave Dictionary of Transnational History* (2009). They state that transnational history deals with the "links and flows," the "people, ideas, products, processes and patterns that operate over, across, through, beyond, above, under, or in-between polities and societies" (XVIII).

Jürgen Kocka's (2003) approach demonstrates the advantages of entangled and comparative history, which is eminently suited to the goals of this book. The strength of the entangled-history approach lies in combining transnational and transtemporal comparisons. On a synchronic level, one considers the events by comparing the Austrian, Israeli, and Austrian Jewish perspectives. On a diachronic level, one compares how the perception of events referred to different, earlier memories and the modes in which it was subsequently reviewed (or not). The approach thereby integrates comparative and transnational elements into a coherent analysis.

Finally, the emerging research field of Jewish international history, which remains a small specialty with nuances, could also be a valuable way to approach Kreisky's role in history. The "Jewish questions" that arise from researching Kreisky are connected to the interrelated, hard-to-resolve issues revolving around emancipation, antisemitism, Zionism, citizenship, labor, capitalism, and anti-Jewish violence, all of which fall under the bigger question of how Jews fit into modern society (Green 2014; Sorkin 1990; Gordon 1964).

LITERATURE REVIEW

There is a certain dissonance both within the international literature and Austrian scholarship between the historiographies of Austria in the twentieth century and Bruno Kreisky. The scarcity of books written exclusively on Kreisky is striking when reviewing the existing literature. Despite his intensive international efforts, colorful personality, and clear visibility compared to other world leaders, his legacy remains vague in literature and international history. Paradoxically, however, it is also interesting to note that Kreisky plays a very different role in works analyzing Austria's foreign-policy heritage. That literature portrays Kreisky as the most dominant post–World War II Austrian figure.

While there are very few historiographical essays on Kreisky, Peter Malina's "'Imagination is More Than Knowledge.' Bruno Kreisky's Life as Biography" (1994) and Oliver Rathkolb's "A New Historiography of Bruno Kreisky" (2016) stand out. Malina focuses on a biographical examination of Kreisky, which serves as a mirror of Austrian society and one's own perception of history. In contrast, Rathkolb critically surveys books and essays written about the former chancellor.

One of the more comprehensive and significant documents in the existing literature is Bruno Kreisky's autobiography, included in *The Struggle for a Democratic Austria: Bruno Kreisky on Peace and Social Justice* (2000) (edited by Matthew Paul Berg, in collaboration with Jill Lewis and Oliver Rathkolb). The English version sums up the three volumes of the German edition. It is a crucial text that enables us to grasp Kreisky's attitudes and complex personality, his relationship to his Jewishness, the State of Israel, and Zionism, the way he dealt with personal and collective memory, and his foreign policy. However, as an autobiography, it is subjective by nature. Therefore, one must read carefully between the lines to see how his past and personality influenced his policies. Herbert Pierre Secher's biography of Kreisky, *Bruno Kreisky, Chancellor of Austria: A Political Biography* (1994), also handles Kreisky's ambivalent and often-confrontational relationship with his Jewishness, Jews, and Israel. The collection of articles in *Die Ära Kreisky: Schwerpunkte der österreichischen Außenpolitik* (1983, edited by Erich Bielka, Peter Jankowitsch, and Hans Thalberg) explores the dominant and fascinating figure both critically and reflectively. American historian Jacqueline Vansant examines Kreisky's construction of an Austrian identity through his autobiographical texts in her essay "Challenging Austria's Victim Status: National Socialism and Austrian Personal Narratives" (1994). General surveys of Kreisky's active term can be found in former Austrian president Heinz Fischer's memoir, *Die Kreisky Jahre, 1967–1983* (1994), and Gerhard Schmid's book *Die Ära Kreisky: Österreich im Wandel 1970–1983* (1997).

Another exhaustive overview of Kreisky's life and political career can be found in Wolfgang Petritsch's *Bruno Kreisky: Die Biografie* (2011). As Kreisky's longtime personal secretary, Petritsch presents intriguing aspects of Kreisky's personality and speaks of his past while focusing on Kreisky's term as chancellor. Unfortunately, while providing a different and more personal perspective, this book does not seek to account for how Kreisky's intricate personality affected the Israeli-Palestinian conflict or his Jewishness.

Elisabeth Röhrlich's *Kreiskys Außenpolitik: Zwischen österreichischer Identität und internationalem Programm* (2009) discusses and dissects Kreisky's foreign policy in depth, starting with his time in Swedish exile during WWII. This book covers the main events of Kreisky's life and the milestones of his career. It is presented as a straightforward historical narrative, with less of a focus on analysis.

As mentioned before, much of the literature about Kreisky's foreign policy and work in the Middle East is embedded in more general studies on Austrian foreign policy and the Austrian-Israeli relationship. The most accurate and focused such account is *Between Vienna and Jerusalem: Reflections and Polemics on Austria, Israel and Palestine* (1997) by Austrian political scientist John Bunzl, which highlights Kreisky's disputed role in these relations. An additional source that provides a profound deconstruction of the convoluted relationship between the Jewish state and Austria— while led by Kreisky as an assimilated Jew—is Helga Embacher and Margit Reiter's *Gratwanderungen: Die Beziehungen zwischen*

Österreich und Israel im Schatten der Vergangenheit (1998). Embacher and Reiter portray Kreisky's Jewish history, in addition to his Austrian and Israeli pasts, in this analytical treatise. Finally, Oliver Rathkolb evaluates key issues of Austrian politics and history and takes a serious look into its future in *Die paradoxe Republik: Österreich 1945 bis 2005* (2005).

Critical, yet significant and relevant, are Robert Wistrich's *Anti-Zionism and Antisemitism: The Case of Bruno Kreisky* (2007) and *Austrians and Jews in the Twentieth Century: From Franz Joseph to Waldheim* (1992). Wistrich offers us an overview of Kreisky's familial past, his attitude toward his Jewishness, and his relationship to Zionism and antisemitism. Both volumes are highly relevant as they deal with Kreisky's Jewish identity and his sentiments toward related matters in Austria and Israel. However, Wistrich portrays Kreisky in a judgmental, one-sided way and does not consider complexities and contradictions in his personality or his relationship to Israel and his Jewishness. Neoconservative American analyst Joshua Muravchik presents a tendentious look at Kreisky's Middle Eastern policy, as well as his relationship to Israel and his Jewishness in his chapter on Kreisky in his book *Making David into Goliath: How the World Turned Against Israel* (2014). The reflective interview Kreisky gave about his Jewish identity, published in the book *Jüdische Portraits: Photographien und Interviews von Herlinde Koelbl* (1989) by Herlinde Koelbl also provides valuable insights.

When it comes to the Kreisky-Peter-Wiesenthal affair, Tom Segev's comprehensive biography of Wiesenthal, *Simon Wiesenthal: The Life and Legends* (2010), is highly relevant. The study documents the intricacy of the famous Nazi hunter. An earlier book, *Simon Wiesenthal: A Life in Search of Justice* (1996) by Hella Pick, also has interesting pointers about Wiesenthal's work. Ruth Wodak presents an interesting angle of the Austrian victim's doctrine and the Wiesenthal and Waldheim affairs in her systematic analysis of Austrian antisemitism, as featured in *Wir sind alle unschuldige Täter: Diskurshistorische Studien zum Nachkriegsantisemitismus* (1990) (written in collaboration with Peter Nowak, Johanna Pelikan, Helmut

Gruber, Rudolf de Cillia, and Richard Mitten), and "Turning the Tables: Antisemitic Discourse in Post-War Austria" (1991). Finally, *Justice Not Vengeance* (1988) by Wiesenthal himself displays his recollections of the various events evaluated in this book.

In his book *Österreichs Außenpolitik der Zweiten Republik* (2005), Michael Gehler looks at the relationship between Kreisky and Israel in a whole chapter dedicated to this matter. Thomas Riegler supplies a comprehensive overview of Kreisky's Middle Eastern policies in *Im Fadenkreuz: Österreich und der Nahostterrorismus 1973 bis 1985* (2011). Riegler focuses on Kreisky's attitude toward Palestinian terror and his encounters with different Arab leaders, including his multifaceted relationship with Arafat.

In his essay "Victims? Perpetrators? 'Punching Bags' of European Historical Memory? The Austrians and Their World War II Legacies" (2004), Günter Bischof gives a breakdown of Austria's problematic method in dealing with its Nazi past. Andrea Reiter's *Contemporary Jewish Writing: Austria After Waldheim* (2013) examines Jewish writers and intellectuals in Austria, evaluating film and electronic media alongside more traditional publication formats. Karin Stögner points out Kreisky's sensitive relationship with Austria's Nazi past and antisemitism in her essay "Bruno Kreisky: Antisemitismus und der österreichische Umgang mit dem Nationalsozialismus" (2008), beginning with the Waldheim affair and the rhetorical responses by the three most prominent members of the survivor generation—Leon Zelman, Simon Wiesenthal, and Bruno Kreisky.

For the analysis of the 1973 Marchegg incident, the booklet issued by the Austrian Federal Chancellery in 1973, *The Events of September 28th and 29th 1973: A Documentary Report*, provides a detailed account of the Austrian official narrative regarding the events. On the other hand, Paul Thomas Chamberlin's "Schönau and the Eagles of the Palestinian Revolution: Refugees, Guerillas, and Human Rights in the Global 1970s" (2012) uses the Schönau incident to illustrate how it illuminated the contested nature of humanitarian concerns in the 1970s and the Cold War era. Matthias Dahlke's *Demokratischer Staat und transnationaler Terrorismus: Drei Wege zur Unnachgiebigkeit in Westeuropa 1972–1975* (2011) is a detailed assessment of tactical and strategic aspects of the Marchegg event.

CHAPTER 2 :
KREISKY'S JEWISHNESS IN HISTORICAL CONTEXT

BRUNO KREISKY:
JEWISHNESS AND LIFE IN VIENNA

Some argue that, like many other Austrian Jews, Kreisky came from an entirely "assimilated" Jewish home. Recent scholarship, however, makes a sharp distinction between "assimilation" and "acculturation." Assimilation assumes total eradication of Jewish identity and some kind of conversion to the culture's dominant religion (Gordon 1964; Sorkin 1990). This does not apply to Kreisky or his family. They never denied their Jewish background or descent, although they had no ties to official Jewish religious observance. It would, therefore, be more accurate to say that, in complicated ways, Kreisky was a fully acculturated Austrian, albeit one who demonstrated certain patterns of identity and familial loyalties that were identifiably Jewish.

Kreisky's family belonged to the *grossbürgerlich*, the Jewish upper-middle-class from the Czech part of Habsburg Austria. His mother was the daughter of an industrialist, and his father was the director of a textile factory (Wistrich 2007). Like many other Bohemian and Moravian Jewish families, Kreisky's background was liberal in culture, politics, and sensibility. Although his father, Max, was successfully engaged in textile manufacturing, in 1925, a fifteen-year-old Kreisky joined the youth wing of the Socialist Party of Austria. Kreisky, along with many other sensitive Jewish bourgeois youths, was upset by the poverty and violence prevalent in Austria. He jettisoned Judaism as a sixteen-year-old and had his name removed from the rolls of the Viennese Jewish Federation (Secher 1994, 13). In 1927, to his parent's chagrin, Kreisky became a member of the Young Socialist Workers. This was a common occurrence among Jewish bourgeois families within Central Europe (Geller 2019). Many prominent Socialist leaders did not come from proletarian families.

Jews could move freely within the lands of the Habsburg Monarchy and could also—within some never fully defined limits—get involved with and integrate into general society. Kreisky's family opposed Theodor Herzl's Zionism, as did most bourgeois Austrian Jews. This undoubtedly played a role in Kreisky's later attitude toward political issues related to Zionism and Israel (Petritsch 2014, pers. comm.). Kreisky's former secretary, Thomas Nowotny (2020, pers. comm.), thinks Kreisky's negative view of Zionism originated in his bourgeois background, which positively emphasized an *Austrian* national identity. Like other Austrian Jewish families, the Kreiskys believed that one should fully identify with their country of birth wherever one lived. This view was in direct contrast to the Zionist idea, which refers solely to a Jewish nationality and a Jewish homeland.

In Kreisky's generation, one can identify a historical link between young, acculturated Jews and an attraction to universal forms of "fin-de-siècle" Socialism. Turn-of-the-century Vienna was an exceedingly cosmopolitan city at the height of great cultural and intellectual creativity. At the same time, it was rife with nationalist and antisemitic unrest—tendencies that had already begun following the revolutions of 1848 (Schorske 1980). Assimilated and unassimilated Jews constituted a significant presence in the city. In 1910, for instance, 175,318 Jews were living in Vienna (*Beit Hatfutsot*). Kreisky states in his memoir that the acculturated Jews were well-integrated into Austrian society and that he and his family only encountered one or two minor negative incidents related to their Judaism (Berg 2000, 416). Kreisky's longtime secretary, Wolfgang Petritsch, reaffirms this point, saying:

Kreisky regarded the Austrians as a nation with a proud past, and he considered himself as a citizen of the "larger Austria"—referring to the Habsburg Empire. He definitively perceived the intellectual and spiritual Austria as one which was built on the very positive heritage from the Habsburg Empire. It was clear that most Austrian Jewish intellectuals were not born in Vienna but came from the peripheral territories of the empire. Jews did not have a country of their own in the monarchy, so for them the larger Austrian Empire was their real homeland. (2014, pers. comm.)

His family milieu was an example of successful social integration in the multinational Habsburg Empire. This historical period significantly influenced Kreisky's attitude toward Austrian society and, later, the Austrian state. It was this sense of multinational tolerance and cosmopolitan elegance that was so attractive to the Jews of the empire, and that rendered them so loyal to Emperor Franz Joseph (1848–1916). In his memoirs, Kreisky highlights a certain distaste for the Galician *Ostjuden* (Eastern Jews) still living in ghettoes and their visceral attachment to Jewish religious rituals. At the time, there was a certain tension between so-called traditional "ghetto" Jews and modern assimilated or acculturated Jews. For Jews (and, unfortunately, for many non-Jews), this was a defining question of identity during the nineteenth and early twentieth century and was particularly intense in the German Reich and the Habsburg Monarchy (Aschheim 1982).

Although Kreisky was born toward the end of what is known as the great period of fin-de-siècle Vienna, many of the attitudes that he brought to bear on his Jewish background resembled the previous generation's (Beller 1991). The end of the nineteenth and the beginning of the twentieth century combined enormous intellectual creativity with political and national upheaval in Vienna. Jewish intellectuals were very much at the center of many of these issues, attracting admiration—and resentment. (Much of the antisemitism then was linked to these intellectuals' "subversive" thinking.) Luminaries such as Gustav Mahler, Arnold Schoenberg, Stefan Zweig, Sigmund Freud, Theodor Herzl, and Ludwig Wittgenstein, to name just a few, come to mind. Jewish identity became a central problem for most—if not all—of these Jews. The writer Arthur Schnitzler—that incisive and subtle psychological portraitist of bourgeois Vienna and its inner sexual, unconscious impulses—masterfully portrays the confusion and the creativity of these Viennese Jewish intellectuals in his remarkable novel Der Weg ins Freie (1908). As one gentile protagonist in the novel puts it, "Wherever he went, he met only Jews who were ashamed of being Jews, or the type who were proud of it, and were frightened of people thinking they were ashamed of it" (quoted in Wistrich 1989, 595, 606).

It is remarkable how obsessive the question of Jewishness or "the Jewish problem" stood at the troubled center of their psyche and consciousness. With nary an exception, all reflected on and ruminated over this question—whether negatively or positively, constructively or despairingly. Everyone deeply pondering the nature of their Jewish being and seeking avenues of addressing their personal and collective predicaments. It was, undoubtedly, in fin-de-siècle Vienna where the peculiar condition called "Jewish self-hatred" reached not only pathological proportions but was given philosophical expression in the works of Otto Weininger, who committed suicide, and Arthur Trebitsch, whose self-hatred was so violent that he became attached to Nazi views (Gilman 1986; Aschheim 1982). Interestingly in the 1970s, during Kreisky's reign, Yehoshua Sobol wrote a wildly successful play in Israel about Otto Weininger. Mohammad Bakri, an Arab Israeli actor, played Sigmund Freud in a production of the play.

IDENTITY AND COMPLEXITY:
KREISKY'S JEWISHNESS

With this historical background and the reactions of other members of the Jewish-educated classes, it is no wonder that Kreisky's relationship with and connection to his Jewish origins were relatively complex. He acknowledged his roots' influence on his personality and identity, yet he refused to accept that either his Jewish heritage or ethnicity had any notable impact. "I stand by what I have said about a general influence [of my Jewish background] on personality," Kreisky stated, "but it has always been quite alien to me to attribute significance to blood or a blood tie" (Berg 2000, 421). Kreisky expected that "one looks at the religious affiliation, which is in my case my Jewish heritage, as a private thing" (Koelbl 1989, 141). Of those who labeled him based on his Jewish religion, Kreisky said, "I don't allow anyone to consider me as a member of a specific race." Instead, he said that he "grew up as a member of a *Schicksalsgemeinschaft* [community of fate] which didn't have a bad life under the old Austro-Hungarian monarchy" (ibid.). When asked by interviewer Herlinde Koelbl about his views as the "first Jewish Chancellor in Austria," Kreisky immediately corrected her for not addressing him as the "first Chancellor of Jewish descent" (ibid., 142). He stressed that, although he had never denied his background, he did not want it to define him (ibid., 141). In many ways, Kreisky's plight—conditioned, of course, by the particular circumstances of the Austrian situation, especially the post-Nazi period—conformed to Jean-Paul Sartre's classical notion of the dialectics of Jewish identity: "The Jew is in the situation of a Jew because he lives in the midst of a society that takes him to be a Jew" (1948, 72).

When replying to Israeli and Jewish accusations that he was a "self-hating Jew," Kreisky said that they "forget that I very deliberately acknowledge my Jewish descent and regard it as a significant part of the structure of my personality" (Berg 2000, 422). On another occasion, Kreisky added that he was "very happy" about his specific Jewish heritage because it made him receptive to tradition and literature (Koelbl 1989, 141).

To be sure, there is much convolution and ambivalence in Kreisky's manifold statements about his Jewishness, yet it is discernible that he resented what he identified as the Jewish sense of superiority. He perceived the Jewish notion of the "Chosen People" as dangerous and misleading. Kreisky even went so far as to argue that there were many similarities between Nazi race theory and Jewish ideas of chosenness. He held that such beliefs could lead to horrible actions (Embacher and Reiter 1998, 179). In his memoirs, Kreisky explains, "To assume for that reason [that coming from a community of religion and history like the Jewish community has a powerful, formative influence on one's personality] that I must feel a special tie with the Jewish community, through the action of some mystical forces, is really to proceed from a racist assumption" (Berg 2000, 421(.

Kreisky pointed out that people tried to include him in an "imaginary Jewish global community." He insisted that he did not want to be forced into a community of people that he had not chosen "only because Hitler decided to divide humanity into Jews and non-Jews." He wondered what a Tunisian Jew had in common with an *Ostjude* and concluded that it was "Only the religion," as "the Jews are a religious community which became a community of destiny" (Koelbl 1989, 145).

As indicated before, Kreisky resisted the blood-tie theory, which attributes Jewishness to ethnicity rather than cultural heritage. According to one author, Kreisky did not even have his son circumcised (Muravchik 2014, 90). Not all Israeli and Zionist leaders linked Jewishness to race, blood chosenness, and superiority, but for Kreisky, this was the way he perceived the Zionist idea.

Consequently, Kreisky very rarely presented himself as Jewish publicly or officially. Micha Harish, former Israeli minister and member of the Knesset for the Labor Party, remembers one of these rare moments in which Kreisky explicitly and proudly presented himself as Jewish in a loaded and symbolic member (1997). During a meeting between Anwar Sadat, Shimon Peres, Kreisky, and Harish, Kreisky emotionally declared that this was a "big victory of history" because "the President of Egypt and the head of the Israeli opposition and maybe the future Prime Minister of Israel and the Jewish Chancellor of Austria, all met together" (Harish 1997).

Because he opposed the idea of the Jews as a "chosen people" or a race, Kreisky selected his words carefully and often used the term "Jewish faith." However, this could be misleading as the term "Jewish faith" in this context did not refer to the religion of Judaism but to how Austria officially recognized Jewish citizens as "citizens of Jewish faith." He also occasionally commented that there was no such thing as the *Jüdisches Volk* (Jewish people) but instead spoke of "*eine religiöse Schicksalsgemeinschaft*" (a religious community of faith), bound together by religious beliefs and historical developments. "We are all in a very weird and cruel story," said Kreisky. "Thrown in the same pot ... we all needed to prepare for the same destiny." However, the most baffling way that Kreisky approached his Jewishness was that he connected his Jewish heritage to Nazi crimes and alleged that he would not have felt bound to it had Auschwitz not existed. "My knowledge about Auschwitz is the only thing that connects me, unconditionally, to my Jewish heritage," asserted Kreisky. "Without Auschwitz, my relationship to Judaism would not bind me to a specific behavior or attitude. [The memory of] Auschwitz is the destiny of the Jews—also those who think that their Jewish heritage is not very strong cannot escape it" (Koelbl 1989, 142).

When confronted by Elazar Granot, the former leader of the Mapam Party, on his views of the Jewish people, Kreisky responded to his charges by comparing his opinion to how he approached Austrian identity. "I said the same thing about the Austrians," declared Kreisky. "There is no such thing as an Austrian. We are a state, we are a country, but there is no *Volk*. I mean we have got so many cultures coming together and if I say it about Austria, why shouldn't I say it about the Jewish people? ... The only thing that combines them is the same religion but not nationality" (Granot 1997).

"Kreisky mostly denied his Jewishness," Israeli journalist Eldad Beck determines. From the moment he returned from exile in Sweden, he tried to brand himself as an Austrian Socialist leader with no special affiliation to Judaism and certainly not to the State of Israel. "The fact that he was a Jew, who was mostly denying it, led him to hold a very hostile attitude towards Israel," says Beck (2019, pers. comm.).

Kreisky's relationship to his Jewishness was highly ambivalent, says Menachem Oberbaum, the former Israeli journalist who served as *Maariv*'s reporter to Austria in the 1970s. "Kreisky fought fiercely against being labeled as 'Jewish'—he truly hated it," he continues. Oberbaum explains that one could have cursed and attacked Kreisky on any matter, and he would have been apathetic. "The only thing that made him go completely crazy," says Oberbaum, "was when someone referred to his Jewishness" (2020, pers. comm.). This strong objection is at odds with how people close to him perceived Kreisky. As Wolfgang Petritsch notes, "What I loved about Kreisky is that in private conversations and meetings, he was a typical Central European Jew—[from] the way he told jokes, his irony, and his intelligence" (2014, pers. comm.). Oberbaum also shares this view of Kreisky's Jewish personality in private, "I think that, inside himself, he was a true Jew ... I am sure he would not have liked to hear such a thing, but I insist that this is the truth." Nevertheless, Oberbaum says, even though Kreisky was furious when someone mentioned his Jewishness, he was "definitely not an antisemite as so many portrayed him" (2020, pers. comm.).

Oberbaum also shares a personal anecdote that is illuminating. "During the Lebanon War, after I was injured," says Oberbaum, "Kreisky wrote me five personal letters, and one was even handwritten." Oberbaum adds that Kreisky was so discreet that he did not show these letters to his secretary. In one of them, "the most touching," Kreisky wrote, "You know that more than fondness connects … us." Even with all of Kreisky's protestations, it was evident, as Oberbaum puts it, that their special connection was that "he was a Jew and I was a Jew." "He never said it clearly," says Oberbaum, "but it was clear that this was the meaning" (2020, pers. comm.).

While Kreisky had a fraught relationship with his Jewishness, "The deepest relationships he had were with Jews," says Petritsch. "Karl Kahane was his best friend. He loved and admired Jewish intellectuals" (2014, pers. comm.). Furthermore, as Oberbaum (2020, pers. comm.) correctly notes, not only were his closest friends Jewish, but Kreisky was also married to a Jewish woman, Vera Fürth, the daughter of a wealthy Swedish Jewish business-man who had been an Austrian emigrant early in the century (Secher 1994).

Kreisky was also very socially active with members of the Jewish community. The Israeli ambassador to Austria between 1979 and 1983, Yissakhar Ben-Yaacov, reinforces this. Ben-Yaacov recalls celebrating a Passover Seder with Kreisky and the Gertner family, who were close to him. "He was well respected in many Jewish circles in Vienna," points out Ben-Yaacov (2019, pers. comm.). Ben-Yaacov's wife, Priva, adds that Kreisky's Jewish wife played bridge every week with a group of Jewish friends. "Kreisky and his wife were very close socially to some members of the Jewish community," says Priva (ibid.).

Barbara Taufar mentions that Kreisky was the first Austrian chancellor to invite Jewish scientists and artists that had escaped from Nazi Austria back to respectable conventions in Vienna. "It was his way to reconnect the Jewish minds that left Austria to the non-Jewish Austrians," says Taufar (2020, pers. comm.). Even though Kreisky referred to the Jews as a "historical religious community" (ibid.), he valued Jewish ethics more than the Jewish religion.

Beneath the surface of apparent tensions, says Ben-Yaacov, the relationship between him and Kreisky was very "correct."

When facing the public, however, Kreisky insisted that he was the "Austrian chancellor and not the Jewish chancellor" and therefore did not want any too pronounced connections with the representative of the Jewish state. Per Ben-Yaacov, when the international press interviewed Kreisky and asked about his Jewishness, he would respond by insisting that he was a Democrat, a Socialist, an Austrian—"all but say that 'I am Jewish.'" Nevertheless, Ben-Yaacov considers Kreisky "a good Jew" who "saved many Jews from the Soviet Union" (2019, pers. comm.). Like others, Ben-Yaacov observed Kreisky's inconsistencies, though he confirms that Kreisky and his wife were socially very close to some members of the local Jewish community. In fact, most of Kreisky's friends were Jewish. However, the media tended to present him as a "self-hating Jew," says Ben-Yaacov. "I think that when he expressed his views, he was guided by political considerations, with the goal of strengthening his status at home and with Arab nations abroad" (2012, 264).

When it came to his Jewish background, Kreisky "had an armored shield," says Austrian historian Oliver Rathkolb, since Jewishness was Kreisky's "Achilles' heel." He states this was a result of Kreisky growing up in a seriously antisemitic environment, which had existed in Austria for centuries (even though Kreisky claimed that he had only experienced one or two antisemitic slurs personally). "He was so much formed by the interwar period," says Rathkolb. "He also realized that even in his political party he would find antisemitism" (2015, pers. comm.). When Kreisky's name was submitted in nomination at the Annual Party Congress in February 1967, the motion gave rise to a most acrimonious debate concerning his person and credentials. Cutting comments were made about his decidedly non-proletarian background, raising (at least by innuendo) his "Jewish origins" (Secher 1994, 17). Therefore, Rathkolb argues that Kreisky attempted to "contain his Jewish roots," as illustrated in his public presentations when he tried to overcome antisemitism (2015, pers. comm.).

Georg Lennkh, who served under Kreisky in the cabinet, maintains that, although "deep in his heart his Jewishness played a role," it did not influence Kreisky's politics. "He was a classical product of a Jewish-assimilated family that, until the middle of the 1930s, was much more connected to Socialist politics than to their religious identity," explains Lennkh (2015, pers. comm.). Even so, the more Kreisky tried to show that his emotions and Jewish background did not influence his actions and policies, the less genuine it seemed (Embacher and Reiter 1998).

Peretz Merchav, a senior political activist in Israel's left-wing political party Mapam, wrote a report about one of his meetings with Kreisky in Vienna. According to his notes, the meeting began with a long lecture from Kreisky about his Jewishness. He did not deny his origins but asserted that he did not see himself obliged to accept authority or an opinion because of his roots, as "Golda [Meir] believes." Kreisky expressed his disappointment and disapproval with the many demands that he and Henry Kissinger had received "just because they were Jewish," things that no one would have demanded from non-Jews. Kreisky then emphasized that he was the Austrian chancellor and worked according to the Austrian interest and only the Austrian interest.[1]

"Kreisky's Jewishness was demonstrated by his care for the Jewish people around the globe," says Wolfgang Petritsch, who adds that toward the end of Krieisky's life, "his Jewishness became stronger in his awareness" (2014, pers. comm.). Ari Rath, a prominent Austrian Israeli journalist close to Kreisky, verifies that in July 1990, in his final days, "Kreisky asked his physiotherapist to read to him stories from the Jewish shtetl" (n.d.).

"The question of his Jewish identity was always there," says Kreisky's former secretary, Thomas Nowotny (2020, pers.

---

1   Shek to Foreign Minister, telegram, 27 October 1976, (Austria: Diplomatic Relations with Israel on a Governmental Level, 1976), 1.1.1976–31.12.1976, Israel State Archives (Item Reference: 000kcf1/Physical Reference: 8488/1-חצ), 93–95, Jerusalem, Israel.

comm.); it was always on his mind and present in many ways. However, Nowotny insists that, although Kreisky never tried to hide his Jewish identity, it did not impact his policies or politics. It only became an issue when imposed on him, like in the Kreisky-Peter-Wiesenthal affair and the Marchegg event.

Historian Elisabeth Röhrlich (2020, pers. comm.) points to the love letters between Kreisky and Marietta Torberg, the wife of the well-known Austrian Jewish intellectual Friedrich Torberg, as proof of his Jewish complex. Torberg was Kreisky's most significant and serious love affair. Röhrlich highlights the significance of Torberg's Jewish identity being essential to her. (While the relationship's existence is no secret, the letters themselves are part of a private collection at the Bruno Kreisky Archives and are not accessible at this time.)

While important on its own, this background and analysis will illuminate the nature of Kreisky's attitudes and politics. This book will next examine some of the major "internal" Austrian events and dilemmas relating to Kreisky's Jewishness and then investigate his tortured and complicated relations to Israel, Zionism, the Arab world, and the Israeli-Palestinian conflict.

CHAPTER 3: KREISKY AND THE AUSTRIAN "VICTIM'S DOCTRINE"

It is impossible to grasp Kreisky's general politics and Jewishness without considering Austria's historical complicity with National Socialism. This issue became particularly acute because Kreisky was known to everyone as a Jew in the post–world war era. By necessity, he had to deal with how Austria rationalized its past involvement with National Socialism—the claim that they had been the Nazi's "first victim." But what did this "victim's doctrine" consist of?

THE AUSTRIAN "VICTIM'S DOCTRINE"

In 1943, senior diplomats, ministers, and army generals from the Allied forces of World War II met in Moscow to discuss cooperation in their mutual war effort. The "Third Moscow Conference" resulted in the Moscow Declaration, intended to strengthen Austrian identity and weaken German identity in Austria. Regardless, many Austrians, especially among the Social Democratic left, did not accept the declaration before 1945. Prominent figures such as Otto Bauer and Friedrich Adler insisted that Austria should be seen as "German" (Stourzh and Mueller 2018). One of the resolutions in the declaration specifically focused on Austria, stating that "Austria was the Nazis' first victim." This slogan was based on the Austrian interpretation that the 1938 Anschluss had been an act of military aggression conducted by the Third Reich. The resolution also ambiguously pronounced that, alongside its victimhood, Austria possessed a certain degree of responsibility for the crimes committed. While people frequently ignored the latter, the first-victim doctrine became a convenient governing political slogan in Austria for decades to come. The provisional Austrian government answered the Moscow Declaration's accusation that "Austria shares some of the responsibility for its participation in the war on behalf of Hitler-Germany," by claiming "that the Nazi reign of Adolf Hitler's Third Reich led the Austrian people, who had been rendered powerless and were bereft of any free will, into a senseless and pointless war of conquest, which no Austrian ever wanted any part of." Historian Heidemarie Uhl (2006, 41) thinks that it was through these passages in the Declaration of Independence that the so-called victim's theory found its fundamental formulation, its first "antifascist" variant.

The Austrian victim's theory became the foundation for the interpretation of history that was incorporated into Austria's Declaration of Independence, which the Socialist Party, the People's Party, and the Communist Party adopted on April 27, 1945 (ibid., 40). In May 1945, during the early days of the Second Austrian Republic, diplomats and international lawyers constructed a legal document entitled "Okkupationsdoktrin" (Occupation Doctrine). This document explicitly states that Germany had invaded and occupied Austria from March 1938 to May 1945 and that Austria could not be held responsible for the crimes committed by its Nazi occupiers. This "externalization" of responsibility, says Günther Bischof (2004), presented the Austrians as wretched victims while marking the Germans as the sole guilty perpetrators.

The Austrian Foreign Ministry convinced the international community to accept and adopt the document. Such international acceptance resulted in Austria not being forced to pay restitution or reparations (ibid.). Oliver Rathkolb says, "The problem of the mental consequences of the occupation theory in Austrian society was that any form of political responsibility was skirted and the confrontation with fascism became obsolete."[2]

In 1946, the Austrian Foreign Ministry attempted to demonstrate that Austria deserved its liberation based on its strong resistance. Through a documentation project named the *Rot-Weiss-Rot Buch* (Red-White-Red Book), Austrian sought to persuade the Allied governments that opposition to the Nazis had been fierce. Bischof notes that the foreign minister's young secretary, Kurt Waldheim, was part of the team that had collected materials for the book. In the *Rot-Weiss-Rot Buch*, Austria puts a particular emphasis on the "resistance of the Austrian people against their Nazi oppressors," trying to counter the critical international opinion deriving from the images of the triumphant reception of the Wehrmacht in Vienna or the rally at Heldenplatz where Hitler spoke in front of cheering masses. The book says that these were "optical and acoustic delusions" and Nazi propaganda (Uhl 2006, 42). However, their efforts to publish a second volume failed as they could not collect sufficient evidence for such a resistance (Bischof 2004).

Early on, and somewhat contradictorily, the Allied forces desired to punish war criminals and undertook a denazification process alongside the official victim's doctrine. However, after the "Prague Coup" of February 1948, the fear of a Communist takeover was more pressing than that of a revived Nazi detritus (ibid.). Bischof argues that while the Austrian government ended the denazification process, Austrians began to hide their guilt or responsibility by joining the national "victims' collective" (ibid.). The Austrian veterans' organization lobby reasoned that Austrian soldiers in the Wehrmacht had merely "done their duty" and were war victims. Consequently, the Austrian parliament passed resolutions supporting the veterans and their families. Meanwhile,

---

2   Oliver Rathkolb, "Die Wiedererrichtung des Auswärtigen Dienstes nach 1945" (unpublished research report, Austrian Ministry of Science, 1988), quoted in Günter Bischof, "Victims? Perpetrators? 'Punching Bags' of European Historical Memory? The Austrians and Their World War II Legacies," *German Studies Review* 27, no. 1 (2004): 17–32.

the actual victims—the Jews and the resistance fighters—were forgotten and marginalized. As Uhl (2006, 48) contends, the 1961 Eichmann conviction in Israeli court led to Germany coming to terms with its past and the initializing of SS-crime prosecutions before German courts. Witnesses for the prosecution were often mocked at Austrian trials, though, and the perpetrators were disgracefully acquitted.

In the final round of negotiations for the Austrian Treaty in May 1955, the signatories scratched out the third paragraph, based on the Moscow Declaration, that announced, "Austria carries a responsibility for her participation in the war, which it cannot escape." Now that the state was no longer held responsible, individual perpetrators found a convenient cover and hid their involvement (Bischof 2004). The contradictions between the reasoning in the victimization thesis and historical reality are readily apparent. Nevertheless, the claim to victim status based on international law became the central strategy in the negotiations for the treaty. The negotiators argued that since there had been no Austrian state and no Austrian government, there could be no Austrian responsibility for the crimes of the Nazi regime (i.e., "Austrians, but not Austria") (Uhl 2006, 46).

In his book *Austria in the First Cold War, 1945–55* (1999), Günter Bischof (20) provides an in-depth description of Austria's postwar politics. Bischof and most other historians agree that when the Third Reich became "the State" in Austria, Austrians widely accepted it. As a result, the Nazi regime gained legitimacy, while resistance remained unpopular and illegitimate. Furthermore, most Austrians supported Hitler's cause to the bitter end. Despite this, Austrians adopted the victim's theory, which promoted that Austrian statehood had lain dormant during the war. Since Austria had not declared war on anyone, it could not be held legally responsible for German war crimes. Austrians saw themselves as victims, and that was how Austria's "Rip Van Winkle legend" was born: a country blissfully sleeping through seven years of war while Germans committed horrific war crimes. The victim's doctrine was elevated to official state doctrine quickly and quietly in August 1945 (Bischof 1999).

Through representations of Fascism, suppression, resistance, and deliverance, a new form of the victim's doctrine evolved, based on a Catholic connotation, presenting images of a burning St. Stephen's Cathedral as the symbol of visual-memory victimhood. In comparison, the extermination of Austrian Jews was barely mentioned (Uhl 2006, 42–43). Historian Peter Pirker (2020) says that the most significant engagements with the past during the first two decades after the war revolved around the question of *erbrachte Opfer* (sacrifices made) rather than *Opferwerdung* (victimization). On the civil-society level, the competing positions in this debate reflected the views of former resistance fighters' organizations and political opponents of National Socialism on one side and the views of Wehrmacht veterans on the other (ibid., 154).

Many opportunities were missed in the 1960s and 1970s to undo the postwar-memory narrative, lift the conspiracy of silence, and probe the notion of "Austrians as victims." Although there has always been criticism of Nazism in Austria and of Austrian Nazism before 1938 (e.g., Karl Kraus regarding Nazi totalitarianism and Irene Harand regarding Nazi antisemitism) and after 1945 (e.g., Hermann Langbein regarding Nazi war crimes and Erika Weinzierl regarding the opportunism of Catholic bishops in Austria), it was very marginalized and hardly representative. Only following Kurt Waldheim's victory in 1986, after the international community put heavy pressure on Austria, did Austrians begin to publicly reconsider their attitudes to their past. These developments led to Austria officially abandoning the doctrine in the mid-2000s. In her essay "Das 'erste Opfer'" (The "First Victim") (2001), Heidemarie Uhl describes the gradual transformation of the doctrine following the Waldheim debate. This debate revolutionized traditional historical concepts and led to open discourse and past reflection. Pirker (2020, 154) presents a similar hypothesis, stating that although the recognition of sacrifice was crucial to the process of Austria's national formation, the turn toward a victimological memory only occurred following Waldheim's election and his international isolation.

"We no longer follow the 'victim's doctrine,'" confirms Hannah Liko, the current Austrian ambassador to Israel. She says that although there are no fixed talking points, Austria "will not use such formulations anymore." What is more, Liko stresses that Austria recognizes its historical responsibility, and how Austria is dealing with its past today "will remain, regardless of whoever is in power" (2019, pers. comm.).

"When we did our first Independence Day event at the embassy, marking sixty years of Austria-Israel relations, I really wanted Sebastian Kurz (then minister of foreign affairs) to deliver a speech," says Talya Lador-Fresher, the Israeli ambassador to Vienna between 2015 and 2019. Lador-Fresher recalls that Kurz had decided to honor the event with his presence, and he gave a "significant and historical speech" which he opened by denouncing the Austrian victim's doctrine. "All who talk about the 'first victim's doctrine' do not know what they are talking about," said Kurz. "We are responsible." In the first forty years after the war, up until the Waldheim affair, Austria did not deal with its Nazi past, reflects the former ambassador. "People before and during the Waldheim era talked openly against Jews," Lador-Fresher says. "Today, these statements would not be said publicly." In Austria's defense, she says that "one needs not to forget. Even though it took a long time, Austria did its self-reflection on its own. As opposed to the forced 'reeducation' process of Germans, no one forced Austrians to do so—and they still did it" (2019, pers. comm.). However, it must be noted that at least since the late 1960s, the process of coming to terms with the Nazi past in Germany has been both complicated and self-generated rather than coming from outside sources (Rabinbach 1988).

KREISKY AND THE AUSTRIAN "VICTIM'S DOCTRINE"

Kreisky's intricate relationship with his Jewishness and his views on antisemitism can be understood as a result of the traditional Jewish loyalty to the state—or in this case, the Habsburg Monarchy—and as a result of Austria's role during the Nazi period. Even though many of his relatives had been murdered in the Nazi death camps, Kreisky refused to use Third Reich atrocities as a reference point in his career. From the 1960s on, Germans, and most prominently former chancellor of the Federal Republic of Germany Willy Brandt, have tried to deal with their country's dark past. Austria, however, put the subject aside, and no actual process of self-examination and reflection was undertaken.

In 1935, Kreisky was arrested for political reasons and imprisoned for eighteen months for his underground work against the Austrofascist state. This regime was founded by the Christian Social Party, the predecessors of the Austrian People's Party. The Christian Social Party established the clerical, authoritarian state between 1934 and 1938, which suppressed Social Democrats and Nazis (Rabinbach 1983). One could attest that the time Kreisky spent in prison influenced his attitude toward conservative political regimes. In prison, Kreisky met "official Nazis" face to face for the first time. Like him, paradoxically, they were under arrest for their opposition to the "Austrofascist" state. Most of the National Socialists who were fighting the authoritarian Catholic *Ständestaat* (corporate state) were mainly of proletarian origin, and as such, it was easy for Kreisky to identify with them. Kreisky described his time in jail alongside Nazis, and the relationships he had formed with them, as thus: "I had contacts with Austrian Fascists and National Socialists in prison. I was sitting in jail with hundreds of Nazis, Communists and Social Democrats. In prison, you didn't stop your companionship because someone was a Nazi. If someone became sick, we all took care of him because he is a human" (Koelbl 1989, 142).

Kreisky sought to convince the Nazis that antisemitism was a tactical weapon of Fascist movements to deflect responsibility for working-class misery away from capitalist exploiters. One of his cellmates was a Nazi supporter named Sepp Weninger. Kreisky took the risk of swallowing a secret note Weninger wanted to smuggle out of his cell before his captors could see, earning his cellmate's special gratitude. When Germany absorbed Austria into the Third Reich, Weninger remembered his debt and saved Kreisky from the Gestapo. It is fascinating that when Kreisky was arrested in March 1938 by the triumphant Nazis, he emphasized his good relations with his Nazi cellmates. He even wrote to the Gestapo, saying, "I am prepared to provide you [at] any time with the names of currently prominent, well known members of the NSDAP who can testify that during my time as a prisoner I have always shown solidarity toward my National Socialist prison mates" (Wistrich 2007; Muravchik 2014). After the war, Kreisky "lost no time in intervening for his former cellmate, but was unable to save him from execution" (Muravchik 2014, 88).

Austrian diplomat and Kreisky's longtime press secretary Wolfgang Petritsch specifies that Kreisky hated the Austrofascists more than the Nazis after his jail experience. "After being imprisoned by them," says Petritsch, "he was in a cell together with a Communist and a Nazi. He claimed that he saw the 'human face of the Nazi'" (2014, pers. comm.). Kreisky described this incident in detail, saying that it had been because of this that he had remained alive:

Later, when the Gestapo arrested me for "state threatening actions," there was a Nazi doctor, a ridiculous person, who was very kind and who helped and supported me. After two painful months of uncertainty, two SS men came in the night and told me "you are lucky—you were in a cell with X and Y and you have been a good companion. We will give you another chance, you can leave, but you need to promise that you will not stay in Europe." At this point, no

one was talking about gassing but they could have put me
in a concentration camp and then I would have been gassed
later anyway. (Koelbl 1989, 142)

Kreisky perceived the Austrofascists as "the destroyers of Austria,"
says Petritsch (2014, pers. comm.). Until the end, Kreisky was
convinced that his imprisonment had been due to him being a
Socialist and not a Jew (ibid.).

In September 1938, after the Gestapo had persecuted him
because of his political beliefs and Jewish origins, Kreisky fled to
Sweden. There, he engaged in journalism and business. As time
went on, Kreisky was undoubtedly aware of the horrible consequences of the Nazis' Jewish persecution, and he learned of his
relatives' fate—with at least twenty having died in extermination
camps. Nevertheless, Kreisky's *Weltanschauung* (worldview) was
still much too secure and confident then to engage in any kind of
sentimental self-analysis. If anything, it reinforced his conviction
that only his Socialist ideal could create a better world in which
such horrors would not be repeated (Secher 1994, 13). He remained in Swedish exile until 1945. Like Karl Marx and Otto
Bauer, says writer Joshua Muravchik (2014, 87), the young and
affluent Kreisky made himself over as best he could, from a Jew
to a proletarian, spurning the Socialist Students organization for
the Young Workers' Movement to participate more directly in
the class struggle. Of course, Muravchik's perspective is specu-
lation, given that it is impossible to know whether Kreisky deliberately tried to submerge his Jewishness into working-class
consciousness.

Historian Robert Wistrich (2007) comments that Kreisky was
heavily involved in helping Austrian Wehrmacht soldiers in Russian captivity return to their homes in Austria during his Swedish
years. Muravchik even goes so far as to claim that while Kreisky
was in Sweden at the war's end, he "worked day and night to
obtain the release of and favored the treatment for former members of the German Wehrmacht, even Waffen-SS, of allegedly

'Austrian origin' at the very same time when those whose 'Jewish origins' he shared roamed Europe by the tens of thousands in search of food and shelter" (2014, 90). Although it must be noted that other experts have vehemently refuted this claim. Barbara Taufar, for one, insists that it is "absolutely not true" (2015, pers. comm.).

What is true, however, about Kreisky's treatment of former Nazis is that during his diplomatic and political career, he continually distinguished between the "small Nazis," for whom he had some empathy (like his former cellmate), and the brutal, power-seeking elite Nazis (Wistrich 2007). As for the latter, whom Kreisky deemed "criminals that hit poor women, people who gave orders and murdered," he said that he "cannot forgive and would never assist" (Koelbl 1989, 142). Kreisky's conception of "small Nazis" is well demonstrated in his portrayal of his relationship with a former Nazi he had met in jail. "Some Nazis that were in jail with me, I knew very well from before," said Kreisky. "For example, Egon Mueller Klingspor lived in my area. We looked at each other with hatred when we crossed each other, he went to the Nazi marches and I went to the Socialist ones. We saw each other again in prison and became rather good friends. The friendship, if you can call it like that, continues until today" (ibid.).

As previously mentioned, at certain stages, the Austrofascist state appeared to him as a graver danger to Austria than the Nazis. Kreisky tried to understand why people became supporters of Hitler. "The hatred of Dollfuss was stronger than the fear of anything else," says political scientist John Bunzl (1997, 63). The hatred of the Austrofascist dictatorship was more intense than the "differences" with the Nazis.

Kreisky's inability to grasp the enormity of the Holocaust might also explain why he—a Jew—signed on to the postwar Austrian victim's doctrine, which denied the significant Austrian participation and complicity in the Holocaust until the Waldheim affair. A more likely explanation, however, is to be found elsewhere. Former foreign minister Erwin Lanc and other Austrian officials have privately said that Kreisky was so supportive of the doctrine because he knew he would never have gotten to the top of Austrian politics had he not abided by this "national consensus" (Bischof 2015, pers. comm.). After returning from Scandinavian exile in 1945, Kreisky helped sell this legal construct to the world and later administer it. The young, ambitious, and exceptionally talented diplomat first did this as undersecretary of state (1953–59) and then again as foreign minister (1959–66) (Bischof 2004).

Moreover, when Federal President Theodor Körner appointed Kreisky assistant chief of staff and political advisor in 1951, he was apparently involved in the amnesty resolutions for former Nazis. Kreisky received strong hints that either he should adapt the Austrian victim's doctrine—or that he would never succeed in a political career (Petritsch 2014, pers. comm.). Kreisky saw himself as a personal victim of the Nazis, and he became one of the foremost advocates of the Austrian victim's doctrine, believing that he had suffered as many Austrians had.

As a Jew involved in Austrian politics, it was important that Kreisky establish and prove his "Austrianness." For Jews, as a vulnerable minority, this was common. Ludwig Holländer, a member of the German Centralverein (Central Association), comments, "Stepchildren must be doubly loyal and well-behaved" (Gay 1978, 183). Kreisky's wrote his memoirs with this in mind, suggests historian Elisabeth Röhrlich. To show that his ancestors had been loyal servants of the Habsburg Monarchy, Kreisky traced his family's roots to the seventeenth century. He stressed that the reason he had left Austria in 1938 had been due to politics and not his Jewishness. Therefore, he had not been and should not be considered a Jewish refugee. Kreisky also said that he had only left Austria when no other alternative had remained. With his memoirs, Kreisky indirectly reinforces the victim's doctrine as a victim of the Nazi regime. When dealing with Bruno Kreisky's autobiographical texts, says Röhrlich, "we can never completely entangle the narrative that he created and the events as they actually occurred" (2012).

Part of Kreisky's posture was related to realpolitik consider-ations. However, because some twenty of his relatives had per-ished in the Holocaust, Kreisky's role in prolonging the myth of "Austrians as victims" poses one of the most baffling mysteries concerning Kreisky's sense of Jewish self. When challenged about Austria's past, Kreisky would be dismissive, declaring, "When fi-nally grass has grown over one thing, a camel comes along and eats it again away" (*Der Spiegel* 1986). He argued in an interview that he could not have achieved "the moral position" (Koelbl 1989, 144) he had reached in Austria if he had persecuted former Nazis in the guise of a "*Racheengel*" (revenging angel).

Many believed that Austria would finally come to terms with its past during Kreisky's early years in office. People took his elec-tion as a Jewish chancellor with long-term popularity as a positive sign. However, Kreisky's ad hominem attacks on Wiesenthal (see chapter four), the reception of the war criminal Walter Reder by Minister of Defense Friedhelm Frischenschlager in 1985, and the Waldheim affair (see chapter four) made it increasingly evident that Kreisky did not want to publicly confront these problematic aspects of yore (Vansant 1994). In no way did he disturb the more palatable picture supplied to Austria's youth (ibid.). Kreisky said he had not dealt with the Austrian past because the country would "never reach a better world" if it got "stuck in the circle of revenge." He wondered, "What should Austria have done with all the people that didn't do anything besides being Nazis? There were 400,000 people in Austria, maybe even 600,000 when you count all the subgroups of the NSDAP. Should we have persecut-ed these people? We would have never found peace. And there are millions of people who didn't open their mouth[s] although they knew what was happening. Should we have shot all of them? Or what else?" (Koelbl 1989, 144).

This question was a dilemma that characterized the response to Nazism within Austria and Germany and indicated a more general problem. As Jeffrey Herf points out in his book *Divided Memory: The Nazi Past in the Two Germanys* (1997), due to the postwar circumstances, one "could foster either memory and justice or democracy but not both" (7).

Sociologist Karin Stögner thinks of Kreisky as "a key figure in Austrian identity in the Second Republic" (2008, 64) because of his radical discourse of reconciliation when dealing with Austria's past during Nazi rule. Kreisky had a significant role in the repression and denial of Austrian complicity with the Nazis. To accusations that serious war criminals had not been punished during his terms in power, Kreisky would maintain that he knew all the names of the "big Nazis," and the reason why only "a few were acquitted" was because one could not "accept from people, 30 years after the end of the war, to imagine that their fathers were criminals of war" (Koelbl 1989, 144). According to Stögner, Austrians demonstrated their appreciation by giving Kreisky an absolute majority three times in a row. Many regarded him as *le Roi Soleil* (The Sun King) and celebrated that this "alibi Jew" openly expressed what others said behind closed doors. Kreisky provided the Austrians with "what they were looking for: first-hand legitimation to ward off memory and responsibility," summarizes Stögner (2008, 66). Menachem Oberbaum observes that Kreisky being elected numerous times served as an excellent alibi for Austrians. It let them exclaim, "Look at us. You say we are antisemitic? But here we elected a Jewish chancellor." "Many people asked me," says Oberbaum, "how can you say we are antisemites when our elected Chancellor Kreisky is Jewish?" (2020, pers. comm.).

"The 'victim's doctrine' was politically the right thing to adapt in 1943. It was, for the Allies, a good way to treat Austria differently," suggests Georg Lennkh, Kreisky's foreign policy advisor. For Lennkh, it was a way for Austrian politicians to say, "We were not perpetrators and not victims." However, Lennkh believes that by 1955, Austria should have more explicitly dealt with this "historical falsification." They did not do so because, as he puts it, "life was going on, and Austria was dealing with catching up with the United Nations and other international affairs." Thinking about the Holocaust at that time was not politically expedient, Lennkh attests.

When Kreisky became chancellor, "he made mistakes in perhaps being a bit too sloppy in choosing people for his government," says Lennkh. "I think Kreisky could have been more careful, but this was a situation in which one had to act quickly and choose people according to their present status rather than their problematic past" (2015, pers. comm.). Lennkh notes that Kreisky ended up appointing five ministers with a Nazi past. Interior Minister Otto Rösch had even been active in neo-Nazi activities after the war. Somewhat problematically, Kreisky publicly defended his appointments, claiming that because of his past as a refugee and a political prisoner, he could forgive former Nazis once they had become reliable democrats (ibid.).

Kreisky's personal assistant, Margit Schmidt, defends Kreisky, claiming that he did not know about the Nazis in his government. "The complicating clash of interests influenced one another," says Schmidt. "The trade unions and the federal system—everyone wanted power. As a leader, Kreisky needed to make compromises, and one of the ministers with whom he was not even acquainted was recommended by a fellow politician. Only later did it emerge that he was a former Nazi." Another consideration behind Austria adopting the victim's doctrine was the possibility that it would have to pay heavy postwar reparations otherwise. This, Schmidt says, "was a very pragmatic attitude, aided by the fact that this was supported by the superpowers" (2014, pers. comm.). "He simply did not see himself as the person who could or should open this Pandora's box," adds Barbara Taufar (2020, pers. comm.).

"I think Kreisky in a way believed that because he was Jewish, he was allowed to use the 'victim's doctrine' whenever it worked for him in Austrian politics," says Elisabeth Röhrlich. In terms of bringing Nazis to court and legal prosecution, the Kreisky administration was reluctant, slow, and did not do very much, she continues. Kreisky thought that his background and the fact that the Nazis had murdered most of his family during the Holocaust gave him particular legitimacy and allowed him to "take care of Austrian politics and do what he thought was good for Austria." He was not someone who said, "Well, we have to get rid of this victim's myth," says Röhrlich (2020, pers. comm.).

Röhrlich goes further, stating that Kreisky knew that this narrative was unfortunately untrue—and perhaps even worthy of his resentment. Nevertheless, he did not hesitate to invoke it for political reasons. In terms of his personal, familial, and Social Democratic experience, Kreisky was shrewdly aware of how cynical politics worked. This hit home for him when local Austrian Social Democrats had shown no interest in having their exiles return to Austria. It really upset Kreisky, says Röhrlich. Nevertheless, Kreisky curiously exploited his repression of the past to build a new form of politics. "There were so many people in Austria who voted for the Nazis and if we exclude them now we will not be able to form a stable democracy," he justified. Kreisky publicly supported the doctrine, but Röhrlich believes that "in private conversations, he would probably talk otherwise" (ibid.). This remains an enigma, however. There is no evidence in his memoirs or press interviews that there was a distinction between his public statements and private convictions.

KREISKY AND ANTISEMITISM IN AUSTRIA

It is necessary to state that Austrian antisemitism did, indeed, exist. Total denial would have been difficult with the continuing prevalence of antisemitism in Austrian society. Kreisky's pronunciations of this matter were hardly consistent with other personal and political attitudes that he had expressed. "I am still allergic to the label 'Jew,'" said Kreisky. "If in England or in America it is mentioned that someone is a Jew or of Jewish origin, this is not normally intended to stigmatize him. Here [in Austria] it is different, and, even if this bit of information is presented in the most innocent way, to me it feels like a survival from the Hitler years. In this sense, the yellow patch is still with us even today" (Berg 2000, 416).

Kreisky was disturbed by this kind of antisemitism, which also appeared in the 1970 election campaign. There, the ÖVP blatantly urged voters to choose the Catholic conservative Josef Klaus over Kreisky. Klaus, it was said, was *"Ein echter Österreicher"* (a true Austrian). The aim of such coded language, Kreisky said, was apparent: because of his Jewishness, *he* could not be considered a true Austrian (ibid., 419). Many years later, when Kreisky was asked about this campaign, he responded that he had "never tried to hide or apologize for his descent, it is clear what he was. Everybody knew it, and obviously it didn't play a role for 75% of the Austrians for many years" (Koelbl 1989, 145). Even with Kreisky's claim that "the circumstances that I am a Jew would not hinder me from winning the trust of the masses" (ibid., 144), in his meetings with politician Micha Harish (1997), he admitted how insulted he was by the campaign. As elsewhere, Kreisky's ambivalences and inconsistencies remain striking.

From her conversations with Kreisky, Barbara Taufar infers that he was deeply hurt by Austrian opportunism and antisemitism. Taufar mentions Kreisky's visit to Carinthia in the late 1970s, a trip that he made, ignoring the warnings he had received about the growing number of Nazi supporters who might put him in danger there. He refused to believe that an actual threat existed, says Taufar (2020, pers. comm.), and was shocked and deeply hurt when he was physically and verbally attacked. Once again, we are faced with a certain inconsistency, for in his interview with Koelbl (1989, 141), Kreisky maintained that he had never suffered because of his Jewish heritage.

"Austria was always an antisemitic country. Modern Zionism might not have succeeded had not Herzl lived in Vienna and saw its anti-Jewish sentiments," remarks Uri Avnery (2015, pers. comm.), an Israeli writer, politician, and peace activist. In 1979, public surveys in Austria revealed that twenty-five percent of the Austrian population born after 1945 held antisemitic and anti-Roma preconceptions (Ben-Yaacov 2012, 235). Avnery insists that this did not interest or bother Kreisky very much. "He was very popular despite his Jewishness, and he preferred to ignore the antisemitism," says Avnery (2015, pers. comm.). Kreisky viewed Austrian antisemitism as "much more dangerous for non-Jews than for Jews." "The 60,000 Austrian Jews who were deported and murdered were the first," said Kreisky, "but in the end it also came to the Austrians. 60,000 Jews were killed, but also 400,000 Austrians" (Koelbl 1989, 148). Undoubtedly, Kreisky found it difficult to come to grips with the specificity and particular nature of the Holocaust.

Whether he publicly admitted it or not, Kreisky's roots did seem to play a role in his decision-making process. In the 1960s, he could not conceive of the idea that he would be able to rule in a still-antisemitic Austria, his great patriotism notwithstanding. When former Austrian president Rudolf Kirchschläger teasingly asked him whether he was already expecting to become federal chancellor of Austria, Kreisky replied without hesitation, "Come on, you don't believe they're going to elect a Jew to be Chancellor" (Wistrich 2007, 3). Reaffirming this point, Petritsch recalls a speech that Kreisky gave in 1980 at the memorial for the failed coup against Hitler on July 20, 1944, in Berlin. "Kreisky movingly spoke about his twenty-two relatives who perished in the Holocaust," says Petritsch. "It was there that he reiterated his commitment to Israel. The Jewish state as a consequence of Hitler's destruction of the European Jewry, as he put it. A rare public occasion, but he stated it out of his personal conviction. In Austrian politics, Kreisky never thought that he could become Number One. Antisemitism was too deeply ingrained in his opinion" (2014, pers. comm.).

When Kreisky was asked about the Austrian collective responsibility for the crimes committed during the Nazi period, he detailed his perspective on the matter: "One can measure a nation that was involved as much as the Austrians according to different principles. For example, the minimal principle which means in a biblical way—if there is only one righteous amongst you, your town should not be destroyed. Or one can judge a nation according to the maximal principle, which means that one needs to include everyone who is guilty. Then you get inevitably to the collective guilt thesis but I cannot acknowledge such a collective guilt, not when it should justify collective punishment" (Koelbl 1989, 142).

Petritsch adds that Kreisky was well aware of the Austrian antisemitic tradition. And, while he resented it, of course, as Petritsch stresses, he was also realistic. Kreisky believed that the descendants of Nazis should be well educated to become democrats and find inclusion in society. "One could not practically exclude 20 percent of the population," says Petritsch (2014, pers. comm.). "One should not think that it is enough to do a forced re-education for denazification," explained Kreisky (Koelbl 1989, 148). Instead, there was the need for a profound and deeply democratic change, one that would come from within (ibid.).

Taufar says that although Kreisky understood that antisemitism had survived in postwar Austria, he tended to ignore it for a long time. His realization as to its extent only began when Jörg Haider and Kurt Waldheim came "out of their holes" (Taufar 2015, pers. comm.) as they attained political power in the 1980s. Many Socialists who had worked closely with Kreisky when he had been chancellor were eager to cooperate with the new antisemitic public figures. His close Social Democratic associate Peter Jankowitsch even acted as foreign minister when Waldheim was president. It was then, in October 1983, that Kreisky resigned after the Socialists had lost their absolute majority.

Taufar describes the problematic atmosphere during those days: "Suddenly, all Austrian embassies in the world got an official telex from the Austrian Foreign Ministry with the order to send a report with the names and functions of the most important Jewish journalists of each country whom they would have to treat 'differently' and try to influence." Only two Austrian ambassadors denied the request from Vienna. The ambassador to Sweden, Dr.

Ingo Mussi, who also had been an ambassador in Israel prior, "rejected such special treatment of Jewish journalists." So, too, did Dr. Erik Nettel in France. Ambassador Nettel called the general director of the Foreign Ministry and told him how dangerous such a request was, and he would not obey it. These developments, notes Taufar, "showed how suddenly, after Kreisky resigned, the atmosphere totally changed" (2015, pers. comm.).

There is a highly moving and revelatory conversation about how Kreisky felt about these developments between Taufar and Kreisky as he lay dying. The conversation occurred after Taufar had decided to convert to Judaism and move to Israel. "I told him about my decision to emigrate from Austria," says Taufar. "It was a hard decision for me, and I had given it much thought. I realized that I just couldn't handle the negative direction in which our beloved country was going and that Austrian antisemitism was rising again. Kreisky looked at me with tears in his eyes and in his soft voice whispered, 'We just didn't learn anything. Anything.' ... We sat there and cried together. It felt as if we were crying more for Austria's fate than for ourselves" (ibid.).

This intimate and touching scene demonstrates Kreisky's deep disillusionment and could even be viewed as a kind of sad admission that somehow his life's work was a failure. But as with other incidents discussed in this book, it is hard to tell how to interpret this event: Was this last-minute confession the real Kreisky, and, if so, what does a statement so close to death tell us about the man? There is no definitive answer to this, and it is precisely in these ambivalences and the ways in which Kreisky managed them that the interest—and perhaps his own creativity—lies. These can be seen in his fraught policies and his responses to local and international politics. We shall now examine this in two illustrative cases.

CHAPTER 4:
POLITICAL SCANDALS

THE KREISKY-PETER-WIESENTHAL AFFAIR:

Background

Simon Wiesenthal (1908–2005), the famous "Nazi-Hunter" (Pick 1996), was a longtime active member of the Jewish Community of Vienna and a supporter of the ÖVP (Rathkolb 2005). His tense relationship with Chancellor Bruno Kreisky soon became known to the world through the "Kreisky-Peter-Wiesenthal affair." This dispute became notorious and appeared in international and national newspapers for weeks. The quarrel emerged in 1975 following Austria's election period and Wiesenthal's revelation that the Freedom Party of Austria's (FPÖ) chairman, Friedrich Peter, had a Nazi past. Kreisky defended Peter, demonstrating a certain degree of understanding for Nazi perpetrators again, and he accused Wiesenthal of being motivated by political interests. The reasons for this dispute were, of course, more complicated. As such, this public clash between two dominant Austrian Jews, Wiesenthal and Kreisky, serves as an excellent showcase to illustrate the Austrian chancellor's complicated relationship to such "Jewish" questions.

Simon Wiesenthal was born in 1908 in Buczacz, Galicia, and trained as an architect (Levy 1995). He described himself as a Zionist but not a religious Jew in any formal sense (Pick 1996). Following the Nazi invasion of the Soviet Union in July 1941, Wiesenthal was arrested and imprisoned in several concentration camps, ending up in Mauthausen, where he was liberated in 1945 by the United States Army (ibid.). In 1961, Wiesenthal moved to Vienna and began a long career in collecting information from around the world, seeking perpetrators, and putting them on trial. He repeatedly criticized the Austrian authorities' disinterest in his investigations and prosecutions of Nazi perpetrators (ibid.).

The enmity between Kreisky and Wiesenthal did not emerge out of the Kreisky-Peter-Wiesenthal affair. It began in 1970, when Wiesenthal took Kreisky to task for including five former Nazis in his cabinet. These Nazis included Hans Öllinger, a former member of the SS, and Otto Rösch, who had also been active in neo-Nazi activities after the war (Petritsch 2011). Kreisky's biographer Wolfgang Petritsch contends that Kreisky sought a large coalition and thus included these questionable personalities (ibid.).

Wiesenthal sent the information about their Nazi past to the German magazine *Der Spiegel,* which published the story and quoted several of Wiesenthal's accusations. In its May 25, 1970, edition, *Der Spiegel* cited another source that had called Öllinger a member of the "NSDAP from the first hour." The magazine harshly criticized Kreisky for protecting his minister. Petritsch (2011) alleges that this was the origin of the lifelong hatred between Kreisky and Wiesenthal. Kreisky dismissed Wiesenthal's accusations, considering them politically motivated since Wiesenthal was a supporter of his party's political rival, the ÖVP. Sarcastically, Kreisky commented that he was waiting for Wiesenthal to accuse him of being a former member of the SS as well(ibid.).

Later, in 1975, Kreisky very controversially decided to turn to the right-wing FPÖ in order to form a coalition should his own party fail to achieve an absolute majority of seats in the National Council (ibid.). A few days before the election, due to the potential formation of a coalition between the Social Democratic Party (SPÖ) and the FPÖ, there existed the possibility that Peter would be appointed vice-chancellor. This was an alarming situation. President Kirchschläger then invited Wiesenthal for a consultation about this matter, and Wiesenthal provided him with new details about Peter's SS past. This appeared to be unusually dramatic as reports circulated that the president had begun to cry upon reading some of the documents (Levy 1995). Wiesenthal proclaimed that the president had promised to prevent such an eventuality.[3]

Thankfully, Kreisky's noticeable majority made a coalition unnecessary. Despite this, on October 9, four days after the elections, Wiesenthal hosted a press conference in which he revealed the "Dossier Peter." He said that Peter had withheld crucial parts of his autobiography in his official resume (Wodak et al., 1990). From the material submitted to the press, it became unmistakable that Peter had served in the Fifth Company of the Tenth Regiment of the First SS Infantry Brigade, which had been involved in the murder of more than ten thousand civilians, including some eight thousand Jews (ibid.). Peter could not explain why he had hidden that reality from the public. As Wiesenthal relates in his memoirs, he came to this discovery mainly by chance. Because he did not want to influence the result of the elections, he chose to reveal this information afterward. While allegedly not wanting to sway the political outcome, Wiesenthal deemed it crucial that the information reach the general public so that some kind of honest confrontation with the Holocaust could take place (Sporrer and Steiner 1992).

Austrian television tried to conduct a discussion between Wiesenthal and Peter. The latter, who had initially agreed to participate, later changed his mind and agreed only to a telephone interview. In the interview, Peter accused Wiesenthal of being an "enemy of Austria." His defense consisted of the claim that he had merely been a simple twenty-one-year-old soldier when he had served. In response to the interviewer's sarcastic question

---

3   Peled to Yaish, telegram, 13 October 1975, (Austria: Office of Prime Minister Yitzhak Rabin, 1974–77), 20.4.1974–3.10.1977, Israel State Archives (ISA in short notes) (Item Reference: 000wl1q/Physical Reference: 4212/9-א), 148–49, Jerusalem, Israel.

("And what did the 'simple soldier' do in the unit?"), Peter very angrily replied that he had fought for the homeland and that it was not his fault that the "homeland" in question then had been Germany and not Austria. He did not respond to the question asking him why he'd only just admitted that he had been part of an SS unit.[4] In a telegram, Israeli deputy ambassador to Austria Michael Peled reports his impressions of the interview to his supervisors: "On the one hand, Wiesenthal's appearance was dignified and restrained. Peter's response, on the other hand, was hysterical and furious."[5]

Kreisky's Response

Chancellor Kreisky decided to defend Friedrich Peter publicly and assertively in response to Wiesenthal. The clash around Peter was soon to be known as the Kreisky-Peter-Wiesenthal affair. On November 10, 1975, Kreisky held a press conference in which he accused Wiesenthal of being the leader of a "Conservative Jewish Mafia." This Mafia sought not to take down Peter but to defeat Kreisky. It was time, he said, to finally put an end to such a "character assassination," which had no place in a civilized country. "As one who lost twenty-one members of his family who were murdered by the Nazis," declared Kreisky, "I have the moral right to denounce Wiesenthal's actions. Thirty years after the end of the Second World War, it is time, once and for all, to erase the past."[6] Kreisky went further. Wiesenthal, Kreisky implied (without any supporting evidence), could have been a Nazi collaborator himself (Petritsch 2011). Moreover, by his actions, Wiesenthal risked a new wave of antisemitism. It was questionable even, Kreisky added, that Wiesenthal should have received Austrian citizenship (Böhler 1996). "Wiesenthal and I have nothing in common," announced Kreisky at the press conference. "Mr. Wiesenthal, I insist, had a different relationship to the Gestapo than I had. ... My

---

4 Peled to Yaish, 13 Oct. 1975, (Austria: Rabin, 1974–77), ISA, 148–49.

5 Peled to Yaish, 13 Oct. 1975, (Austria: Rabin, 1974–77), ISA, 148–49.

6 Peled to Yaish, 13 Oct. 1975, (Austria: Rabin, 1974–77), ISA, 148–49.

relationship to the Gestapo is unambiguous: I was its prisoner, its detainee. And was interrogated. His relationship is different, as far as I am aware" (Wiesenthal 1988, 367).

These accusations caused Wiesenthal to sue Kreisky for libel (Böhler 1996). Later, however, Wiesenthal decided to withdraw this lawsuit. In his memoir, Wiesenthal gives three reasons for this decision. The first reason is that his wife, Cyla, suffered grievously as these events and accusations unfolded; it even led to some death threats. Secondly, he took into consideration that the Viennese religious community feared a continuation of the conflict would encourage a new wave of antisemitism. The final reason concerns Austrian-Israeli relations. With Austria's central location, there was some apprehension that this dispute would endanger the passage for Jews emigrating from the Soviet Union to Israel through Austria (Wiesenthal 1988).

Historian Ingrid Böhler (1996) suggests another ironic reason: perhaps antagonistic circles would enjoy such public demonstrations of Jewish disunity. This would contribute to an already-negative stereotype of Jewish people in Austrian society.

However, this did not mark the end of the conflict. Ten years later—three years after leaving office and thus losing parliamentary immunity—Kreisky again accused Wiesenthal of being a Gestapo collaborator. Wiesenthal sued again (Petritsch 2011). Kreisky was found guilty of defamation and had to pay a fine of 270,000 Austrian shillings. Kreisky died nine months after the trial. The antagonism between the two men remained (ibid.).

In his memoirs, Wiesenthal describes his emotions around these events accordingly: "I was a leper in my new home, and the very thought that I had survived Hitler prevented me from emigrating from Austria" (1988, 366). Many in Austria attacked Wiesenthal, and almost no one came to his aid. The office of the Jewish Historical Documentation Center, which he headed, was forced to move to another location due to right-wing agitation (Wiesenthal, 1988). In cases where Wiesenthal did receive assistance, it came from ÖVP-affiliated circles or victims' associations such as the Österreichische *Widerstandsbewegung* (Austrian resistance movement) (Wodak et al. 1990).

Public Response to the Affair

The affair became a central topic for the Austrian press, with most articles being critical of Wiesenthal. For example, the *Kronen Zeitung*, edited by Hans Dichand, harshly condemned him and noted that the judicial authorities had dealt with the case of Friedrich Peter years ago without any outcome. The only case to be investigated, the newspaper announced, had been the "Wiesenthal Case" (Böhler 1996, 505). The *Kronen Zeitung* also claimed that Wiesenthal was the source of Austria's bad reputation (Levy 1995, 309). However, Wiesenthal did receive enthusiastic support from the publisher and editor in chief of the newspaper *Profil*, Peter Michael Lingens. In October 1975, Lingens published a favorable four-part series entitled: "Who is Simon Wiesenthal" (ibid., 507).

Wodak et al., in their book, *Wir sind alle unschuldige Täter: Diskurshistorische Studien zum Nachkriegsantisemitismus* (1990), analyze the various antisemitic stereotypes employed by the *Kronen Zeitung* and *Die Presse* in this case. Most revolved around accusations of Jewish infamy and Jewish world conspiracy. They also assess the terminology used by the papers. Both used the term "Causa Peter" only three times; Wiesenthal's name, conversely, appeared fifteen times. The implication was that Wiesenthal was responsible for this scandal. The journalist Gerhard Steininger wrote in the newspaper *Salzburger Nachrichten* that Wiesenthal's intervention in Austrian politics removed every possible moral justification for his actions. What is more, he was responsible for the antisemitic outbreaks (Böhler 1996, 506). Only one organization supported Wiesenthal, the nonpartisan organization of resistance fighters, and their support barely received newspaper coverage. They did, however, receive some television and radio coverage. Peter's party united behind him. The chairman of the ÖVP, Josef

Taus, was the only leader who responded moderately and called for an investigation of Wiesenthal's accusations.[7]

The then Israeli ambassador to Vienna Avigdor Dagan refers to the usually pro-Israeli *Kronen Zeitung* columnist Staberl, who similarly wrote a critical piece about Wiesenthal in one of his telegrams.[8] Following the publication, Dagan met with Staberl for a long, private conversation. There, Dagan received some troubling insights regarding Austrian responses to the events. To quote Staberl:

> There is no journalist that can write against his readers. The *Kronen Zeitung* has 1,600,000 readers. 1,400,000 of them are against Wiesenthal. ... For me, Peter, as any other person who was in the SS, is a criminal and it does not matter in which unit he served. However, no person in Austria is interested in what had happened thirty or forty years ago. Those under 30 years old do not even know what the SS is. It is unrealistic to believe that Wiesenthal's actions can change anything. In fact, the result is the opposite. If Wiesenthal would have come with this information before the elections, Peter would have received even more votes.

According to Staberl, the most problematic aspect of Wiesenthal's actions—whether intended or not—was that he had damaged Austria's image in the world. Ambassador Dagan concludes his confidential report by stating that after this conversation, he feared that the Austrians would try to close Wiesenthal's offices and that his life was in danger.[9]

---

7 Peled to Yaish, 13 Oct. 1975, (Austria: Rabin, 1974–77), ISA, 148–49.

8 Dagan to Shek, telegram, 15 October 1975, (Austria: Office of Prime Minister Yitzhak Rabin, 1974–77), 20.4.1974–3.10.1977, Israel State Archives (Item Reference: 000wl1q/Physical Reference: א-4212/9), 145, Jerusalem, Israel.

9 Dagan to Shek, 15 Oct. 1975, (Austria: Rabin, 1974–77), ISA, 145.

Kreisky, Antisemitism, and the Kreisky-Peter-Wiesenthal Affair

The Kreisky-Peter-Wiesenthal affair was a scandal in which two of Vienna's most prominent Jews fought over exceedingly delicate matters. However, it appeared to most people that this was not a conflict between two Austrians but an inner-Jewish rivalry. As a result, this affair is an excellent case study for Jewish integration—or its opposite—in postwar Austrian society and Kreisky's role in that complex.

Kreisky's rhetoric against Wiesenthal, another prominent Jewish figure, essentially rendered it possible and legitimate for the Austrian media to openly express antisemitic claims. Wiesenthal became a persona non grata, which allowed many sections of Austrian society to unite in a feeling of solidarity while downplaying their Nazi past (Wodak et al. 1990). "The attacks of the Jewish Chancellor on Jewish groups was [sic] unprecedented and added oil to the antisemitic fire which exists in Austria all the time. Antisemitic circles regarded Kreisky's attacks as massive support of them and their accusations regarding a 'Jewish Mafia,'" says Israeli deputy ambassador to Austria, Michael Peled.[10] In a telegram, Ambassador Dagan also expresses his shock and dissatisfaction with Kreisky's reactions, which, he argues, directly contributed to the antisemitic atmosphere. "I expected antisemitic responses to come from Austrian actors following Wiesenthal's press conference," says Dagan. "However, I did not expect Kreisky to use the same words that antisemites used. Kreisky's reaction was so hysterical and horrible that, with all due respect to Kreisky, whom you know that I do respect more than most Israelis, it would be hard to forget it in the future."[11]

The affair had obvious negative, long-term effects on Simon Wiesenthal's reputation. The dispute became another breaking point in his complex life story. In an interview, Wiesenthal ex-

---

10   Peled to Yaish, 13 Oct. 1975, (Austria: Rabin, 1974–77), ISA, 148–49.
11   Dagan to Shek, 15 Oct. 1975, (Austria: Rabin, 1974–77), ISA, 145.

plained that there would be no further trials against Austrian Nazi perpetrators in Austria; they would be wholly integrated into Austrian society (Sporrer and Steiner 1992). Wiesenthal remained forever an outsider in Austrian society. He sarcastically stated that there had always been great Jews in Vienna who had tried to be "more Austrian than the Austrians" (1988, 369), but unfortunately, this had been accompanied by a pinch of antisemitism.

The Jewish Community
and the Kreisky-Peter-Wiesenthal Affair

The Israelitische Kultusgemeinde Wien (Jewish Community of Vienna) distanced itself from the so-called "immigrant" Wiesenthal, fearing that the antisemitism directed against him and his "avenger image" would have repercussions against all Austrian Jews. Consequently, Wiesenthal remained isolated within the Jewish community (Wiesenthal 1988, 370). The Jewish Community of Vienna explicitly pointed out that Wiesenthal's Jewish Historical Documentation Center was not a part of the official religious community. Furthermore, on the same day that Wiesenthal held his press conference, the president of the Austrian-Israeli Society, Otto Probst, announced that Wiesenthal's actions had not been useful as he had "nothing concrete in his hands" (Embacher 1995, 356). As a result, Wiesenthal felt abandoned by Viennese Jews in his fight to expose Nazi crimes. He now alleged that he had become the conscience of the Jews (Böhler 1996). Wiesenthal admitted his disappointment, explaining that, while he had never demanded support from the Jewish community, he had expected it in such a situation (Pick 1996, 269). The conflict also had disquieting political overtones. Jews who sympathized with the SPÖ even saw Wiesenthal as an agent of the ÖVP and interpreted his criticism of Kreisky as electoral support for the ÖVP (Embacher 1995).

Ariel Muzicant, former president of the Jewish Community of Vienna, mentions that his father, a prominent Austrian businessman, had attempted to bridge the gap between Wiesenthal and

Kreisky two years before the affair. However, he had failed, saying that "he had never seen so much hatred between people. They both truly despised one another." As Muzicant states, Kreisky once again showed, in the way he had handled the affair, that he "hated Israel and the Jews." Muzicant points out that members of the Jewish community often wondered "how these actions were possible for someone from a Jewish origin" and that Kreisky had a "serious problem with his Jewish background and hated being reminded that he was Jewish." Muzicant concludes, "He had an anti-Jewish paranoia" (2018, pers. comm.).

Israel and the Kreisky-Peter-Wiesenthal Affair

In contrast to the general Israeli policy in which Israeli politicians actively got involved in Austrian-Israeli matters and criticized Kreisky's policies, the Kreisky-Peter-Wiesenthal affair led to a different approach. The Israelis considered this conflict a domestic Austrian matter involving two "unpleasant men" that did not concern Israel.[12] "We must stay out of this business and I suggest that you do not discuss this with the Austrian embassy," writes Ambassador Dagan to his superiors via telegram.[13] Nevertheless, it was Dagan who suggested that the Israeli press be encouraged to denounce Kreisky's actions. This was no easy task, Dagan complains, as "Wiesenthal phones us every day, the journalists ask us what we think, the Jewish community is split and its leadership is acting in a disgraceful manner."[14]

Immediately after Kreisky responded to Wiesenthal's accusations, Ambassador Ze'ev Shek, the deputy general director of Europe at the Israeli Ministry of Foreign Affairs, ordered Dagan to respond only if asked, using the following talking points: Israel emphasizes unequivocally that there is no time limitation to Nazi crimes; Wiesenthal's documentation center is an institution that runs independently; all its publications are theirs and theirs alone;

---

12 Peled to Yaish, 13 Oct. 1975, (Austria: Rabin, 1974–77), ISA, 148–49.
13 Dagan to Shek, 15 Oct. 1975, (Austria: Rabin, 1974–77), ISA, 145.
14 Dagan to Shek, 15 Oct. 1975, (Austria: Rabin, 1974–77), ISA, 145.

and Israel does not want to get involved in the personal argument between Kreisky and Wiesenthal.[15]

The deputy director-general of the Israeli Ministry of Foreign Affairs responsible for Europe, Gershon Avner, had already expressed his discomfort with the Kreisky-Wiesenthal confrontations in 1970. In a confidential telegram to the Israeli ambassador in Vienna, Avner asks to officially reach out to Kreisky and explicitly point out to him that the affair should not be connected to Austrian-Israeli relations; he suggests to refrain from exclaiming, "We Israelis, because we are Jewish, support Wiesenthal's work." Due to Israeli interests, Avner writes, "we must see to it that there is a clear separation between the Kreisky-Wiesenthal conflict and Israel." According to Avner, Israeli strategic interests needed to overcome "intellectual and emotional accuracy," and therefore, Israel could not be seen as supporting Wiesenthal. "What we demand is a separation of the cases without taking an official stand as an Israeli embassy in that matter," says Avner.[16]

To be sure, the Israelis were also critical of Wiesenthal. "As we know, Wiesenthal is a problematic figure and not necessarily pleasant," reports Israeli deputy ambassador in Vienna Michael Peled.[17] In his telegram to the Foreign Ministry, Peled refers to the proximity of Wiesenthal's press conference to the elections as "a tactical error" and that no harm would have been done if he had revealed the new facts one or two months later. The Israeli diplomat connects Kreisky's anger to Wiesenthal's desire to prevent a Social-Liberal coalition. However, writes Peled, after it was clear that Kreisky did not need to form such a coalition,

15   Shek to Dagan, telegram, 14 October 1975, (Austria: Office of Prime Minister Yitzhak Rabin, 1974–77), 20.4.1974–3.10.1977, Israel State Archives (Item Reference: 000wl1q/Physical Reference: 4212/9-א), 150, Jerusalem, Israel.

16   Avner to Shek, telegram, 4 September 1970, (Austria: Diplomatic Relations with Austria on a Governmental Level, 1970–71), 1.1.1970–31.12.1971, Israel State Archives (Item Reference: 0002ysm/Physical Reference: 4556/30-חצ), 294, Jerusalem, Israel.

17   Peled to Yaish, 13 Oct. 1975, (Austria: Rabin, 1974–77), ISA, 148–49.

it was "unclear why Wiesenthal revealed the information specifically when he did so."

Eventually, after the Austrian government's meeting on October 21, 1975, Kreisky delivered a statement to the press on the Kreisky-Peter-Wiesenthal affair.[18] Out of the blue, and without any evident context, he declared that a kind of "mysterious racism" existed and that "it has not been scientifically proven that the Jewish people exist. There is a unity in belief, in which, at certain times and certain conditions, brought it to a unity in destiny. However, those who do not believe in the existence of the Jewish race are taken out of the 'group.' This is an intolerant and hidden racism." Kreisky added that, since 1970, Wiesenthal had attacked him "in the service of Israel."

As a result of these comments, the Israeli press continuously attacked the Jewish Austrian chancellor. Kreisky's statements also shocked the Israeli diplomats who had said before that it would be better not to comment on the Kreisky-Peter-Wiesenthal affair. On October 22, 1975, Ambassador Dagan wrote a telegram back to the Jerusalem headquarters asking to change the Israeli response. "Until now, my position was that we must not get involved in any way or take a public stance on the Peter-Wiesenthal affair," Dagan says in the telegram. "Kreisky's statements yesterday, prevent us from continuing with this line. He has turned the affair into an anti-Zionist attack and even explicitly mentions Israel. It is easily possible to understand his words as a clear hint that we [Israel] are part of Wiesenthal's Mafia."[19]

Dagan suggests that the best way to act would be to receive an official order from the Israeli government, urging him to arrange a meeting at the Austrian Foreign Ministry, as Israel could

18   Peled to Office of Minister of Foreign Affairs, telegram, 22 October 1975, (Austria: Office of Prime Minister Yitzhak Rabin, 1974–77), 20.4.1974–3.10.1977, Israel State Archives (Item Reference: 000wl1q/Physical Reference: 4212/9-א), 142, Jerusalem, Israel.

19   Dagan to Shek, telegram, 22 October 1975, (Austria: Office of Prime Minister Yitzhak Rabin, 1974–77), 20.4.1974–3.10.1977, Israel State Archives (Item Reference: 000wl1q/Physical Reference: 4212/9-א), 141, Jerusalem, Israel.

not ignore Kreisky's statement. At such a meeting, Dagan would accentuate to his counterparts that although Israel viewed the matter as an internal Austrian one, "we are surprised and worried by the Chancellor's words which refer to Zionism and Israel and demand a clarification of this part of his statements."[20]

Dagan continues his report by sharing notes from his private conversation with Steiner (probably Ludwig Steiner, former political director and deputy secretary-general of the Austrian Ministry of Foreign Affairs), who told him that "he and his friends are surprised by the lack of 'Jewish response' to the Peter Affair and especially to Kreisky's position." He pressed that he did not necessarily mean Austrian Jewry but, instead, referred to the lack of an Israeli response. "His hint was clear and I think he is correct," says Dagan.[21]

The Israeli response came shortly after Ambassador Dagan's telegram. On October 23, 1975, the deputy general director for Europe, Zeev Shek, shared with the ambassador Israel's action plan in response to Kreisky's statements.[22] "We shall work in three different fields," Shek announces in this message.

First, Austrian ambassador Johanna Nestor was summoned to the Foreign Ministry in Jerusalem. At this meeting, Shek expressed his "surprise" and asked for clarifications on Kreisky's statements about Israel. Shek continued, saying that the Israelis did not rely on the Austria Press Agency's (APA) text about Kreisky's allegations. "We do not want our relations with Austria to deteriorate. Nevertheless, it is clear that the publication of the text has caused many negative public opinion reactions," stated Shek. Ambassador Nestor claimed that she had not received the official version and had only learned about it through the Israeli press. She also said that Austria did not want the situation to deteriorate and that she had already mentioned that the affair might harm the atmosphere

---

20 Dagan to Shek, 22 Oct. 1975, (Austria: Rabin, 1974–77), ISA, 141.

21 Dagan to Shek, 22 Oct. 1975, (Austria: Rabin, 1974–77), ISA, 141.

22 Shek to Dagan, telegram, 23 October 1975, (Austria: Office of Prime Minister Yitzhak Rabin, 1974–77), 20.4.1974–3.10.1977, Israel State Archives (Item Reference: 000wl1q/Physical Reference: 4212/9-א), 138–39, Jerusalem, Israel.

prior to the planned 1975 meeting between Israeli prime minister Rabin and Kreisky.[23]

Second, Shek explains that the World Jewish Congress and
B'nai B'rith were beginning to tackle Jewish and racism issues,
which was to be encouraged.

Third, the Foreign Ministry should try to guide and brief the
press on this issue, although Shek was skeptical about the degree
to which this message could be controlled.

All these objections were secondary to concerns like continuing moving Jewish immigrants from Austria, Austria voting with
Israel on the "Zionism is racism" resolution in the United Nations, and the bilateral relations between Israel and Austria. These
were the main goals of Israeli policy. "We must separate between
diplomatic actions and the public campaign," writes Shek. "This
would help Kreisky to back off, should he wish to do so or at least
minimize the Israeli connection in his conflict with Wiesenthal.
It is vital that these important interests not be harmed by esca-
lating the argument on the bilateral level." Simultaneously, Shek
includes that Israel would "settle the bill with Kreisky" on the
Jewish matter through the Jewish organizations and the papers.
"We are aware of Kreisky's sensitivity to any Jewish or Israeli matter, but the Schönau experience shows us that despite the verbal
deterioration, Kreisky did not dare to touch the movement of
Jewish immigrants," says Shek. "Indeed, he had even improved his
stance on this matter."[24]

One day after the described meeting between Shek and
Ambassador Nestor, Chancellor Kreisky unexpectedly phoned
Ambassador Dagan. Dagan reports this call in a highly classified telegram addressed directly to the Israeli minister of
foreign affairs, Yigal Allon, and Prime Minister Yitzhak Rabin.[25]

---

23 Shek to Dagan, 23 Oct. 1975, (Austria: Rabin, 1974–77), ISA, 138–39.

24 Shek to Dagan, 23 Oct.1975, (Austria: Rabin, 1974–77), ISA, 138–39.

25 Dagan to Shek and Office of Minister of Foreign Affairs, 24 October 1975,
(Austria: Office of Prime Minister Yitzhak Rabin, 1974–77), 20.4.1974–
3.10.1977, Israel State Archives (Item Reference: 000wl1q/Physical Reference: 4212/9-א), 135–37, Jerusalem, Israel.

Kreisky's reaction is depicted in a very critical manner by the Israeli ambassador: "Kreisky phoned me while I was at home and for 20 minutes he erupted in a way that could not be described other than on the edge of insanity." Dagan portrays Kreisky's method of communication as an "unstopped flow of attacks and slanders."

On the procedural level, Kreisky expressed his protest by noting that Shek, "a bureaucrat at the Foreign Ministry[,] will demand clarifications from a foreign Prime Minister." Shek needed "to learn how to act" appropriately, and Kreisky wondered whether "Israel is such a young state that they do not know in its Foreign Ministry what is allowed and what is not." Kreisky continued that Israel did not know what it was doing "when it protects Wiesenthal." He repeated the public accusations he had previously made about Wiesenthal's connection to Israel. "Wiesenthal is despicable and remained alive only because he was an agent of the Gestapo," said Kreisky, "and today he is not only an agent for Israel but also of other countries." He alleged that he had documentation to prove these accusations and was eagerly looking forward to presenting them in court.

Ambassador Dagan answered, saying that Israel considered the Kreisky-Peter-Wiesenthal affair an internal Austrian matter and assured him that Israel had no intention to intervene. He added that while, contrary to Kreisky, one should always pursue Nazi war criminals, there was no reason for Kreisky to involve Israel in this particular situation.

Kreisky responded by claiming that he had not attacked Israel. All he had said, Kreisky attested, was a marginal notation arguing that the "Israel people" existed but not the "Jewish people" and that the scientific proof of this could be found in a book written by the Jewish author Ignaz Zollschan.

Dagan, in turn, said that he knew Zollschan and thought him a "good Zionist." "I do not think that his books prove the non-existence of the Jewish people but the conversation that we are holding is diplomatic and not ideological," commented Dagan. The

Israeli ambassador did not understand why Kreisky had used this example or needed to include Israel in his attacks on Wiesenthal.

Kreisky denied mentioning Israel and asserted—without substantiation—that he had "just quoted Wiesenthal who in 1970 told Golda Meir that Kreisky must be liquidated because as a Jew he must serve Israel and he did not." Kreisky aggressively added, "This is all the Hutzpah that the Jews think that they can demand from any person of Jewish origin. In such a case it is permitted to say anything." Kreisky railed that Wiesenthal constantly provoked him due to his nationalism. He then put forward a warning to "all those who ignore the contemptibleness of Wiesenthal." They should know that he would not withdraw "but turn to war and it will be 'a new Schönau' and definitely not a happy one."[26]

At this point, Kreisky suddenly raised the topic of his mentally disabled brother, who lived in Israel. (See chapter six for more details.) He alleged that his brother, Paul, had been missing for a month, and "horrible things were being done to him." He suspected that Paul had been forced to leave Israel—"probably to Holland," where "Wiesenthal had many friends and was now being held in order to be used in the right moment against him."

Recounting this episode in the telegram, Dagan says that at that moment, Kreisky "reached the limit of mental sanity." Therefore, Dagan decided to shorten the conversation by assuring Kreisky that Israel had no interest in deteriorating its relationship with Austria. Moreover, the two agreed to meet the following week to discuss a few open questions. "I suggest to wait with this diagnosis and with a suitable therapy until after our meeting on Monday," writes Dagan. Kreisky ended the conversation, stating that whatever he had said had been said in "good spirit"—as he had done "many good deeds to Israel." Ambassador Dagan felt that Kreisky knew he had made a "serious error" and was afraid of the consequences.[27]

---

26   Dagan to Shek and Office of Minister of Foreign Affairs, 24 Oct. 1975, (Austria: Rabin, 1974–77), ISA, 135–37.

27   Dagan to Shek and Office of Minister of Foreign Affairs, 24 Oct. 1975, (Austria: Rabin, 1974–77), ISA, 135–37.

Shortly after, on October 27, 1975, Dagan met with Kreisky. He congratulated Kreisky on his electoral victory but mainly wanted to clear the air around the Kreisky-Peter-Wiesenthal affair.[28] He thanked the chancellor on behalf of the foreign minister for Austria's pro-Israel stance on the anti-Zionist resolution at the United Nations. After a short while, Kreisky started to read from a large file with all sorts of reports concerning Wiesenthal's past and his connections to the Gestapo. As Dagan recounts, he stopped Kreisky after a few minutes and said, "although it is interesting, it is not connected to us." Kreisky then repeated all that he had previously told the ambassador on their phone call, to which Dagan replied that he would not get involved in an ideological discussion on the Jewish problem. "We both definitely remember these discussions in our days at the youth movements," said Dagan. "Now we are holding a diplomatic dialogue and I hope that you are interested not less than us in purifying the atmosphere." Dagan suggested calling Kreisky's secretary into the room and deciding on a joint statement that would end the deterioration of the situation. Kreisky immediately agreed, and "we sent the message to the press through APA," recalls Dagan.[29]

The chancellor and the ambassador addressed the press with a joint statement following the meeting.[30] Kreisky announced that the attacks against parliament member Peter should be viewed only as an internal Austrian matter. He also clarified that he had never doubted the right of the State of Israel and the existence of its people. Austria, as it had done in the past, would work to find a peaceful resolution to the Middle Eastern conflict.

---

28   Dagan to Shek, telegram, 27 October 1975, (Austria: Office of Prime Minister Yitzhak Rabin, 1974–77), 20.4.1974–3.10.1977, Israel State Archives (Item Reference: 000wl1q/Physical Reference: 4212/9-א), 129–30, Jerusalem, Israel.

29   Dagan to Shek, 27 Oct. 1975, (Austria: Rabin, 1974–77), ISA, 129–30.

30   Dagan to Shek, telegram, 27 October 1975, (Austria: Office of Prime Minister Yitzhak Rabin, 1974–77), 20.4.1974–3.10.1977, Israel State Archives (Item Reference: 000wl1q/Physical Reference: 4212/9-א), 131, Jerusalem, Israel.

On December 17, 1975, Ambassador Dagan again met with Kreisky to discuss various matters.[31] According to Dagan's account, most of the meeting dealt with "rational matters" concerning potential Israeli dialogue with the Palestinians and the Arab world. At the end of the discussion, Kreisky brought up the Kreisky-Peter-Wiesenthal affair again. Dagan writes, "It is hard to imagine the change in the way he talked." Suddenly Kreisky spoke "without any sense or reason and barely let me respond. He did not stop complaining, was angry and miserable. He complained about the Israeli press and continued with talking about 'all the evil that the Jews have done.'" Dagan, Kreisky declared, had no idea how much he had suffered from "the Jews." Kreisky blamed Wiesenthal for receiving numerous letters from various Jews that had a "Nazi Style." He repeated all the accusations against Wiesenthal again. However, he accused him of being an "American agent" instead of an Israeli or a Gestapo one this time. He provided details about his brother's situation and claimed that he was not convinced that Wiesenthal was not connected to his disappearance. "I shall continue my struggle against Wiesenthal and the editor of *Profil*, Lingens," said Kreisky. Dagan then decided to cut him off and repeated the requests for not involving Israel in Austrian and Austrian Jewish affairs. Kreisky responded that he was "not afraid of growing antisemitism as in the United States it is much more poisonous than in Austria." In addition, he promised not to involve Israel in the affair.[32]

Although the notion that Wiesenthal was "an American agent" is bizarre enough, Kreisky's charges that he was in some way a Gestapo agent are even more so. Historian Tom Segev visited the Bruno Kreisky Archives to see Kreisky's sources regarding the allegation around Wiesenthal and the Gestapo. He reports the following:

---

31 Dagan to Shek, telegram, 17 December 1975, (Austria: Office of Prime Minister Yitzhak Rabin, 1974–77), 20.4.1974–3.10.1977, Israel State Archives (Item Reference: 000wl1q/Physical Reference: 4212/9-א), 107–109, Jerusalem, Israel.

32 Dagan to Shek, 17 Dec. 1975, (Austria: Rabin, 1974–77), ISA, 107–109.

I was there to see on what Kreisky based his claims. I was treated in a very honorable way. They brought three pieces of newspaper articles, which hardly seemed serious evidence. I asked again [about] what Kreisky knew about Wiesenthal, to which they replied that such evidence was confidential. At that point, I stated that I would write that they were hiding evidence. The reason for this, they claimed, consisted of the fact that other people's personal information was present. I then said, by all means, hide the names, to which, absurdly, they claimed to have no budget. I replied that I would pay! They finally agreed, and so I did. I waited for the material to reach me for three months. Eventually, when it arrived, I saw that 90 percent of it was based, no less, on letters Kreisky received from Nazis and antisemites, mostly from South America and other countries! (2020, pers. comm.)

Segev adds that this evidence was unsuitable for a newspaper article, let alone a chancellor. Furthermore, the letters were written *while* the conflict with Wiesenthal took place. Moreover, Kreisky had thought that relevant, damning evidence could be obtained from an old couple in Vienna. However, when the Austrian secret police had interrogated the couple, they had found no credible evidence whatsoever. The whole accusation had amounted to nothing and had been, unmistakably, libelous, Segev confirms (ibid.). Segev's version must be the prevailing one because American analyst Joshua Muravchik's claims—that Kreisky's allegation against Wiesenthal came from the intelligence service of Communist Poland—remain unsubstantiated.[33]

In the Kreisky archive box concerning the Wiesenthal case, Segev also found reports by the secret police of Wiesenthal's actions

---

33 In a report on Wiesenthal, the Austrian news magazine *Profil* reported as early as the end of October of 1975 that the Austrian state security policy was in possession of materials produced by the Polish intelligence service and that these documents contained charges of collaboration (see Muravchik 2014; footnote 19).

immediately after his release from Mauthausen. What is more, Segev discovered copies of Wiesenthal and his wife's claims for reparations from Germany in the same box. These documents included intimate and personal health details. Segev wondered how these documents came to be there and surmised that Wiesenthal had been a "target" of Austrian intelligence from early on. (Ironically, the same Austrian sources never discovered that Wiesenthal had worked in the Mossad for ten years, as Segev reveals in his book.)

When Segev's book about Wiesenthal was published in 2010, Austrian president Heinz Fischer said on TV that it was wrong that Wiesenthal had been tracked but added that all people had been similarly tracked. Nevertheless, it is troubling that this highly personal information was available and on Kreisky's desk at a moment of political conflict.

Kreisky's actions in the whole affair are highly puzzling and pose some interesting questions: What was Kreisky's decision-making process, and how did it lead to his sometimes nonsensical reactions to the series of events? What motivated Kreisky in the first place to involve himself in such an intensive way, especially when it concerned him only indirectly? What were the reasons for Kreisky's hostility toward Wiesenthal? What was Kreisky's contribution to the rapid displacement from Peter's Nazi past to Wiesenthal's within the Austrian public debate? Would Kreisky have reacted similarly had the accusations been made public by someone other than Wiesenthal? Finally, why did Kreisky involve Israel in the affair? Many of the answers to these questions remain unclear yet deserve consideration.

Prior to analyzing Kreisky's role in the affair, we must consider that Wiesenthal, too, was a highly complex and contested personality in his own right—and Kreisky was well aware of this. Although Tom Segev's comprehensive 2010 biography of Wiesenthal recognizes his many impressive achievements, it does not ignore his somewhat-egomaniacal character and tendency to exaggerate and make accusations, which were at times unfounded. Segev also notes that Wiesenthal sometimes presented different versions of the same events. This inclination toward "untruth," Segev suggests, flowed from what he calls Wiesenthal's "survivor guilt," as well as from a temptation to provide well-told stories. Like other Holocaust survivors, there was an occasional urge to indulge in fantasies, such as his rescue from the camps and exaggerating his suffering. There are legitimate reasons to doubt Wiesenthal. Furthermore, as Segev (2020, pers. comm.) states, Vienna was a hive of gossip in which everyone told stories about everyone else. It was quite easy to invent tales about people. In the same way, Kreisky could have heard similar rumors about Wiesenthal.

Within a short time, there was consensus in Austrian discourse, which transformed the "Peter affair" into the "Wiesenthal affair" and finally into the "Kreisky-Peter-Wiesenthal affair." The discussion focused on a distraction: whether or not Wiesenthal was a pleasant person and whether or not he should have revealed the relevant information at a later point. All this, however, ignored the real issue at hand: that of Peter's past. Ambassador Dagan refers to this in a secret telegram to his Jerusalem headquarters.[34] "It was horrifying that the reactions were that 'one must forget and end the account,'" writes Dagan. "I do not see that the primary question which is discussed is whether a person with a problematic past has a place in political life. The reactions revealed the Austrian fear of awakening their 'Skeletons in the closet.'"

Former Israeli *Maariv* journalist to Vienna Menachem Oberbaum, who developed close relations with the chancellor, suggests that Kreisky's support of Peter mainly was related to his basic political needs. "He was a politician, and he needed the people's support," says Oberbaum. "As chancellor, he needed to act accordingly" (2020, pers. comm.). As is well known, in the aftermath of World War II, many former Nazis were living and

---

34   Dagan to Director of Europe Department, telegram, 14 October 1975, (Austria: Office of Prime Minister Yitzhak Rabin, 1974–77), 20.4.1974–3.10.1977, Israel State Archives (Item Reference: 000wl1q/Physical Reference: 4212/9-א), 147, Jerusalem, Israel.

working in Austria, and because of this, says Barbara Taufar, "no one could form a government without them." Taufar similarly portrays Kreisky's actions as ones based on his political needs. "The issue with Peter was connected to domestic politics," says Taufar. "Kreisky wanted to retain power, and as the conservative party had done previously, he took people into his government who had an SS past. This was a controversial subject, but that is politics" (2020, pers. comm.). Kreisky believed, on a political level, an attack on an implacable pursuer of Nazi war criminals would not harm his popularity with the Austrian electorate. On the contrary, it would reinforce his image as a patriotic Austrian (Wistrich 2007, 12). Historian Günter Bischof (2004) says that Kreisky's defense of Peter was undoubtedly a political move and was intended to keep from reawakening Austria's complicated, hibernating memory of the war.

Georg Lennkh points out another perspective. He thinks that the press blew the Kreisky-Peter-Wiesenthal affair out of proportion. He alleges that when Kreisky became chancellor, he was perhaps a bit sloppy with his appointment of cabinet ministers, but it was not aimed at "clearing Nazis." "He made this alliance with the Freedom Party," says Lennkh. "I think Kreisky could have been more careful choosing people for his government. However, he definitely did not intend to appoint Nazis. Although he protected Peter, I do not think he was happy with his choice" (2015, pers. comm.).

Even so, Oberbaum emphasizes the emotional "Jewish" aspect that characterized the Kreisky-Wiesenthal confrontation: "The true fight between the two started mostly because Wiesenthal always reminded Kreisky that he was Jewish" (2020, pers. comm.). Kreisky's former secretary, Thomas Nowotny, reinforces this point, saying that Kreisky resented people who referred to his Jewishness to "push him to pro-Israeli policies" (2020, pers. comm.). This, he says, produced very emotional reactions in Kreisky. He did not want his "Jewishness" to be a factor in formulating Austrian policy.

The rivalry between Wiesenthal and Kreisky had deep roots. Kreisky referred to Wiesenthal as an *Ostjude*, a negative term used to describe Yiddish-speaking Jews from Eastern European countries who had immigrated to Germany and Austria. Kreisky held that there was "nothing in common" between the highly acculturated Jews of America and Western Europe, the *Ostjuden*, and the Sephardic masses from Islamic lands. The closest phrase one could use was "a community of fate," a term borrowed from Otto Bauer and widely used by the Nazis (Wistrich 2007, 13). Tom Segev supposes that Kreisky regarded Wiesenthal "not just as a political opponent but rather as an enemy, because Wiesenthal was a threat to his Austrian identity" (2010, 285). Furthermore, Kreisky had problems with Wiesenthal's center, which was a "reminder of the blackest hole in their history" for Austrians (Wistrich 2007, 11).

Both Kreisky and Wiesenthal used their biographical background in the Austro-Hungarian Monarchy to establish their Austrian patriotism and loyalty to the Austrian state. However, there was another factor at play here. Most critics acknowledge that Kreisky's outburst against Wiesenthal was connected to a deep anxiety about the assimilated Jews' loss of status, one that conjured up the confrontation between Eastern and Western Jews in the nineteenth century (Reiter 2013, 20).

Kreisky's view of other Jews in Austria confirms the theory that he made a distinction between *Ostjuden* and Western Jews. In his memoirs, he speaks fondly of the Austrian ambassador to Sweden after 1945, Baron Winterstein, an aristocrat of Jewish descent. Although the two were political rivals, he refers to him in the following fond terms: "He belonged to that group that one called the 'Jewish barons,' of which there were a great number in Austria, without caring about whether they were baptized or unbaptized" (ibid., 21).

Menachem Oberbaum, who considered himself a close friend of both Wiesenthal and Kreisky, recalls that in his private meetings with the chancellor, it was apparent that talking about

Wiesenthal was taboo. This was linked to Kreisky's issues with being labeled Jewish, as discussed in the introduction. According to Oberbaum, it "drove Kreisky mad" when others reminded him of his Jewishness, and Wiesenthal had done that on many occasions. "All his life, Kreisky fought to be considered as an ordinary Austrian and not as a Jew," says Oberbaum. "Then comes this person and tells him—[it doesn't] matter what you do—you will stay Jewish" (2020, pers. comm.). Oliver Rathkolb says Kreisky demonstrated an extreme emotional sensitivity whenever Jewish or Israeli issues were raised. This was especially the case with Wiesenthal, says Rathkolb, where Kreisky "went out of control." "He always feared that his Jewishness [would] be shown to the Austrian people, and he [would] become a target of antisemitism again," analyzes Rathkolb. "He thought that Wiesenthal was pushing him to his Jewishness and that the Austrians would attack him due to his Jewishness" (2015, pers. comm.).

For all that, Kreisky still chose to publicly deploy his background as a Jew and one who had lost many family members in the Holocaust at that. In this instance, he utilized this truth to denounce Wiesenthal's actions and—with somewhat twisted logic—to "erase the past once and for good." He also referenced this "past" when debating Jewish, Israeli, or Palestinian issues in general. This served him to counter the criticism that he denied his Jewishness.

Historian Elisabeth Röhrlich (2020, pers. comm.) has shown that Kreisky always pointed to this personal background when discussing his relations to Israel. Kreisky's justifying narrative, per Röhrlich, went like this: "Yes, I have a Jewish background, and most of my family members died in the concentration camps, but I lived in Vienna in the time between wars, and I even became friends [with] Nazis in the prison. The fact that I have a Jewish background doesn't change the fact that the Austrofascist state was a bigger enemy than the Nazis" (ibid.).

In a 1975 press conference, Kreisky mentioned his relationship with the Gestapo—as a former prisoner—to legitimize his claims regarding Wiesenthal's collaboration with the Nazis. Which, as discussed above, were found to be fictional by the Austrian court. Such claims could not have been made by a non-Jewish person without being marked as antisemitic. As a Jewish victim of Nazism, Kreisky's allegations against other Jews seemed more objective, unbiased, and rational, regardless of the terminology he employed. However, it must be noted that his terminology, at times, resembled that of outspoken antisemites.

Kreisky's Jewish sensitivity was heightened when he dealt with criticism directed against him by Israeli politicians and various American Jewish leaders. However, his behavior and reactions in the Kreisky-Peter-Wiesenthal affair were disproportionate and extreme, almost pathological. This was more than simple personal rivalry. Röhrlich says, "Kreisky just hated Wiesenthal—the way he was, his methods" (ibid.).

However, this does not explain why the popular Austrian chancellor spent so much of his time and energy on Wiesenthal's comments, as judgmental as they may have been. Menachem Oberbaum compares Kreisky's behavior to an Israeli prime minister who would start a war against a local, critical opposition leader in a small and irrelevant town. "This was an insignificant event, which Kreisky made into a big fight just because Wiesenthal had touched on a sensitive point in Kreisky. He could and should have ignored the whole thing," says Oberbaum (2020, pers. comm.). Rathkolb suggests that Kreisky's behavior, when it came to such matters, was "completely irrational" (2015, pers. comm.).

When reading the reports of the Israeli diplomats, it seems that Kreisky was keen on raising these sensitive topics, even when his Israeli counterparts were willing to overlook Kreisky's dramatic accusations against Wiesenthal and his alleged connection to Israel. In the delicate relationship between Israeli leaders and Kreisky, it was usually the Israelis who raised their concern and publicly criticized Kreisky when they thought he had done something that was against their agenda. In this case, however, the Israelis did not publicly oppose the chancellor. One could argue that Kreisky's eagerness to involve Israel in this affair came from an emotional connection and a desire to receive Israeli support for his claims. Alternatively, it is possible to look at this as a kind of delusion for Kreisky in which there was a global Jewish conspiracy aimed against him where Wiesenthal was fantasized as an agent of foreign Jewish powers.

THE WALDHEIM AFFAIR:

Background

In 1986, former Austrian diplomat, statesman, and ÖVP member Kurt Waldheim (1918–2007) decided to run for the office of Austrian president. Waldheim, who had served as the United Nations' secretary-general between 1972 and 1981, did not win an absolute majority in the first round of the election. In the second round, he ran against the SPÖ candidate, Kurt Steyrer. During that period, several serious allegations were raised accusing Waldheim of war crimes, which he had supposedly committed during World War II as an officer in the German Army and an active member of the Sturmabteilung (SA). Waldheim was harshly criticized by several Austrian politicians, especially Chancellor Fred Sinowatz (SPÖ), but most of the attacks came from abroad. The World Jewish Congress (WJC) led the international opposition to his candidacy. Waldheim's party, the ÖVP, responded by using antisemitic language, which appealed to Austrian voters who favored him. Ultimately, Waldheim won the election. All the while, Waldheim denied any involvement in war crimes, claiming that he had done nothing but "his duty as a soldier." He may have been victorious in Austria, yet his unclear war role isolated Waldheim in the international community, and he was even banned from entering the United States. The Austrian government's commission, which had been formed to investigate the allegations, found that Waldheim must have known about the war crimes, but there was no tangible evidence as to his personal involvement (*Encyclopædia Britannica*).

The Waldheim Affair and Austria Dealing with Its Past

As the WJC exposed more facts about Waldheim's wartime activities, Austria's problematic relations and methods of dealing with its Nazi past became unmistakable and more publicly visible. The Waldheim affair was the catalyzer that brought Austria's relationship to its past under intense scrutiny for the first time (Bunzl 1995). However, for many Austrians, the allegations against Waldheim were interpreted as Jewish attacks against a highly respected Austrian diplomat. What is more, this fundamentally challenged the country's collective image of victimhood. As a result, Waldheim was defended not only by his own political party but also by most of the national media. The 1986 campaign was seen as the struggle to keep "Austria's founding myth," that the country was the first victim of National Socialism, intact. Waldheim said that the criticism against him was threatening to "discredit an entire generation" of "old fighters" (ibid., 15).

Waldheim's presidency was seen by many as a representation of Austria's unwillingness or inability to confront its role in the Third Reich and produced much international critique. Nevertheless, it also resulted in gradual, domestic critical approaches. In Austria, the controversy led to outspoken opposition against Waldheim by several intellectuals and artists (Bunzl 1995). The group, who protested Waldheim's candidacy in frequent demonstrations, steadily raised awareness of Austria's complicity within the Third Reich. Certainly, challenging the governing consensus and raising Austrians' consciousness about their war-crime contributions were two difficult tasks. These debates continued well into the 1990s.

Kreisky's defense that Austrians had not been involved and his insistence that foreign forces were spreading lies about Waldheim's past demonstrate the absurdity of Austria's post-1945 victim's approach, which was becoming increasingly implausible (Bischof 2004). Merely "having done one's duty" was a weak excuse that was no longer simply accepted by everyone without question, says Austrian historian Günter Bischof (ibid., 23). He adds that international pressure finally forced Austrians to confront the dark side of their World War II past (2004). Had it not been for international pressure in the late 1980s following the Waldheim affair, Austrians still might be living with their "conspiracy of silence," even though many of them had been perpetrators of and accessories to Hitler's war crimes (ibid.). The former Israeli ambassador to Vienna, Talya Lador-Fresher, shares this view: "In the first forty years, until the Waldheim affair, Austria did not deal with its Nazi past. ... People in the Waldheim era talked openly against Jews. The reflection and change had begun then" (2019, pers. comm.).

The Austrian Jewish Community and the Waldheim Affair

Public discourse about Jews in Austria became a serious cause for concern for the Austrian Jewish community in the wake of the Waldheim affair. While antisemitic sentiments had been openly expressed by members of the government almost forty years earlier, during the meetings of Austria's Council of Ministers (immediately after 1945), times had changed. Hostile, anti-Jewish expressions were considered public political taboos after 1945 in Austria.

However, as scholar Ruth Wodak (1991) correctly asserts, while the bon ton of Austria praised the Jews who contributed to Austrian culture and displayed pride for their Jewish friends, many expressed their dissatisfaction with the fact that they were not allowed to criticize individual Jews. Non-Austrian Jews were described as "dishonorable," or worse.

Antisemitic Stereotypes during the Waldheim Affair

Wodak (1991) identifies four main antisemitic stereotypes that were frequently used in 1986, the year Kurt Waldheim ran for the office of Austrian president:

1. *Christian antisemitism*: The mass media in 1986 portrayed Jews as the murderers of Christ and as traitors according to a longtime prejudice.

2. *The "dishonest" or "dishonorable" Jew and the "tricky Jews"*: Terms that originated with Judas's betrayal of Christ, along with economic stereotypes, were repeatedly used when referencing the actions taken by the WJC in the course of the Waldheim debate.

3. *The Jewish conspiracy*: The "campaign" against Waldheim was portrayed as part of the Jewish control and domination of the international press, banks, political power, and capital—all part of a Jewish world conspiracy.

4. *Jews are privileged*: The Jews who had "emigrated" before the Holocaust and therefore had been able to avoid a far worse fate did not have a legitimate reason to complain. According to these accusations, Jews who had not been in concentration camps did not have a justifiable claim regarding the past.

Wodak analyzes such antisemitic terminology in terms of inclusion and exclusion. The judgment concerning "insiders" and "outsiders," or "them" and "us," was combined with descriptions used for the WJC. The *Neue Kronen Zeitung* describes the organization in an article from April 2, 1986, like this: "That whippersnapper, General Secretary Singer ... the private club with that bombastic name, World Jewish Congress."

The directors of the Jewish Community of Vienna conducted a press conference on June 18, 1986, where they presented a collage of statements by the ÖVP regarding Jews and Jewish organizations. One such statement mentioned Jewish organizations' "untrustworthy and dishonorable methods." Another talked about the "dishonorable members of the WJC ... full of hate." More examples included lines like, "Lies—deception and breaking promises—having no culture and simplistic and unfounded hate. The crying of the puppets of the WJC motivated by hate and the need for admiration. Assassins. Mafia of slanderers," (Wodak 1991, 71).

Karl Hödl, then the vice-mayor of Linz, compared "Waldheim's persecution" by the WJC to the Jews handing over Jesus to the Romans in a letter to Edgar Bronfman (WJC president in 1987). The conservative Austrian media similarly demonized the WJC and considered the group the leader of an international Jewish conspiracy against Waldheim and Austria. They also viewed the critical reporting of the international media, often referred to as the "East Coast Press," as dominated by an all-powerful Jewish lobby (Bunzl 1997).

Kreisky and the Waldheim Affair

By 1986, Bruno Kreisky had already retired from political and party activities, but his passions and prejudices involving Jewish issues never waned. Thus, early in the Waldheim debate, he adopted a public stance and accused the WJC of "exaggerated interference," alleging "some Austrians of Jewish origin" of having had a Nazi/Fascist past. Later in the campaign, Kreisky gradually kept his distance from Waldheim, whose candidacy for the United Nations' secretary-general position in the 1970s he had strongly supported. Social scientist Otmar Höll (1994) says that Kreisky's attacks mirrored his ambivalence regarding his own Jewish descent, as well as his complicated relationships with Israeli politicians and politics and with Austrian Jews over almost his entire lifetime.

Waldheim's election campaign did not only trigger antisemitism but also divided Austrian Jews, says author Andrea Reiter (2013). Per Reiter, the Waldheim affair caused a division between Austrian Jews (i.e., the generation of survivors and their descendants) and instigated a rift within the group of survivors themselves. Reiter compares the reactions of three prominent Austrian Jews to Waldheim's candidacy: the Jewish Welcome Service director Leon Zelman, "Nazi hunter" Simon Wiesenthal, and Bruno Kreisky. What appeared at first sight to be a disagreement between men affiliated with different political parties, explains Reiter, was far more complicated. Despite their differences of opinion about Waldheim, the three prominent Austrian Jews' reactions were guided by their complicity with the status quo in postwar Austria. All three, says Reiter, were united by their view that Waldheim's Jewish critics "allegedly fomented public demonstrations of antisemitism" (ibid., 11). Journalist and diplomat Barbara Taufar suggests that Kreisky criticized the WJC because he had never liked the organization. She adds that Kreisky had never liked Jews who were full of chutzpah and had considered the leaders of the WJC as such. "Kreisky loved Austria and did not like the interference of the WJC in an Austrian affair," says Taufar. "One must not forget that they had been fighting Kreisky all his career" (2020, pers. comm.).

Furthermore, Kreisky still believed that because of the large number of former Nazi Party members in Austria, former Nazis had to be reintegrated into Austria and its decision-making mechanisms (Reiter 2013). In her comprehensive research of antisemitism during the Waldheim affair, Wodak determines that the Austrian press exploited Kreisky's reaction to the Waldheim affair (1991). Kreisky's accusations legitimized the argument that the WJC had "interfered in Austria's internal affairs," says Wodak (1991). As in the Kreisky-Peter-Wiesenthal affair, instead of discussing Waldheim's role in the war, discussions were shifted to whether it was legitimate for "outsiders" to intervene in Austrian issues. The fact that these ideas were put forth by a Jew gave justification to others and opened the door for criticism (Bunzl 1997).

On March 25, 1986, the news program *Mittagsjournal* was supposed to talk about the WJC's press conference, which had not yet taken place, and dissect the accusations about the ÖVP's presidential candidate's past. However, Wodak points out that the WJC's claims were trivialized in the program. Kreisky was the first Austrian politician to be quoted, and he stated the following:

> First of all, I knew nothing about any of the things being asserted about Dr. Waldheim as a person. However, if I had known, I would certainly not have withheld my recom-

mendation in this case, because it all happened a long, long time ago. And he was a young man … but that is not what it is all about at all. The point is, that certain groups, albeit very small ones, are interfering in the Austrian campaign … with both candidates in an improper way in my opinion. I am not prepared to tolerate this. But these groups have been fighting me for decades. (Wodak 1991, 374)

To Wodak (1991, 375), Kreisky served a three-fold purpose: as the "alibi Jew" (his words, thus they carry more weight); as a former chancellor and Socialist; and, finally, as a world-wise, traveled diplomat, he was certainly someone who could estimate Waldheim's worth.

After the press conference, Waldheim was interviewed by the *Abendjournal* and asked to address the allegations against him. "Yes, I categorically deny these accusations," said Waldheim. "The former chancellor Kreisky has also already explained that these accusations by the World Jewish Congress have to do with, and I quote, 'monstrous baseness'" (ibid., 76). Waldheim continued to justify his actions as "doing one's duty," like many other Austrians in service of the Wehrmacht. By quoting Kreisky, says Wodak, Waldheim shifted the responsibility for the defamation away from him.

On March 25, 1986, the newspaper *Neue Vorarlberger Tageszeitung* wrote an article stating, "The Judenrat [Jewish council] wants sippenhaftung [kin liability]: Everybody will face the consequence. … The WJC threatens with a kind of liability in case Kurt Waldheim will be elected President, actions will be taken against him and every Austrian for the six following years" (Wodak et al. 1990, 38). On the same day, the press also reported on that Kreisky had claimed that the WJC interference was "bad" and that their accusations against Waldheim were "monstrous baseness." This statement by Kreisky was likewise the headline in many other Austrian newspapers and journals. In this context, Kreisky's statements seemed to be aimed mainly to substantiate the central claim against the WJC, maintaining that their allegations were all "defamations."

Through his remarks, Kreisky suddenly received acclaim from newspapers that previously had been highly critical of him. The *Tiroler Tageszeitung*, for example, used the following headline: "Kreisky to the World Jewish Congress: Improper." Then he was quoted in detail: "It is absolutely improper to express yourself in this way. Such threats are not common among serious people in the West. And in addition, criticizing a state that has been the only one to allow Russians of Jewish origin to pass through it" (ibid.).

The *Neues Volksblatt* headline simply said: "Kreisky: Improper Interference by Jewish Circles!" The article continued with Kreisky's quote: "The anti-Waldheim campaign of the Jewish World Congress is an outrageous one, a stupid interference in our election campaign. ... If I had run for the presidency, they would have attacked me even more" (ibid.).

Austrian historian Oliver Rathkolb says Kreisky did not realize that public discourse in Austria had begun to change during the Waldheim affair. "Two years after Waldheim was elected, I talked to Kreisky, and he told me that he feared that the open discourse about Waldheim's past would bring back antisemitism," recalls Rathkolb (2015, pers. comm.). "In reality there was a new generation, and when Waldheim came into power, the young generation revolted against this narrative of recent Austrian history," says Barbara Taufar (2020, pers. comm.). According to Rathkolb, Kreisky did not comprehend these changes and feared that discussions about the 1940s and 1950s would have adverse effects. Although he understood that Waldheim was a problematic figure, he disapproved of the debate. "He considered reviewing the past as a job for historians and not politicians," says Rathkolb (2015, pers. comm.). In the end, the open debate led Austrian society to slowly rethink its victim's doctrine and investigate its past. It took between ten and fifteen more years for Austrians to officially accept the changes (ibid.).

Waldheim and Wiesenthal

Wiesenthal's actions during the Waldheim affair present an interesting contrast to how he handled the Peter case and illustrate an unlikely similarity between Kreisky and Wiesenthal. Instead of criticizing the problematic presidential candidate as before, Wiesenthal criticized the WJC in this case. Leon Zelman—the founding editor and publisher of the journal for culture and politics *Das Jüdische Echo*, a co-founder of the Jewish Welcome Service, a Socialist, an admirer of Kreisky, and someone who had known Wiesenthal since soon after they had both been liberated—distrusted Wiesenthal. He was convinced that Wiesenthal supported Waldheim due to "obvious party considerations." Zelman and Wiesenthal had had a previously strained and distrusting relationship. Much politicking on both sides took place, and the motivations of each remain dubious.[35] However, it was also Zelman who was informing the WJC of the documents about Waldheim's past. Wiesenthal was aware of these investigations and was surprised that he had not been contacted (Reiter 2013, 16).

Eli Rosenbaum, the Israeli American litigator who directed the WJC investigation that resulted in Waldheim's Nazi past being exposed, sheds light on why Wiesenthal was not involved. In his book, *Betrayal: The Untold Story of the Kurt Waldheim Investigation and Cover-Up* (1993), Rosenbaum (48) reveals that his principal informant, whom he calls "Karl Schuller," ordered him not to consult Wiesenthal because of his aversion to Kreisky. Per Wiesenthal (1998, 386), the WJC's main reason for engaging in the campaign was to gain publicity. Wiesenthal, like Zelman, blamed the antisemitism in Austria on the WJC's interference and especially on an interview in *Profil* in March 1986. In that interview, WJC director Elan Steinberg and WJC secretary-general Israel Singer warned Waldheim and Austrians "should they elect him as their president" (ibid.).

---

35   For a detailed exposition of this strange relationship, see Andrea Reiter, *Contemporary Jewish Writing: Austria after Waldheim* (Milton Park: Routledge, 2013), 11–14.

In the wake of this interview, the ÖVP's slogan, "We Austrians will choose whom we want," became extremely popular. Wiesenthal doubted "that officials of a Jewish organization actually have the right to prompt, to provoke these antisemitic reactions unnecessarily." He went on to say, "Two young Jewish functionaries, who live in the USA, are by no means justified in this, whereas we Austrian Jews are the ones who have actually been affected" (1988, 387). The Jewish Community of Vienna, an organization that had disagreed with Wiesenthal in the past, shared his opinion on this matter. Its president, Paul Grosz, "denied to any outsider the right to teach us how we should fight antisemitism on our home ground" (Reiter 2013, 16).

When Wiesenthal was asked to check documents about Waldheim in 1971, he claimed that there was no indication of his involvement in any war crimes. Andrea Reiter refers to Tom Segev, who suspects that Wiesenthal took for granted what Waldheim had told him about his past. In 1979, Yad Vashem asked Wiesenthal to scrutinize documents once again. In the course of this research, Wiesenthal learned from a French archive that Waldheim had actually lied but decided not to reveal this information (Reiter 2013). As a result, Segev states that Wiesenthal did not have much choice but to fight the WJC and others who attempted to disclose Waldheim's past because he worried about his own credibility. According to Segev, this attempt to save face even led so far as to Wiesenthal acting as a "kind of confidential advisor" (2010, 371) to the Waldheim campaign team.

CHAPTER 5 : KREISKY AND THE 1973 MARCHEGG INCIDENT

This chapter will focus on the 1973 Marchegg incident. This incident is significant because of its intrinsic interest and worth highlighting because of how it has receded in historical memory but also highly relevant to this book because of what it reveals about Kreisky.

Among other things, the incident is ideally suited to analyze the following:

- Almost every aspect of Kreisky's complex and entangled relationship to questions of Austrian domestic politics and their connection to dilemmas of morality

- Connections to Kreisky's Jewishness

- Kreisky's views on Zionism

- Kreisky's dealings with the State of Israel

- Kreisky's views on the Palestinian question

- Kreisky's views on terrorism

- Kreisky's emotional relationship with Israeli leaders

BACKGROUND TO MARCHEGG INCIDENT

By 1973, during Kreisky's first term as chancellor, Austria was a transit point for emigrating Soviet Jews, the largest remaining Jewish population in Europe. This was exceptional as Austria was the only European country that permitted the operation of organized transit camps for masses of Soviet Jews on their way to Israel. Moreover, as a neutral country—at least in Austrian self-perception— Austria saw itself as uniquely suited to serve as an immigration corridor in both the Cold War and the Arab-Israeli conflict, mainly for humanitarian reasons. The Schönau Castle, near Vienna, had been transformed into such a transit point in 1965. Between 1965 and 1973, more than 70,000 Jews passed through the camp.

On September 28, 1973, three Jewish emigrants and one Austrian customs official were taken hostage on a train at the Austrian-Czechoslovakian border by the Syrian-based Palestinian Arab terrorist group as-Sa'iqa. Along with demanding free passage to an Arab country, as-Sa'iqa confronted the Austrian government with an ultimatum to close the Schönau transit camp or else they would execute the hostages. The Austrian government rejected the terrorists' demand to be allowed to leave the country by air along with their hostages. However, despite this refusal, the Austrian government decided to stop operations at Schönau that same day. In December 1973, the Schönau Castle Jewish transit camp was permanently closed and replaced by the Lower Austrian Provincial Red Cross Aid Station for Refugees and Other Transients.

It is surprising that although this historical event holds much significance, it has not been widely researched and has hardly played a role in scholarly discourse. For various reasons (that will be discussed in this chapter), little of this incident has remained in Israeli, Austrian, and Austrian Jewish historiography.

JEWISH IMMIGRATION THROUGH AUSTRIA

Before discussing the Marchegg terrorist incident, it is crucial to contextualize The Jewish Agency for Israel's "humanitarian operation" undertaken at Schönau Castle prior to the terrorist attack. Rescuing Soviet Jews and bringing them to Israel during the 1970s should be seen as part of the international movement toward human rights and humanitarianism in the 1970s. The pre-terrorist Schönau operation might, indeed, be an overlooked episode of this 1970s humanitarianism. According to professor of history and law Samuel Moyn (2010), the 1970s were a turning point in human-rights history. It was then that human rights began to be exploited and employed as a legitimizing political claim by new entities, such as non-governmental organizations. In this context, human rights were most often interpreted as individual protection against the state and proffered by supranational or international organizations. The journal *Human Rights Quarterly* (2014) demonstrates how the human-rights movement achieved unprecedented global prominence between the 1960s and 1980s. The activities of the Soviet dissidents who attracted worldwide attention with their heroism in facing down a totalitarian regime were central to this effort. A thorough examination of the Marchegg event and its aftermath could, consequently, also contribute to a better understanding of Cold War history in the 1970s and the role of human-rights discourse within that history.

In the first years of the Bolshevik Revolution, Jews had complete access to all educational, vocational, political, economic, and cultural opportunities provided by the Soviet systems. Although Zionism, the Hebrew language, and the Jewish faith were repressed, this was part of an anti-religious Communist ideology that also oppressed other political ideologies (Gitelman 1982). Following World War II, in which two million Soviet Jews died, an explicitly anti-Jewish campaign was launched in the Soviet Union. This led to the closing of nearly all Jewish cultural facilities by 1948. Moreover, leading Jewish cultural figures were murdered in the purges of 1952 (Gilboa 1971). Until Joseph Stalin's death in 1953, Soviet Jews were singled out and not allowed to assimilate into Russian society. They were denied equal educational, political, and vocational opportunities. Until 1971, the Soviet Union officially denied the possibility of emigration. Aside from an insignificant amount of slave laborers, prisoners of war, Nazi collaborators, and people who simply took advantage of wartime chaos to flee the Soviet Union after the war, movement out of the Soviet Union was prohibited (Gitelman 1982).

In 1952, Israel established Nativ (the Liaison Bureau), a governmental liaison organization that maintained contact with Jews living in the Eastern Bloc during the Cold War and encouraged *aliyah* (immigration to Israel). This organization reported directly to the Israeli prime minister. Lowa Eliav, who was responsible for bringing Soviet Jews to Israel in the late 1950s, explains that the unit aimed to establish contact with as many Jews as possible to bring them to Israel. "Being Israeli diplomats, we had full diplomatic relations with the Soviet Union—we could send diplomats, first secretary, second secretary, third secretary," says Eliav. "And the people we sent there, those people from the 'unit,' were especially engaged in what I call trying to map Jewish life in the Soviet Union" (1997).

There were many attempts by individuals and interest groups to raise awareness of the conditions of Jews in the Soviet Union. For example, on May 1, 1964, a thousand students gathered across from the Soviet Mission to the United Nations in Manhattan to demonstrate against the Soviet ban on baking matzos, among other anti-Jewish measures. This demonstration—the first of many to come—marked the beginning of the struggle to free Soviet Jewry (Halevi 2010). In December 1970, nine Jews and two non-Jews were tried in Leningrad for attempting to hijack a plane to flee the Soviet Union. Two were sentenced to death, while the others were harshly punished. This received much global attention, and it placed the emigration of Soviet Jews on the agenda of world politics. As a result, a few months later, one thousand Jews were permitted to leave for Israel, which turned into a steady stream after March 1971 (Gitelman 1982).

As the plight of the Soviet Jews became an international human-rights cause at the start of the 1970s, a combination of political agitation and international criticism led Moscow to ease its restrictions on emigration (Chamberlin 2012). The original decision to allow emigration, beginning in March 1971, resulted from internal and external pressure for a more liberalized policy. Another reason for Soviet decision-makers to change their policies regarding Jewish emigration was the need to expand trade relations with the West to receive economic and technological aid and amend strategic arms limitation agreements. As a result, between 1971 and 1980, over three hundred thousand Soviet citizens immigrated to Israel, the United States, the Federal Republic of Germany, Canada, Australia, and other countries in Western Europe and Latin America (Gitelman 1982).

The American Jewry campaign ("Let My People Go") became one of modern history's most successful protest movements. This quarter-century-long campaign eventually led the United States Congress to adopt the Jackson-Vanik Amendment in 1974 (Halevi 2010). This amendment, sponsored by Senator Henry Jackson, a strong advocate of human rights, made foreign trade between the United States and the Soviet Union conditional upon the Soviet Union relaxing restrictions on Jewish emigration. Western and Soviet leaders did not foresee the quick escalation and the great magnitude of the emigration movement. To be sure, motivations for immigration ranged from personal to ideological (Gitelman 1982).

Between 1968 and 1986, 270,199 Soviet Jews immigrated to Israel, the United States, and elsewhere through Austria, a neutral region in the Cold War and the only country to offer transit through its territory (*Beit Hatfutsot*). In 1965 The Jewish Agency for Israel, the largest Jewish organization worldwide, leased the Schönau Castle near Vienna and converted it into the first stopover point for immigrants on their way to Israel to facilitate the immigration movement.

The Schönau compound was comprised of a four-hundred-acre Habsburg estate, containing a twelfth-century castle and a nineteenth-century hunting lodge. The premises were surrounded by barbed-wire fences and armed guards (Chamberlin 2012). Schönau rapidly received much attention in Israel, Austria, and around the world. Palestinians and other Arab countries viewed it as an undermining of Austria's neutrality in the Arab-Israeli conflict, an attempt to alter Israel's demographic balance, and a way to push the Palestinians aside. By 1973, seventy thousand Jewish emigrants from the Communist Bloc had passed through the camp (Bachleitner 2018).

Former president of the Jewish Community of Vienna, Ariel Muzicant, places this migration in a long tradition of Austria acting as the first stop for refugees. In 1945, for instance, many displaced persons stopped in Austria on their way to the United States or Palestine. Later, Austria received Hungarian refugees in 1956 and Czech refugees in 1968, says Muzicant. "It was natural to give the Jews from the Soviet Union the option," summarizes Muzicant (2018, pers. comm.).

The official Austrian guideline for treating refugees is best illustrated in a booklet published by the Austrian government in the wake of the Marchegg event (*Events of September 28th and 29th 1973*, 7–8). The document begins by stating Austria's moral and universal responsibility: "As a permanently neutral State, Austria feels a special obligation to offer refugees or emigrants asylum or the right of passage regardless of nationality, religion or political persuasion." The document then references previous waves of immigration to Austria: "Reception has been granted to the refugees and displaced persons of the immediate post-war years, to refugees later in 1956 (Hungary) and 1968 (Czechoslovakia) and to all people who, previously or since then, have come to Austria because they feel personally under pressure or because they feel political persecution" (ibid., 7). It also details the legal grounds from which Austria derived its refugee policies, which included the Geneva Convention of 1951 on the legal position of refu-

gees and the Austria Federal Act on Refugees' Residential Rights
(Asylum Act) of March 7, 1968. According to the report, since
1945, around 1,650,000 displaced persons, emigrants, expellees,
and refugees had been "accommodated in the widest sense of
the word" and treated by integration programs, which had cost
the Austrian state some 3,600 million schillings (ibid.). Between
1956 and September 1973, states the report, 196,653 Jews had
come to Austria from Eastern Europe under this arrangement.
Of these, 74,336 had come from the Soviet Union (ibid., 8). The
freedom of these immigrants to choose their final destination is
emphasized in the document. "Any of these Jewish people emigrating from Eastern Europe who have passed through Austria
and decided due to personal reasons to stay in Austria are allowed
to stay here while they make the necessary arrangements," says
the document. "A number of them chose to remain in Austria"
(ibid.).

The former head of the liaison bureau Nativ, Naomi Ben-Ami,
who had passed through Schönau on her way to Israel as a young
child herself (only days before the Marchegg event), explains that
Austria was the only realistic transit option for many Soviet Jewish immigrants. The trains came from West Ukraine to the borders of Czechoslovakia and Hungary, where they could not stop.
It was, therefore, not possible to establish a camp there. "The
only country on the border was Austria," she says. She also states
that neither Austria nor Israel wanted the camp to be placed
where it was. However, "there were no other feasible options,"
she concludes (2020, pers. comm.). Golda Meir emphatically
shared that thought. At a government meeting, she declared that
"what I would really want is that no Jew will need to pass through
Austrian soil."[36]

---

36   Protocol of Government Meeting, top classified protocol of the Israeli,
3 October 1973 (Protocol of Government Meeting), 3.10.1973, Israel State
Archives (Item Reference: N/A as it was sent by email directly by the director
of the archive, Hagai Tsoref), 31, Jerusalem, Israel.

KREISKY AND JEWISH IMMIGRATION

While it is well known that Bruno Kreisky was the chancellor during the Marchegg event, his prior involvement concerning Jewish emigration from the Soviet Union should be similarly noted. In 1953, Kreisky was appointed undersecretary in the Foreign Affairs Department of the Austrian Chancellery, responsible for immigration issues. Former Israeli minister, prominent politician, and the founder of the National Religious Party Yosef Burg describes Kreisky's proactive role. "Much before Kreisky was the Chancellor, he was the chief negotiator with the Soviets, on behalf of Austria," says Burg. "In the 1950s he was involved with Lowa Eliav, working with The Jewish Agency, enabling Jewish immigration through Austria" (1997).

At the end of the 1970s, Professor Ilan Knapp was part of an intimate group responsible for Jewish immigration through Vienna under Chancellor Kreisky. Knapp recalls his trips to Moscow to discuss the logistics with the Soviet authorities. Knapp says that Kreisky allowed Jewish immigration through Vienna throughout his terms as chancellor, serious risks aside, purely due to his "Jewish conscience" (2019, pers. comm.).

Talya Lador-Fresher, who served as the ambassador of Israel to Vienna between 2015 and 2019, goes even further and claims that the credit for the masses of Soviet Jews who came through Austria should go to Kreisky. However, she bemoans that "instead of remembering the myriad of Jewish immigrants who came, ... what people unfortunately remember from the Marchegg event is the 'glass of water' incident" (2019, pers. comm.). (See p. 98, Kreisky & Golda Meir.)

"Kreisky always used to say that he would never forget his time as a refugee," recalls Menachem Oberbaum (2020, pers. comm.). Oberbaum says that Kreisky's past as a refugee in Sweden led to his feelings of responsibility toward other refugees. There were two competing agencies for immigrants in Vienna: The Jewish Agency and the Hebrew Immigrant Aid Society (HIAS). The Jewish Agency helped bring immigrants to Israel, while HIAS assisted with their transfer to the United States. Kreisky objected to The Jewish Agency's pressure on people to immigrate to Israel. He firmly believed in "free decision making," referring to the desired immigration destination (Berg 2000, 457). According to political scientist Fred Lazin (2020, pers. comm.), in various interviews, Kreisky was incredibly proud that he had allowed free entry to Austria and had enabled immigrants to choose where they wanted to go. Politician Yossi Sarid reprehends the Israeli attitude toward Kreisky on matters connected to Jewish immigration. "When Kreisky assisted the refugees coming from the Soviet Union," says Sarid, "he was praised in Israel, but after a minute, when he was critical, everything was forgotten" (1997). Nevertheless, Kreisky achieved several goals concerning Jewish immigration, according to *Der Spiegel*: first, a close relationship with the United States and the United Nations; second, a high international moral standing point; third, a certain "letting go" of the Austrian past; and finally, the attainment of good international public relations (Dahlke 2011, 192).

TERRORISM IN AUSTRIA

Middle Eastern terrorism formed the single most virulent brand of political violence in Austria. The Marchegg incident in 1973 was just the first of several such incidents. It was followed in 1975 when a group of international terrorists calling themselves "Arm of the Arab Revolution" occupied the Organization of the Petroleum Exporting Countries (OPEC) headquarters in Vienna. All OPEC ministers were taken hostage. The government agreed to the terrorists' demands and allowed them to leave with the hostages. In 1981, Heinz Nittel, president of the Austria-Israel Friendship Society and a leading Viennese Social Democrat, was killed by the Palestinian Abu Nidal Organization, a terror squad. Later that year, Abu Nidal terrorists attacked a Viennese synagogue, which resulted in the tragic killing of three people (Riegler 2011).

Akin to other matters, Kreisky's attitude toward terrorism was multifaceted. As historian Thomas Riegler explains, "While ... condemning terrorism, Kreisky was careful when applying the term" (2011, 71). Kreisky distinguished two forms of terrorist violence. He referred to the first of these as "terrorism for its own sake" when describing Italian or West German left-wing extremism. Kreisky thought this sort of terrorism was extremely damaging to a democratic society and could lead to a dictatorship. However, there was another kind of terrorism for Kreisky, which he approached with a sense of understanding (Riegler 2011).

Kreisky described his understanding of these terrorist acts in an interview with the Austrian magazine *Profil*: "Terrorism is one of the political weapons of the underground, of illegality. ... They are cruel and I reject them without constraint. ... But there are dictatorships, in which underground movements are fighting for freedom and democracy, and occasionally by means of employing terrorism" (ibid., 431). To Kreisky, this sort of violence, often marked the start of a political movement or a subsequently respectable political career. To highlight this point, Kreisky frequently brought up the example of Nobel Peace Prize winner and Israeli prime minister Menachem Begin, who had fought both British occupation forces and Arabs in the 1940s (Riegler 2011).

Kreisky contended that sometimes the terrorists of today are the peace partners of tomorrow, and he worked accordingly. Former minister Erwin Lanc reaffirms this, saying, "Kreisky repeatedly mentioned that people have the right to defend their existence by all means, and if they are not able to do it at home because of lack of military power, then he can understand the reason that they operate in the international arena" (2017, pers. comm.).

KREISKY'S ANTI-TERRORISM POLICY

Although Kreisky's official and public anti-terrorism policy was clear, political scientist John Bunzl (1997) points out that the attitude of the Austrian authorities was not uniform or consistent. According to Bunzl, the Austrian authorities under Kreisky acted in a circumstantial manner and drew different national and international conclusions from their experiences. Kreisky set a consistent priority to "save human lives at all costs," which overrode all other considerations. He insisted upon avoiding bloodshed in all circumstances and firmly rejected counterviolence and the policy of "no compromise." In his memoir, Kreisky (2007) says that no government has the moral right to risk the lives of hostages and that fighting terrorists who hold hostages means risking people's lives in vain. He argues that combating terror with more force is absurd and only leads to escalation.

Instead, Kreisky stressed the importance of addressing the political, social, and economic causes of terrorism. Riegler (2011) explains that Kreisky's approach was an excellent example of understanding terrorism as an expression of grievances by the weak or disenfranchised and was shaped by the interaction of political and social forces.

Kreisky's policy could perhaps be summed up by his response to a journalist who had asked him if his preoccupation with the Middle Eastern conflict had drawn radical elements to Austria. Kreisky, attempting to argue the success of his policy, said that hundreds of thousands of Soviet Jews had emigrated through Austria for fifteen years without one bomb exploding. When confronted about his dialogue with the terrorist groups, Kreisky responded, "I would talk to the devil if I could achieve something positive" (ibid., 449). Nevertheless, Kreisky's policies resulted in much domestic and international criticism.

However, how to deal with terrorist organizations was a question throughout Europe. In the 1970s, Austria, Germany (Bohr, Latsch, and Wiegrefe 2012), Italy (Hof 2018), Switzerland (Foulkes 2016), and perhaps others entered into informal and secret agreements with the Palestine Liberation Organization (PLO). These agreements were aimed at protecting these countries against terrorism. In 2008, former Italian president Francesco Cossiga confirmed an agreement of "don't harm me and I won't harm you" between the Italian government and the Popular Front for the Liberation of Palestine, and with the PLO (Klein 2008). Christian Democratic prime minister Aldo Moro, who approved of this agreement, was later murdered by Italian terrorists.

While the agreements between these countries and the PLO were kept secret, Kreisky did not try to hide his connections with the PLO. On the contrary, he was the first Western European leader to publicly accept the legitimacy of Palestinian leadership and its positions, which only a short period later became the mainstream position of the West in general and Europe in particular.

Despite this formal recognition, Palestinian extremist groups continued terrorist attacks to promote their messages. One consequence of these terrorist attacks that is still present nowadays was the founding of specialized police forces to deal with such threats. Following the massacre at the Munich Olympic Games by the Palestinian terrorist group Black September in 1972, Willy Brandt ordered the formation of the GSG 9 anti-terror special unit. It took the Austrian authorities a couple of years to establish a similar unit. As Erwin Lanc explains, "We were convinced that we must build up a counterterrorist force in case of future terrorist attacks in Austria, and therefore we formed a unit, which was called Gendarmerieeinsatzkommando—also known today as the EKO Cobra. The goal was to educate the members of this group as a sort of 'mad dogs' behavior, which is not usual in civil police service" (2017, pers. comm.).

KREISKY'S DECISION TO CLOSE THE
SCHÖNAU TRANSIT CAMP

Kreisky was aware that the presence of the Schönau camp posed a significant security threat to Austria. Moreover, the camp had become almost a kind of tourist attraction and a site of pilgrimage for prominent Israeli and Jewish guests, such as ministers, diplomats, and other officials (Riegler 2011).

In June 1972, in reaction to various threats to Jewish institutions and Austrian intelligence recommendations, an order to form a centralized Austrian security force was issued to protect Schönau: the Wachkommando Schönau/Triesting. However, the threats continued: In January 1973, three Arabian men were caught in Vienna, and three others were found on their way to Italy. All were members of the Black September Organization, a group planning an attack on Schönau. In their interrogation, the Austrians found a detailed map of Schönau, which had already been sent to Beirut. Following these events, Austria strengthened the security around the camp (Dahlke 2011).

Nevertheless, the intimidations continued. In February of that year, a man with a foreign accent telephoned the offices at Schönau, threatening that there would be an attack. In June, a suspicious vehicle was seen in the vicinity of the Schönau camp. In September, a message from the Austrian mission abroad reported that four men, assumed to be Syrians, were planning to leave for Algiers. From there, they were planning to fly to Vienna on September 6, 1973. According to Austrian security forces, their purpose was to attack the Schönau camp around September 10 or 11, 1973. In addition, an anonymous telephone call was made to the gendarmerie station in the nearby town of Günselsdorf by someone claiming to be a member of the Black September Organization. He warned of an imminent bomb attack (*Events of September 28th and 29th* 1973, 21).

Because of these various threats, at least four Israeli workers at Schönau carried weapons. The presence of an armed enclave under the administration of an Israeli government semi-official agency in the heart of Austrian territory raised questions about state sovereignty and humanitarian operations on foreign soil. There was a fear that Schönau was being transformed into a de facto piece of sovereign Israeli territory (Dahlke 2011). Kreisky accused the Jewish Agency of acting in a disrespectful and demanding way—as if they were "extraterritorial" and not under Austrian jurisdiction. He referred to their activities in the camp as "a thorn in my foot" (Berg 2000, 457). In concert with his ideological position, he also had a problem with their alleged *rassenstandpunkt* (racial viewpoint) (Dahlke 2011, 194). The Communist Party of Austria went so far as to say that Schönau was a "human smuggling center" and a "Zionist spying center" (ibid., 193).

Austria's former foreign minister Rudolf Kirchschläger complained that his government had been concerned for some time about the "over-organization" of the flow of Soviet Jews through Austria. He believed that the Israeli government's control of Schönau Castle made it "almost foreign territory and a target for Arab terrorists and therefore a threat to Austrian security." Finally, Kirchschläger attested that "the facility represented a violation of Austrian sovereignty" (Chamberlin 2012, 690). In light of these facts, there is no doubt that the Austrian government had considered closing the facility prior to the 1973 Marchegg attack.

When the Austrian government ultimately decided to close the Schönau camp in return for the hostages' release, it led to massive criticism of Chancellor Kreisky. The central claim was that he had given in to terrorists' demands. However, Kreisky tried to justify his decision by focusing on the human-life aspect of his choice. "My guiding principle in politics was to protect human life at all costs," said Kreisky, "and I acted upon this principle from the moment that I became embroiled in the hostage affair" (Berg 2000, 454). Writer Matthias Dahlke (2011, 207) states that Kreisky's political concerns were visible in his decisions even more clearly than the humanitarian aspect. He attests that Kreisky had feared that his policies would have been held culpable if an Austrian had died in such an attack.

Kreisky defended his decision at an Austrian government meeting on the eve of the attack. "If we let the terrorists fly with the hostages," said Kreisky, "people will say that I risked the life of an Austrian." Kreisky stressed that his decision to prohibit Jewish immigration by closing the camp had been a hard but necessary one. "We must prohibit the transfer, with heavy heart," said Kreisky, "but we cannot guarantee their safety any longer and we must think about the Austrian people" (ibid., 211). Kreisky insisted that the only alternative to closing the camp was allowing the terrorists to leave with the hostages.

Minister of Justice Christian Broda affirmed that Kreisky had told his ministers that Austria should not consider the Israeli government's stance on the issue. Regardless, says Dahlke (2011), the transcripts of the meetings reveal that the Israeli stance was certainly considered in the discussions. In the official Austrian statement announcing the camp's closure, the safety of the immigrants is mentioned as the main reason for the decision: "Considering the fact, that the security of Soviet Citizens emigrating in groups from the Soviet Union to Israel could be endangered while transiting through Austria, the facilities granted up to now or in future for this purpose such as the temporary accommodations of these persons in the camp of Schönau will have to cease."[37] It is important to note the terminology used to describe them. They are referred to as "Soviet Citizens" with no reference to them being Jewish.

In Kreisky's statements on Austrian radio that same evening, he reiterated his concern for the immigrants' safety considering recent events, stating, "The government has come to the conclusion that the lives of the four people held by the two Arabs

---

37   Kidron to Dinitz, telegram, 30 September 1973, (Vienna: September–December 1973), 1.9.1973–31.12.1973, Israel State Archives (Item Reference: 000w3z1/Physical Reference: 7037/15-א), 406, Jerusalem, Israel.

were in genuine danger. ... The Austrian government was not prepared to risk the lives of the three Jewish citizens of the Soviet Union" (*Events of September 28th and 29th* 1973, 82). In another radio broadcast, Kreisky explained that "once people are dead, they cannot be brought back to life. Everything else can be arranged or made good—for me, this is the only criterion." Kreisky assured listeners that Jewish immigration would continue and criticized those who claimed otherwise. "We are not preventing emigration; we are not forbidding people to pass through Austria," Kreisky stressed. "We are only discontinuing certain facilities. ... we shall continue to grant transit to all people with a valid visa, or who do not need one, wanting to pass through Austria, as we have done for years. Anything else that people may say means that they are over-dramatizing the situation" (ibid., 83).

Another factor for Kreisky's stance in the negotiations was that he knew that the Austrian legal system's most severe punishment would not be enough to deter the terrorists. "When the terrorists shoot the hostages," said Kreisky, "we can only sentence them to lifelong imprisonment, but in the next operation they will be released. They know that! In reality, they are not risking a thing! I don't really understand why they would like to commit suicide. They know what a small risk they are taking" (Dahlke 2011, 207).

On October 1, 1973, the Israeli ambassador to Austria, Yitzchak Patish, sent a telegram to the director-general of the Ministry of Foreign Affairs and Prime Minister Golda Meir.[38] Patish reports on the interview that Minister of Justice Broda gave on Austrian television. Broda asserted that the decision to close Schönau had been unilaterally decided by the Austrian government and not as part of an agreement with the terrorists or the Arab ambassadors. Broda's version was different from that of the gendarmerie head at Schwechat Airport, who had claimed Kreisky himself had suggested that Schönau be closed.

---

38   Patish to Dinitz, telegram, 1 October 1973, (Vienna: September–December 1973), 1.9.1973–31.12.1973, Israel State Archives (Item Reference: 000w3z1/Physical Reference: 7037/15-א), 381, Jerusalem, Israel.

In his comprehensive and detailed book *Im Fadenkreuz: Österreich und der Nahostterrorismus 1973 bis 1985* (2011), Thomas Riegler analyzes the Arab ambassadors' active roles in the negotiations process; roles which went far beyond being mere mediators. According to Riegler, the Lebanese, Iraqi, and Egyptian ambassadors attended a meeting at the Austrian Foreign Office on the afternoon of September 28, 1973, where they were asked to assist in conducting the negotiations with the terrorists. Shortly later, they went to the "field" to negotiate with them directly. However, just then, the terrorists made a new demand: "Austria must immediately end the transfer of Soviet citizens." In his book, Riegler speculates why this demand was only made then, what influence the ambassadors had on the terrorists' demands, and what their political influence was. Keeping in mind that Kreisky had thought about shutting down operations in Schönau before, one can assume that he had a major role in the decision-making process.

Nevertheless, Ilan Knapp, who worked closely with Kreisky on Jewish immigration a few years after the Marchegg event, attests that Kreisky's decision to close Schönau was primarily politically motivated. He points out that the Schönau camp was in the district of Wiener Neustadt in Niederösterreich, which was populated by many Nazis and their supporters, who resented that the camp operated there. To Knapp, Kreisky needed the support of that population for the 1975 elections as it was the largest support group of the Social Democratic Party. "Kreisky was not sure that he would gain the majority again in 1975, and he therefore needed those votes," says Knapp. "He wanted to give them something and therefore closed the camp" (2019, pers. comm.). In a similar vein, Dahlke (2011) alleges that public opinion was the main cause for Schönau's closure. Kreisky wanted the focus and symbolism of the place removed.

Conversely, Kreisky's assistant, Margit Schmidt, claims that the primary motivation for Kreisky was that he always sought to solve matters without bloodshed and wanted to save lives at all costs. Closing the camp, Kreisky reasoned, would be the least problematic alternative. Nevertheless, in line with some other explanations, Schmidt also recalls Kreisky viewing Schönau as a problem even prior to the events because The Jewish Agency ran it, and people were "denied the option to choose their destination" (Schmidt 2014, pers. comm.).

According to Austrian diplomat Wolfgang Petritsch, Kreisky went so far as to say, "I cannot have this prestige position that I do not give in to terrorists. Also, as a politician, I can give in to demands that are immoral if it saves lives" (2014, pers. comm.). Erwin Lanc maintains that Kreisky did not want to close Schönau before the event in Marchegg. In Lanc's estimation, the concrete question for Kreisky, in this case, was: "Shall we risk the life of the Jewish emigrants or close Schönau? The answer was clear to Kreisky" (2017, pers. comm.).

This view is shared by Kreisky's former secretary, Thomas Nowotny, who says that Kreisky could not bear the thought of people dying and was not willing to sacrifice the hostages as Helmut Schmidt of Germany had done. Per Nowotny, "He decided in favor of life." He remembers Kreisky's resentment against the "extraterritorial enclave that made sure the refugees went only to Israel." Even so, Nowotny says that Kreisky "perhaps would have wanted to change some things that he resented but did not actually think of closing it" (2020, pers. comm.).

Despite all that, Petritsch (2014, pers. comm.) says that Kreisky did not know much about the camp's operations. Only upon examination did he find out that The Jewish Agency forced the immigrants to go to Israel. Kreisky wanted the Jews who arrived in Vienna to see it as "the first stop in the free world" (ibid.) and to decide where they wanted to go from there. In fact, after Kreisky closed Schönau, people could choose not to go to Israel for the first time, says political scientist Fred Lazin (2020, pers. comm.). Lazin explains that the rabbi of the Satmar, the anti-Zionist Hasidic dynasty, worked at persuading the immigrants to continue to America. However, even independently of that activity, Lazin points out, most Jews desired to go to America and not to Israel.

THE POLITICS AND SYMBOLISM OF IDENTITY: BRUNO KREISKY MEETS GOLDA MEIR

Israeli prime minister Golda Meir, "The Iron Lady" of Israel, was a pioneering Zionist leader. She held some of the most important positions of power prior to the establishment of the State of Israel, during its critical years of formation, and finally, as it reached the pinnacle of Israeli political power. She was a highly regarded figure throughout the world—indeed, she was considered an icon by many.

In her article "Golda Meir and Bruno Kreisky—A Political and Personal Duel" (2018), Kathrin Bachleitner provides an insightful analysis of the relationship between these two prominent (Jewish and Socialist) heads of state. She states that Austria's diplomatic support for Israel in the wake of the 1967 Six-Day War and its key role as a transit hub for Eastern Jewish emigrants helped improve the relationship between the two countries to new levels. In 1972, the *Jerusalem Post* described these relations as the "best ever." Similarly, in his interview with the Israeli Socialist newspaper *Davar*, Kreisky referred to the bilateral relations as "excellent" (Petritsch 2011, 233). There were various points of commonality between the two leaders. Both had served as foreign ministers before being elected prime minister and chancellor, and both were active members in the Socialist International. They had met several times at the United Nations and in other Socialist platforms prior to Kreisky's election in 1970. In June 1972, at the Socialist International meeting, Meir spent eleven days in Vienna. According to the Austrian ambassador in Tel Aviv at that time, this was Meir's most extended stay in any foreign country besides the United States (Bachleitner 2018).

On September 30, 1973, one day after the events in Marchegg concluded, Meir visited Strasbourg to address the Parliamentary Assembly of the Council of Europe. Immediately after landing in France, Meir delivered a speech at the downtown Synagogue of Peace. Some 2,500 members of the local Jewish community attended. In her thirty-minute speech—delivered in Hebrew and translated into French—Meir referenced Austria's decision to close Schönau. She highlighted Austria's "great tradition of humanitarianism" and thanked it for its actions. "We have not forgotten," said Meir, "and we remain grateful for what Austria has done to help these people in the past." At the same time, she urged the Austrian government to change its decision and keep Schönau open, stating, "Our hope is that this was a momentary, temporary decision, based perhaps on a misunderstanding" (Smith 1973). Despite her general criticism of the Austrian decision, Meir "went out of her way to avoid starting an acrimonious public debate with Dr. Bruno Kreisky, the Austrian Chancellor," indicates Terence Smith in his special report to the *New York Times* (ibid.).

However, Meir's tone changed drastically in her speech to the Council of Europe the following day. Discarding her prepared notes, she was determined to bring up the recent events in Austria. "I have here my prepared address, a copy of which I believe you have before you," said Meir. "You will forgive me if I break with protocol and speak in an impromptu fashion. I say this in light of what has occurred in Austria during the last few days" (Avner 2009). With dramatic words and gestures, Meir described the Arab terrorists' efforts to attack Israelis and Jews in Europe, noting that they threatened Jews there due to their unsuccessful attempts to harm them in Israel. She continued by cynically averring that she "well understands" the feelings of a "European Prime Minister" who believes that "he has nothing to do with this" and asks himself, "Why has our territory been chosen for activities of this kind?" In Meir's conclusion, she attacked the Austrian decision to close Schönau and accede to the terrorists' demands. "Any government which strikes a deal with these killers does so at its own peril," she proclaimed. In effect, Meir directly accused Kreisky of giving in to the terrorists' ultimatum.

She stressed that this was unacceptable to her, stating that "[t] errorism has to be wiped out." She went on to say "There can be no deals with terrorists. What about this terrible thing which happened in Vienna? Is that a deal? Otherwise, I do not know what happened. ... There is a great victory throughout the terrorist organizations and the radios of the Arab states—and rightly so from their point of view. This is the first time that a government has come to an agreement of this kind" (1973). According to Meir's advisor and speechwriter, Yehuda Avner, the audience reacted to the speech enthusiastically, and "the ensuing applause told Golda Meir that she had gotten her message across to a goodly portion of the European Council, so off she flew to Vienna" (2009).

Immediately following the event in Marchegg, but prior to her speech at the Council of Europe, Meir requested an immediate meeting with Kreisky in Vienna. Kreisky hesitated at first, wanting to see whether there was any common ground for such a discussion based on her upcoming speech. He then only agreed to meet Meir after her return from Strasbourg (Bachleitner 2018). Once the meeting was scheduled, Meir shortened her trip to Strasbourg and made her way to Vienna. In hindsight, this meeting is the most memorable element of the Marchegg event.

Avner describes the first minutes of the meeting—when Meir entered the chancellor's office—in detail:

> Ushered into the presence of the impeccably dressed, bespectacled, heavy-set man in his mid-60s whom she knew to be the son of a Viennese Jewish clothing manufacturer, she extended her hand, which he shook while rising with the merest sketch of a bow, but not budging from behind the solid protection of his desk. "Please take a seat, Prime Minister Meir," he said formally. "Thank you[,] Chancellor Kreisky," said Golda, settling into the chair opposite him, and placing her copious black leather handbag on the floor. "I presume you know why I am here." "I believe I do," answered Kreisky, whose body language bore all the signs of one who was not relishing this appointment. (2009)

The meeting put Kreisky's fraught and entangled relationship with Israel, Austrian politics, and his own Jewishness on display in a remarkable fashion. There was something archetypical in this meeting between two great Jewish and socialist personalities and the gulf in attitudes toward Jewishness and Israel that divided them.

In fact, as the meeting began, Kreisky outlined the differences. He delineated the conflicting approaches of Israel and Austria to solve the Israeli-Palestinian conflict and interact with Arab countries, among other foreign affairs. Kreisky mentioned that he had continuously stressed in his meetings with Arab leaders that their relations with European countries depended much on forming their relations with Israel (Kreisky-Meir Meeting Protocol 1973, 130). At the same time, Kreisky demanded an explanation for the personal accusations and the critical articles about his policies that had been circulating, which had often described him as a "traitor who betrayed Jewish matters and the Jewish people."

The two also discussed different ways of dealing with terrorism. While Meir advocated for what she saw as the successful Israeli doctrine of forcefully combating terrorists, Kreisky insisted that "the war on terrorism will not solve the terrorism problem." In an apparent show of incomprehension, Meir responded that "she did not know of another way to combat terrorism" and critically wondered, "What kind of world is it where Jewish lives do not matter?" (ibid.).

Kreisky countered that his decisions during and following the incident in Marchegg had resulted from his desire to "save Jewish lives." He reiterated his commitment to protecting the hostages and mentioned that his conscience would not allow him to tolerate the "loss of human lives." While noting the security concerns in Schönau, Kreisky argued that the Jewish immigration route was solely a technical matter. He also pleaded for other countries to assist in enabling Jews to leave the Soviet Union or for the United Nations High Commissioner for Refugees to sponsor the operations at Schönau.

These statements did not convince Meir. Nevertheless, as historian Tom Segev (2006) points out, her arguments concerning Kreisky's actions against Jewish immigration were ultimately irrelevant. Because from the start, Kreisky said that he would allow Jewish emigration from the Soviet Union to continue to pass through Austria on their way to Israel (ibid.). When Meir understood that the discussion had reached a dead end, Kreisky, seeking to elicit some empathy from Meir, addressed her in English. "It might be that my way is not the way to fight terrorism, however, yours is not either. ... Let us assume that the hostages would have been murdered—what would I be accused of? I would be asked why did I not allow the terrorists to leave with the hostages to an Arab country. In this case I would have needed to respond and say that that it would result in their certain death" (ibid.).

However, the gulf between them remained, for Meir did not respond to Kreisky. Instead, the conversation ended there. To somewhat soften the antagonism, Kreisky asked Meir how long she intended to stay in Vienna. When she told him that she would be leaving that same evening, he promised to make sure that an Austrian minister would escort her.[39]

The Israeli protocol summary of the meeting from October 2, 1973, highlights Kreisky's practical offers for the continuation of Jewish immigration through Vienna and Meir's response to these offers.[40] However, it only vaguely mentions the differences in their approach to handling terrorism, including Meir's accusation of Kreisky mishandling the Marchegg event. Although the official protocol does note some disagreements, it gives the impression of a somewhat-civilized discussion. As such, this written ver-

---

39 Kreisky-Meir Meeting Protocol, 2 October 1973, (Prime Minister's Office: Office of Prime Minister Golda Meir, 1973–74), 1.9.1973–30.6.1974, Israel State Archives (Item Reference: 1418909/Physical Reference: 7245/16-א), 141, Jerusalem, Israel.

40 Kreisky-Meir Meeting Summary, n.d., (Prime Minister's Office: Office of Prime Minister Golda Meir, 1973–74), 1.9.1973–30.6.1974, Israel State Archives (Item Reference: 1418909/Physical Reference: 7245/16-א), 128–129, Jerusalem, Israel.

sion stands in stark contrast to several other far more dramatic descriptions of the meeting, which portray it as explosive and symbolic of the divergences between these two titans.

Yehuda Avner (2009), who escorted Meir to many of her meetings, leaves little doubt about the adversarial nature of the encounter. He comments that what started as a dialogue between political opponents with shared views proceeded into a "nasty cut-and-thrust duel between antagonists." Avner confirms that Meir not only accused Kreisky of "betraying the Jewish people" but also of encouraging "more hostage-taking." In reaction, Avner says, Kreisky's brows drew together "in an affronted frown."

"I cannot accept such language, Mrs. Meir. I cannot," answered Kreisky.

"You have opened the door to terrorism, Herr Chancellor," replied Meir. "You have brought renewed shame on Austria. I've just come from the Council of Europe. They condemn your act. Only the Arab world proclaims you their hero."

Looking uncomfortably still, Kreisky said in an expressionless tone, "Well, there is nothing I can do about that." And then, per Avner, Kreisky uttered with the hint of a shrug, "You and I belong to two different worlds."

"Indeed we do, Herr Kreisky," responded Golda Meir in a voice cracked with sardonic Jewish weariness. "You and I indeed belong to two very, very different worlds." Then she rose, picked up her handbag, and made for the door (ibid.).

In an interview with the British journalist David Yallop, Kreisky said that Meir had begun to bang her fists on his desk during the meeting. "The noise she was making was so loud that it was impossible for me to understand any of what she was saying," he accused. When he had refused Meir's request to reopen Schönau, Meir had begun calling his behavior "antisemitic." Now, it was Kreisky who banged his fists on the table, loudly reminding Meir of his own Jewish roots (Bachleitner 2018, 32). Apart from the apparent difference in ideological viewpoints, Hagai Zoref (2019, pers. comm.), head of the Documents and Commemoration Department at the Israel State Archives, notes a specific personal angle that Meir brought to the conversation. For Meir, Soviet Jewish immigration was not only of national significance but also of personal importance since she was born there and had worked on the issue of Jewish immigration from the 1950s on.

Regardless of which description of the meeting is the more accurate, both Kreisky and Meir walked out of the chancellor's office to a scheduled press conference, offended and angry. When Kreisky held the door open to the room where journalists had already gathered, Meir refused to join. Kreisky's comment on their "different worlds" had seemingly reduced her to a most uncharacteristic silence. Israel's ambassador to Vienna, Yitzhak Patish, recalls that Meir appeared "muted and withdrawn" and that no one had "the courage to disturb her" (Bachleitner 2018, 32).

Instead of staying for the press conference, Meir rushed directly to the Vienna Airport on her way back to Israel. There, she pointedly boarded a plane with a group of Soviet Jewish emigrants. Many journalists awaited her at the Ben Gurion Airport five hours later upon landing. "I think the best way of summing up in a nutshell the nature of my meeting with Chancellor Kreisky is to say this: He didn't even offer me a glass of water," she declared. This quote became the most, and perhaps only memorable, "sound bite" of the Marchegg incident and its aftermath.

Former Israeli prime minister and president Shimon Peres (1997) describes how the "glass of water" affair contributed significantly to Kreisky's negative image in Israel. That statement, says Peres, was deeply hurtful to Kreisky, who was proud of his Viennese hospitality and was well known for it. Kreisky even addresses the "glass of water" story in his memoirs. According to him, it was "a total fabrication." Meir "left my office in a rage. I had more reason to be annoyed by her displays of tactless behavior than she did" (Bachleitner 2018, 32).

Many years later, Lowa Eliav, who was very close to Kreisky, discussed the matter with him. "What about this glass of water?" asked Eliav. "I don't know what to do with it," Kreisky replied, "because the whole world knows that I did not give Golda Meir a glass of water. I wanted to give her coffee or cakes and I even offered her a shower. She never wanted coffee or tea or anything." Eliav supposes that Meir's statement was made simply because she "hated his guts and hated Jews who were anti-Zionists. She definitely hated Bruno Kreisky" (1997).

The reference to offering Meir a shower is also supported by Kreisky's personal assistant, Margit Schmidt:

> Kreisky asked me to take good care of Golda Meir as she had come in a complicated and indirect flight. Behind his office was a shower and a small bed where one could lie down. We discussed whether she would like to eat, and whether she keeps Kosher—we talked about the matter for a long time in order to make all as comfortable as possible. She came from the airport with her security guards into my office and I asked, if she would like anything before she entered the room with the Chancellor. "Negotiations, negotiations!" She wanted to portray Kreisky in a negative way to the world press. That was it. (2014, pers. comm.)

Israeli ambassador Patish, who was present throughout the entire visit, connects this incident to the general atmosphere during the meeting. "The air was tense and nobody thought about water or coffee," says Patish. "It was a very brief meeting." However, the encounter soon escalated into a diplomatic incident that left both political leaders angry. Meir described her feelings following the meeting in a highly emotive and provocative fashion, using implicit Holocaust terminology. "I felt as though my mouth were filled with ashes," Meir declared. "We belonged to different worlds? The things that Kreisky had said to me just went round and round in my head" (Bachleitner 2018, 34).

Perceptions of the encounter and its aftermath vary greatly, and personal, political, and ideological dimensions are deeply intertwined in them. Journalist and diplomat Barbara Taufar (2020, pers. comm.), for example, suggests that Meir's resentment at Kreisky's decision resulted from the simple fact that Kreisky wanted the Jewish immigrants to have a choice as to where they should go. For Meir, this was a blatantly non-Zionist viewpoint, and it was this that "motivated her hatred for Kreisky" (ibid.).

Ariel Muzicant, on the other hand, argues that Kreisky's demeanor was not logical. "Besides his inner circle, no one else understood his behavior," he says and adds that "Meir was extremely offended." Muzicant speculates that Kreisky's reacted in an illogical way because "he had a constant problem with Israel, with its representatives, and with the Jews" (2018, pers. comm.).

Interestingly, Golda Meir's accounts of the incident differed too: on October 3, 1973, she convened a government meeting to report on her visit to the Council of Europe and her meeting with Kreisky. Most ministers participated. There, surprisingly, her report of Kreisky was far more tempered, balanced, and moderate than her public statements or the reports made by some of the media and her advisors. Perhaps her public pronouncements were politically and emotionally motivated, while her confidential reporting was more realistic and to the point.[41]

As Meir recollected, after Kreisky had thanked her for her visit, he had commented on the Israeli press's harsh criticisms of him concerning the "Jewish matter." He had asserted that although he was not a Zionist and had never been religious, he had never denied his Jewish descent and had always appreciated the extraordinary achievements of Israel.[42]

Kreisky had noted that a few days before their meeting, he had addressed the directorate of the Socialist Party and the Workers Union. There, he had explained the necessity of enabling Jewish immigration from Russia to Israel as that was the only way to leave the dictatorship. Meir said that Kreisky had

41   Protocol of Government Meeting, top classified protocol of the Israeli, 3 October 1973 (Protocol of Government Meeting), 3.10.1973, Israel State Archives (Item Reference: N/A as was sent by email directly by the director of the archive, Hagai Tsoref), Jerusalem, Israel.
42   Protocol of Government Meeting, top classified, 3.10.1973, ISA, 3.

reported this to show that he had devoted thought and time to the matter. However, Kreisky also pointed out that the Arabs perceived Jewish emigration from the Soviet Union as a serious threat. He also observed that Austria was becoming a "blood arena" of Arab terrorism precisely because Jewish immigration proceeded from there.

In Meir's retelling, Kreisky had claimed that the terrorists had asked the Austrians to cancel the transit visas of groups and individuals, but the Austrians had refused. Finally, after hours of persuasion, they had come to an agreement. However, Meir commented that there was no such thing as an individual transit visa. On top of that, Kreisky had criticized the goings-on around Schönau. It had become a kind of "tourist landmark," which had been unacceptable and was another reason for the proposal to open a new camp under the supervision of the United Nations.[43]

Meir also shared her responses to Kreisky at the meeting. She had told him that Israel was shocked by his decision to close the camp and that Israelis were stunned by the "great victory" of the terrorists and Austria's acceptance of their demands. "If Kreisky thought that Schönau was a dangerous place, it was natural that he would discuss it with us," said Meir. "Perhaps he would have convinced us to find alternatives."[44]

Meir added that the news about the transit camp's closure had appeared in the international press before the Israeli ambassador had been informed. Kreisky had not denied this. Instead, Kreisky had told Meir that he had received "hundreds and thousands of letters and telegrams" thanking him for saving the lives of four people, while the Israelis had not said a word. Meir had responded by proclaiming, "We also appreciate life in general, and Jewish life in particular, but the question is how many Jews will lose their life the next time?"[45]

---

43   Protocol of Government Meeting, top classified, 3.10.1973, ISA, 5.

44   Protocol of Government Meeting, top classified, 3.10.1973, ISA, 6.

45   Protocol of Government Meeting, top classified, 3.10.1973, ISA, 7.

Meir had then mentioned to Kreisky that Sadat had sent his envoy to thank him for his deeds. Kreisky verified this and explained that Austria had strong relations with Egypt and that the envoy had previously been an ambassador in Austria. Possibly to soften the blow, Kreisky had also admitted that he had had "nicer conversations" in his life.[46]

Meir highlighted Kreisky's concrete suggestion that, while Jews would continue to pass through Austria, Israel had to find other countries that would be willing to "share the burden."[47] The movement of immigrants would not immediately stop, and Kreisky was not "closing Schönau tomorrow." Despite this, Meir had been told that because of "anger and agitation," the minister of the interior had ordered the camp's closure "the following day."[48]

In a remarkably empathic manner, Meir described Kreisky as pretty "dispirited" due to the confessional nature of the discussion around Jews, Jewishness, and Austria. For all that, she believed Kreisky felt that his party members and the professional unions supported him, and there were *goyim* (gentiles) who thought that he had executed an astonishing humanitarian act. Therefore, this event could not be interpreted as a great victory for the terrorists.

"I refused to join him at the press conference, as I did not want to place myself in an argument with him on his home ground and in front of journalists," explained Meir. "On the way to the airport, I heard parts of the press conference which was broadcast live." She summarized his words to the press as: "This Schönau cannot continue; we must find other places for this burden of transferring Jews; what is happening in the world [i.e., the criticism against Kreisky] is hurting him."[49]

In conclusion—and in retrospect—Meir determined that she did not regret her trip to Vienna; it had not harmed her or Israel's honor. Once again, though, her resentment and anger at Kreisky

46   Protocol of Government Meeting, top classified, 3.10.1973, ISA, 7.
47   Protocol of Government Meeting, top classified, 3.10.1973, ISA, 7.
48   Protocol of Government Meeting, top classified, 3.10.1973, ISA, 8.
49   Protocol of Government Meeting, top classified, 3.10.1973, ISA, 9.

emerged. "When there is someone who is about to bring a decree upon the Jews," said Meir, "it is no shame to come and discuss this with him."[50]

In a protocol of the meeting, Minister of Tourism Moshe Kol expresses skepticism about Meir's trip given Kreisky's "Jewish Complex." That complex, Kol says, also extended to Meir. He points out that both Kreisky and Meir were leaders of the Socialist Party. However, despite this similarity, Kreisky's status in the world was perceptibly lower. It was, therefore, not possible for Kreisky to "surrender" to a Jewish prime minister in his home. Nevertheless, Kol praises Meir for her "mental courage."[51] Deputy Prime Minister Yigal Allon assesses that changing Kreisky's mind on Schönau was unlikely. Schönau "became a symbol of Kreisky's prestige."[52]

The rest of the meeting was mainly devoted to examining practical ways of continuing immigration, both through Austria and through alternative countries. The ministers also expressed their views on how to handle the Austrian decision. Some supported a boycott of Austria, while others called for "quiet diplomacy."

---

50   Protocol of Government Meeting, top classified, 3.10.1973, ISA, 9.
51   Protocol of Government Meeting, top classified, 3.10.1973, ISA, 14.
52   Protocol of Government Meeting, top classified, 3.10.1973, ISA, 20.

KREISKY, SCHÖNAU, AND THE INTERNATIONAL COMMUNITY

Kreisky's handling of the Marchegg incident led to massive international criticism, especially in Israel, the United States, and the Netherlands (Riegler 2011).[53] In Israel specifically, Kreisky's decision to close Schönau drew an almost inordinate amount of negative public attention in the first week of October 1973 (Dank 1984). An extreme example can be found in the virulent words of Minister of Labor Yosef Almogi:

> "Kreisky, with his cynical expressions, betrayed the humanitarian way, and his surrendering to terrorism would reflect on his possible future actions. ... 15 years ago, when I was the secretary of MAPAI, I met him in the Socialist International. He was the most unpleasant person there, especially in regard to Judaism and Zionism. I think that in this case he proved himself as a Jewish Kapo. ... What he has done to us is an act of a Kapo and we must fight it. ... His actions were disgraceful."[54]

In the United States and Europe, mass demonstrations were held. In London, New York, and Los Angeles, thousands protested Kreisky's decision. At the same time, consumers boycotted Austrian products (Dahlke 2011). American Jewish organizations expressed their shock and outrage over Vienna's move and called for an immediate reversal of the decision. "This yielding to the blackmail of Arab terrorists is immoral and unbecoming a sovereign state," one telegram would say. The secretariat of the radical "Jewish Defense League" threatened to unleash a worldwide terror campaign against Austria (Chamberlin 2012).

---

53 The Netherlands was a close ally of Israel during those years, and they handled consular matters for Israel in Moscow, including entry or transit visas for Soviet Jews wishing to emigrate.
54 Protocol of Government Meeting, top classified, 3.10.1973, ISA 31.

President Richard Nixon criticized Kreisky publicly. He also phoned Kreisky and—like the Israelis—contended that "one just cannot negotiate with terrorists" (Dahlke 2011). Nixon openly appealed to Kreisky to "reconsider his decision for this fundamental reason that goes far beyond his country, and even ours, and that is that we simply cannot have governments, large or small, give in to international blackmail by terrorist groups" (Pick 2000, 124).

German officials in Washington testified that Nixon's harsh approach had mainly been influenced by domestic politics and the fact that the matter meant much to many Americans. While the State Department was more understanding of the complexity of the Austrian situation, it also agreed that Kreisky had gone "one step too far" (Dahlke 2011). While it declined to comment on Austria's decision, the State Department announced its regret that "terrorist actions should succeed in placing additional hurdles in the way of persons exercising a basic human right of emigration" (Chamberlin 2012, 600).

In the United States Senate, the reactions concerning Kreisky's decision over Schönau were overwhelmingly negative. A Senate resolution describes the camp's closure as "an outrage against humanity" (Pick 2000). It called upon the president to take immediate and determined steps to "impress upon the Austrian Government the grave concern of the American people and urge them to reverse their decision and permit group travel from the Soviet Union through Austria."[55] Senator Henry Jackson decried Austria's decision as giving in to intimidation and the most serious and short-sighted concession to blackmail (Chamberlin 2012). House Minority Leader Gerald Ford joined the condemnations of Kreisky. "I am deeply disappointed that the Austrian government would yield to the blackmail practiced by Arab terrorists," said

---

55   Israeli Embassy in Washington to Ministry of Foreign Affairs, telegram, 1 October 1973, (Vienna: September–December 1973), 1.9.1973–31.12.1973, Israel State Archives (Item Reference: 000w3z1/Physical Reference: 7037/15-א), 347, Jerusalem, Israel.

Ford. "I hope that the Austrian Cabinet will reconsider and will rescind this unfortunate decision."[56]

The State Department updated their Israeli counterparts on their diplomatic moves. In an urgent telegram sent to Prime Minister Meir, the Israeli diplomats in Washington explained America's actions. According to a report on the matter, the United States ambassador in Vienna was expected to meet Kreisky to express his concern with what had happened. He would thank the Austrians for allowing the continuation of movement through Austria and hoped they would find a way to "set aside the agreement made under duress." The report goes on to say that the United States ambassadors in the United Kingdom, Germany, Denmark, and the Netherlands would all convince their local governments to pressure Kreisky. However, the State Department asked Israel to keep this information strictly confidential to give Austria the option to change its decision.[57]

According to the writer Matthias Dahlke (2011), the United States tried to utilize the close relationship between Kreisky and Willy Brandt by asking Brandt to intervene in this decision. This, however, proved unsuccessful. Dahlke says that only one week after Nixon's dramatic criticism of Kreisky, Austria still took part in secret negotiations in Washington that dealt with the USSR and the oil crises. Kreisky remained relevant in international politics, while Nixon's criticism was confined to the domestic sphere (ibid.).

Of course, the Arab states and their public welcomed Kreisky's decision and supported his position (Embacher and Reiter 1998). There were also some in the Western world that

---

56   Israeli Embassy in Washington to Ministry of Foreign Affairs, telegram, 30 September 1973, (Vienna: September–December 1973), 1.9.1973–31.12.1973, Israel State Archives (Item Reference: 000w3z1/Physical Reference: 7037/15-א), 402, Jerusalem, Israel.

57   Evron to New York, Strasbourg, Washington, London, Bonn, Copenhagen, Hague, and Vienna, telegram, 1 October 1973, (Vienna: September–December 1973), 1.9.1973–31.12.1973, Israel State Archives (Item Reference: 000w3z1/Physical Reference: 7037/15-א), 363, Jerusalem, Israel.

supported Kreisky. Senator J. William Fulbright, the chairman of the Senate Foreign Relations Committee, demonstrated this support in a glowing letter. "I wish to offer my sincere congratulations for your courage and good judgment," writes Fulbright. "Some of the small countries with long experience, such as Austria and Denmark and Sweden, have produced the wisest leaders in our world today. ... In a brief exchange on the Senate Floor a few days ago, I attempted to support your right to act in the interest of your own country. I just wanted you to know that there are some of us who admire your wisdom and courage" (Dahlke 2011, 225).

Nevertheless, the overwhelming international reaction was negative and highly critical. Unsurprisingly, Austria's reactions to this criticism were not long in coming. As Erwin Lanc, Kreisky's minister of the interior, reports, Kreisky resented that while leaders of countries like the Netherlands were denouncing Austria, when asked to build immigration camps in *their* territory, they "all suddenly disappeared." Lanc asserts that nobody wanted to take on the responsibility that Austria had taken upon itself. "After the Marchegg event, we understood the danger in running such activities in Austria," recalls Lanc. "We knew that we could not be completely sure that we could stop terrorist activities in time, but it was clear that we would continue with the immigration through Austria, and we did" (2017, pers. comm.).

POST-SCHÖNAU: KREISKY AND THE CONTINUATION OF JEWISH IMMIGRATION THROUGH AUSTRIA

It was crucial to Kreisky to emphasize that his decision to close Schönau did not prevent future Jewish immigration through Austria. In several interviews with the Israeli media, Kreisky repeated this message. In one instance, he clarified this to television reporter Ron Ben-Yishai, saying, "I should like to make it quite clear, that as far as the question of free and unimpeded transit through Austria was concerned, no concessions were made to the terrorists, who had demanded that transit should be completely barred" (*Events of September 28th and 29th* 1973, 40).

At a luncheon for visiting Soviet parliamentarians on September 28, 1973, Kreisky reemphasized his government's moral duty regarding immigration. "Austria is committed to the principles of democracy and humanity," Kreisky stressed, "and I should like to make it quite clear—today especially—that everything which has happened and which might happen will make no difference to our fundamental attitude, to our laws or to our tradition of humanitarian practice. ... Austria will remain a country which offers asylum to everyone who feels persecuted and which provides anyone who wishes to travel through Austria to another country with the opportunity to do so" (ibid., 42).

Schönau proved less of a surrender than was assumed by many observers at the time. Later, it became apparent that the camp's closure did not affect Kreisky's willingness to provide transit facilities for Soviet Jews. Instead, it took several weeks before it became apparent that Kreisky had never intended to close the doors on the emigrants from the Soviet Union (Pick 2000). The Schönau camp was closed on December 12, 1973. A short while after, following Kreisky's instructions, the Austrian Red Cross set up a new camp in Wöllersdorf, and Jewish emigration from the Soviet Union continued. In 1974 alone, twenty thousand Jewish migrants passed through Austria (Bachleitner 2018).

This was only appreciated by Israel retrospectively, for, at the time, Meir refused to trust Kreisky (Berg 2000, 473). "In the following months, she had to recognize that she had been wrong," Kreisky said later with satisfaction, boasting that he was the only politician in Europe that Meir "couldn't blackmail" (Bachleitner 2018, 40). Meir's spokesperson, Meron Medzini, concedes that the Israeli prime minister may have been "a little hasty in her judgment" (Pick 2000). In her memoirs, Meir herself admits, "To be quite fair, I must note that although I don't believe there is ever a good enough excuse for knuckling under to terrorism, the Austrian decision was not altogether unreasonable" (Bachleitner 2018, 40). She realized that "far from halting the influx of Soviet Jewry, four weeks after the Schönau terrorist attack, the emigration from Russia reached the highest monthly quota recorded" (Pick 2000).

ISRAELI REACTIONS
TO THE SCHÖNAU INCIDENT

While international reactions to Kreisky's decision to close Schönau were negative, they were particularly strong in Israel. The hostility at times approached that of personal animosity, even hate. Throughout the country, people organized anti-Austrian demonstrations with Kreisky at their center. These all suggested that Austrian policies were based on its Nazi past. The mayor of Jerusalem, Vienna-born Teddy Kollek, sent Kreisky a letter calling upon him to retract his decision. Kreisky's close friend Uri Avnery similarly urged this, for Kreisky's decision "hurts freedom and reminds people of the Anschluss." More empathy was required, suggested Avnery (Embacher and Reiter 1998, 170). The public, too, responded poorly. Various items were thrown at Austrian institutions, joint events were canceled, and hunger strikes were arranged.

The Israeli press repeated a well-known insult: Kreisky was a "self-hating Jew." One newspaper wrote that the "devil knocked on the door, and the Austrians happily opened it." Another branded Kreisky's decision as "a mark of Cain on Kreisky." A caricature appeared in *Maariv,* showing the relaxed terrorists drinking wine and asking cynically why they had not offered to open the gas chambers again (Dahlke 2011). Members of the Israeli Labor Party wrote a scathing letter to Kreisky expressing their astonishment at his choice. Terrorists "had blackmailed Austria," and Kreisky's actions constituted a "betrayal of the Socialist and party values."[58]

The criticism was voiced by both the media and by governmental institutions. The Israeli government conveyed its "astonishment and shock at the unjustified actions taken by the Austrian government which we regard as giving in to the terrorists' demands." Its official statement from September 29, 1973, warns about "encouraging future acts of blackmail and violence and jeopardizing the right of Jewish immigration." However, the statement also includes a positive note, mentioning Austria's actions regarding Jewish immigration in general: "The Israeli government values the humanitarian tradition of the Austrian government for many years on their way to their homeland."[59]

The Knesset, Israel's parliament, was united in its condemnation against the decision, and all parties—besides the Rakach (New Communist List)—announced that they had "heard in shock and horror the Austrian government's decision to stop providing transit services for Jews immigrating to Israel from the Soviet Union." The Knesset called for the urgent cancellation of "the decision that was made under threats of Arab terrorists to murder four innocent people." It warned about the "harsh and fundamental damage to human morality and international law" and called upon the Austrian government to continue to "provide transit services for Jewish groups coming from the Soviet Union to the historical home of the Jewish people."[60]

---

58   Yadlin to Kreisky, 30 September 1973, (Vienna: September–December 1973), 1.9.1973–31.12.1973, Israel State Archives (Item Reference: 000w3z1/Physical Reference: 7037/15-א), 417, Jerusalem, Israel.

59   Kidron to All Embassies, Announcement of Israeli Government, 30 September 1973, (Vienna: September–December 1973), 1.9.1973–31.12.1973, Israel State Archives (Item Reference: 000w3z1/Physical Reference: 7037/15-א), 412, Jerusalem, Israel.

60   Hasbara (Advocacy) to Strasbourg, telegram, 1 October 1973, (Vienna: September–December 1973), 1.9.1973–31.12.1973, Israel State Archives (Item Reference: 000w3z1/Physical Reference: 7037/15-א), 365, Jerusalem, Israel.

Kreisky was well aware of the criticism. In interviews with Israeli television, Kreisky explained his decision-making process, saying that he did not share Israel's mode of dealing with terrorism. "Fighting terrorism with force leads to more terror and an unending cycle which does not bring peace," he pronounced. He also mentioned the events of the 1972 Munich Olympics, which had "played a significant role" in his choice. As Israeli ambassador Patish puts it, "Kreisky did not want Munich again" (Dahlke 2011, 216). "He did not want to be in the shoes of Brandt, who was pushed to act as he did by the Israelis," says Hagai Zoref (2019, pers. comm.) of the Israel State Archives.

As he did so often when faced with the charges regarding his "self-hating" Jewishness, Kreisky responded that while "he was never a Zionist, was never religious; nevertheless, he never denied his Jewish origin."[61] However, even though he did not consider Israel his homeland, he had always acknowledged the importance of a state for Jews. As always, he made it apparent that he considered himself first and foremost an Austrian—albeit an Austrian of Jewish descent.[62]

AUSTRIAN REACTIONS TO THE SCHÖNAU INCIDENT

Reactions to the event in Austria were different from the predominantly negative international and Israeli reactions. Austrians, by and large, approved of Kreisky's decision to close the Schönau transit camp (Bachleitner 2018). Much of this positive support flowed from the fear that their nation faced being transformed into "a secondary theatre of the Middle Eastern conflict" (Chamberlin 2012, 606). The Social Democrats, the Freedom Party, and the Communists also endorsed Kreisky's decision to shut down Schönau. The Communist Party even considered Schönau a spy-

---

61   Protocol of Government Meeting, top classified, 3.10.1973, ISA, 2.
62   Protocol of Government Meeting, top classified, 3.10.1973, ISA, 2.

ing headquarters for the Israeli Mossad. Still, approval was not unanimous. The ÖVP attacked Kreisky, saying he "was playing into the terrorists' hands" (Embacher and Reiter 1998).

Despite this, according to 1973 public polls, most Austrians approved of their government's decision-making process during the event. Letters addressed to the chancellor mainly credited Kreisky for saving peoples' lives by avoiding an Austrian "Munich" (ibid.). "One has to understand Kreisky's status in Austria at that time," says Menachem Oberbaum, who remembers that many Austrians considered the chancellor as "half a God" (2020, pers comm.). Barbara Taufar says that people were perplexed. After all, this was the first Arab terror attack in Austria. "Austrian journalists and politicians were at that time very provincial and did not understand Kreisky, who had a world vision," declares Taufar (2020, pers. comm.), confirming that most Austrians supported Kreisky and his decisions.

The criticism by Israel and other countries was perceived as an unjustified attack on Austria and its sovereignty. Such criticism, indeed, fostered strong patriotic feelings: "We, the Austrians," are united against "the rest of the world" (Bachleitner 2018, 38). The "world," which condemned Austria, was seen by many as an "unfriendly, hypocritical outside world" (Chamberlin 2012, 606). This inward turn of solidarity was hardly an unknown psychological defense mechanism.

Even so, it would be wrong to think that there was a complete agreement of Austrian opinion. The Austrian press, for instance, was divided on the matter. Some papers attacked the decision, arguing that "never before in the history of modern terrorism did a drama with hostages end so disgracefully. ... The government put itself on an equal footing with gangsters and made them bargaining partners" (ibid., 607). Others wrote that the decision to close the camp was "damage that could not be repaired" and wondered, "How could we still believe the claims of the government that the best defense of Austrian neutrality is successful foreign and security policies—that was a warning sign from a distance."[63] However, many others supported the government's decision (Chamberlin 2012) because it had been reached "in the interest not only of Austrian security, but also the security of the Jews" (607). "Kreisky will not change his decision also not under the most massive pressure," heralded a *Kronen Zeitung* headline. "To our Israeli friends—do not raise ghosts from the past because looking in anger at the past will not help us when destiny pushes us again to a confrontation," wrote the *Kurier* newspaper.[64]

Historian Paul Thomas Chamberlin (2012) says that while the press was divided over Kreisky's decision, it was unified in its resentment over international scorn directed toward Austria. The *Kronen Zeitung* argued that had the world's reaction "not been so loud," Austria would have been able to replace Schönau with alternate facilities quietly. A journalist from the *Kurier* decried the notion that in every Austrian decision, its "past is raised" and wondered when that would come to an end (Embacher and Reiter 1998). Minister of Defense Karl Lütgendorf accused the foreign journalists who opposed the decision as being influenced by the Jews who control the international media (ibid.).

On the right of Austrian politics, sympathy for Kreisky took on a different tone: "Kreisky has now proven that he is an Austrian and not a Jew" (Bachleitner 2018, 38). Political scientist Kathrin Bachleitner (2018) suggests that the way Kreisky dealt with Israel during the Schönau crisis led to the Austrian public realizing that their very own Jewish chancellor could—and would—absolve them from the "curse" of their past. There was a recognition that only someone like Kreisky could have decided to close the camp in the face of world criticism.

Golda Meir's visit only strengthened these perceptions. There was resentment against Israeli attempts to interfere with what was

---

63 Lev to Director General of Ministry, telegram, Austrian Press Summary, 1 October 1973, (Vienna: September–December 1973), 1.9.1973–31.12.1973, Israel State Archives (Item Reference: 000w3z1/Physical Reference: א-7037/15), 359, Jerusalem, Israel.

64 Lev to Director General of Ministry, 1 Oct. 1973, ISA, 359.

viewed as an Austrian affair (Chamberlin 2012). Israeli officials were quite aware of the feelings its actions were creating. "The call for boycott and personal attacks on Kreisky bring together the Austrian public around him," one report mentions.[65] According to the Israeli diplomats, the Austrian press saw the United Nations' negative response to Kreisky's request for assistance as a way to avoid sharing the burden and danger that came from allowing Jewish immigration. Kreisky was seen as the heroic leader who "stands up to those who dirty Austria's image in the world." The report concludes that Israeli publications advocating an economic boycott would lead to harsher anti-Israel tendencies.[66]

THE AUSTRIAN JEWISH COMMUNITY'S REACTION TO KREISKY AND THE SCHÖNAU INCIDENT

Surprisingly, little is known (or has been written) about the Austrian Jewish community's response to the Marchegg event. Ariel Muzicant, a prominent leader of the Jewish Community of Vienna, shares some insights about the community's feelings and opinions at that time. "We all felt frustrated by the way Kreisky acted," says Muzicant. Those feelings, he adds, did not only derive from the Marchegg event but from Kreisky's general conduct. "We were protesting, demonstrating, writing letters," he recalls. Muzicant's father, together with approximately one hundred other Jews, left the Social Democratic Party following the event. "We felt betrayed by him," says Muzicant. "The streets were full of anti-Israeli sentiments, which we felt as antisemitic." As to the dialogue between the organized Jewish Community of Vienna and Kreisky's administration, Muzicant professes that "there

---

65 Israeli Embassy in Vienna to Kidron, telegram, 4 October 1973, (Vienna: September–December 1973), 1.9.1973–31.12.1973, Israel State Archives (Item Reference: 000w3z1/Physical Reference: 7037/15-א), 56, Jerusalem, Israel.

66 Israeli Embassy in Vienna to Kidron, telegram, 4 October 1973, ISA, 56.

was no dialogue at all as we were not a factor for him." However, Muzicant admits that in hindsight, things look different. "After the initial anger about Kreisky's decision, which gave into the terrorists' demands, we saw that no one was hurt, that the immigration continued through Austria, and that they opened a new camp," he says. "It was not as terrible as we described it" (2018, pers. comm.). Barbara Taufar states that the initial negative attitude toward Kreisky's decision might have been connected to the Jewish Community of Vienna's prior prejudices about Kreisky. "The Jewish Community was never friendly toward the Socialists and Kreisky," says Taufar (2020, pers. comm.).

The founder and head of the Jewish Vocational Training Center in Vienna, Ilan Knapp, puts forth another reason for the Jewish objection to Kreisky's decision. Namely, the hope that some of those "in transit" Jews would stay and become members of the local Jewish community. This sentiment, however, was not made public for fear that this would rebound against the community. Knapp affirms that most Austrian Jews felt treated as second-class citizens. Anxiety, too, played a role. Thus, Knapp notes that the minority of Jews who did demonstrate against the decision were mainly Jewish university students, themselves members of families who had emigrated from the Soviet Union. "The Austrian Jews did not know if Israel [would] continue to exist in light of the many threats it faced," says Knapp. "Its future was unknown." Knapp insists the reason that Jews decided to stay in Austria—despite their feelings—was related to the fact that "the Marchegg events made them feel that the terrorism which Austria faced was just the tip of the iceberg of what was going on in Israel" (2019, pers. comm.). After all, it was around this time that Israel faced its greatest existential threat yet.

MARCHEGG AND THE YOM KIPPUR WAR

Just one week after the event in Marchegg—on October 6, 1973, Yom Kippur, the holiest day in the Jewish calendar—Egyptian and Syrian forces launched a coordinated attack against Israel, hoping that they would gain back the territory lost to Israel during the 1967 Six-Day War. The attack found Israel unprepared and resulted in more than 2,500 Israelis being killed and thousands wounded. As part of the continuing Cold War, both the United States and the Soviet Union came into indirect confrontation in defense of their respective allies.

Israel's lack of preparedness has been studied extensively. Criticism has mainly been focused on the failures of Israeli Military Intelligence, as mentioned in the reports of the Agranat Commission, the National Commission of Inquiry's investigation on the failings of the Israel Defense Forces. These reports said that the Intelligence Research Unit refused to think beyond its "concept and persistent adherence" to an assumption they had made about Egypt. Their theory was that Egypt would not go to war until it gained long-range fighter planes capable of destroying the Israeli Air Force and Scud missiles that could be used to deter an Israeli strike deep into Egypt. This belief contrasted with the Intelligence Collection Unit's findings, which had detected irregular movements from the Egyptian Army around Sinai and the reinforcement of forces in the northern part of the Syrian Golan Heights. In addition, many testimonies from 1973 emphasized the post–1967 war arrogance, euphoria, and hubris of Israel's decision-makers (Ginsburg 2012).

Following his unexplained death in 2007, the fascinating story of the controversial spy Ashraf Marwan has received wide public attention in recent years. Marwan, the senior assistant to Egyptian president Anwar Sadat, warned Israel on October 5, 1973, that the "war will start tomorrow." However, as riveting as Marwan's story is, it is surprising that in comparison, so little has been written about the Marchegg event and the possibility that the terrorists' actions were a carefully planned distraction to turn attention away from the movement of Egyptian and Syrian forces.

It is unclear if this is what happened. However, what is certain is that from September 28, 1973, to the start of the Yom Kippur War, the Israeli government was mainly focused on the Marchegg event and its aftermath. The Israeli media reported Golda Meir's visit to Vienna, criticized Kreisky's reactions, and discussed the future of Soviet Jewish immigration through Austria. Foreign Minister Abba Eban would later observe that because of the Schönau incident, "historians who read the Israeli newspapers published in the first days of October will be startled to find that there was no hint of any crisis, let alone of imminent war" (Zaretsky 2007, 75). In their book, *Israel's Secret Wars: A History of Israel's Intelligence Services* (1991), historians Ian Black and Benny Morris noted, "Political deception was supplemented by diversions during the countdown to war. The most serious specific feint, which shifted Israeli political and intelligence attention away from the Middle East to Europe for 5 vital days, was the Schönau Affair" (293).

Golda Meir returned to Israel on October 3, 1973. Israel's ambassador to France, Asher Ben-Natan, accompanied the prime minister during her trip to Strasbourg. He tried to persuade Meir to reconsider her trip to Vienna by pointing out that her meeting with Kreisky would not lead him to change his mind. As reported by the Insight Team of the London *Sunday Times*, the diplomat was aware of the "Arab buildup" through secret cables. "Your place," Ben-Natan told Meir, "[is] back home."

Meir, however, disagreed. "The Russian immigrants are so important to Israel," she said, "that if there is a one percent, even half a percent chance, of changing Kreisky's mind, I must try." Tragically, ambassador Ben-Natan's son was one of the first Israeli soldiers killed on the Golan Heights (Insight Team 1974, 108–9).

At the same time, Egyptian and Syrian armies moved their forces toward Israel's borders. Egypt announced a "high state of readiness" along the Suez Canal, and Syria announced a general call-up of reserves. Defense Minister Moshe Dayan, Army Chief of Staff David Elazar, and Director of the Mossad Zvi Zamir noticed signs of disturbance and asked Prime Minister Meir to arrange an immediate meeting of her "Kitchen Cabinet," the term given to her key advisors (McKenzie-Smith 1976).

Henry Kissinger describes the visit of Simcha Dinitz, the Israeli ambassador to the United States, to his office on the last day of September. Dinitz was distraught, and Kissinger assumed that he was concerned about Syrian movements on the Golan Heights border. However, that was not the case. Instead, Schönau was Dinitz's main concern. Dinitz insisted on talking about Schönau, focusing all his attention during the crucial week before the war on Austria, instead of Egypt or Syria (Pick 2000).

Upon her return to Israel, Golda Meir immediately summoned a meeting with Defense Minister Dayan, Chief of Staff Elazar, Deputy Prime Minister Yigal Allon, Minister without Portfolio Yisrael Galili, Air Force Major General Benny Peled, and Brigadier General Arie Shalev from military intelligence, who was representing Major General Eli Zeira, who was ill. At the same time, Shalev was also part of Israel's only intelligence evaluation unit that claimed the two army movements were unconnected. Consequently, he concluded with the following words: "The possibility of an Egyptian-Syrian attack is not, in my personal view, likely, because there has been no change in the Arabs' assessment of the balance of forces in Sinai such that they could go to war" (McKenzie-Smith 1976, 45).

However, the Syrian Army's movement was still not explained. As the "conception" held that Syria would not start a war without Egypt, the Marchegg event was used to explain the unusual movement of Syria. The Egyptian and Syrian military advances were seen as defensive actions in anticipation of Israeli reprisals following the Schönau incident (McKenzie-Smith 1976). It was hypothesized that the Syrians might have known of the raid beforehand and had consequently amassed these forces to deter the almost-inevitable Israeli retaliation.

That same evening, the Foreign Affairs Committee—and later the full cabinet—were summoned to discuss recent events. Those ministers who were not part of the Kitchen Cabinet—and consequently were not present at the earlier meeting—were not notified about the developments along the border. The meeting was dedicated entirely to the Schönau event, and the buildup was not mentioned. As one Israeli minister would remark, "That week, you would have thought Israel's front line was not Suez but the Danube" (Insight Team 1974, 108).

Former member of the Security Committee, Lowa Eliav, describes the abnormality of the situation in an interview. It is unclear whether he is referencing the earlier meeting in which Meir presented a more or less balanced account, but where her harsh words were omitted from the protocol, or whether this was an entirely different meeting. "When Golda returned from Vienna," says Eliav, "she summoned an immediate urgent session. ... We did not know what she was talking about, to what subject she was referring. ... Then she talked for perhaps an hour about how Kreisky received her at his Ballhausplatz number two and how very rude he was." Eliav recalls that the only subject of the meeting was "what a terrible man Kreisky was" and the fact that she had not been given a "glass of water." The meeting was dismissed without mentioning the "whole pile of cables and assessments" that had piled up on her desk, warning that the Egyptians and Syrians were amassing tens of thousands of troops. "She did not even mention this or hint at it," explains Eliav (1997).

PLANNED DECEPTION?

Whether the Marchegg attack was a premeditated diversionary maneuver as part of a deception operation before the Yom Kippur War remains unresolved and ambiguous. No Arab leader has claimed responsibility for the event, and no clear documentation or evidence of any order given by the Syrian or Egyptian government exists. Nevertheless, several clues indicate that the event was planned as a deception.

Colonel (Res.) Dr. Shaul Shay (2018, pers. comm), former head of the Israeli Defense Forces' Military History Department and deputy head of the National Security Council of Israel, says there is no doubt that the Syrian government organized the Marchegg operation to divert Israel's attention as far away from the Golan Heights as possible. In conversations of Egyptian and Syrian tactics of deception, though, no mention of Marchegg can be found. Instead, Shay bases his theory on two main factors.

First, in contrast to other Palestinian organizations, the as-Sa'iqa terrorist group was founded in 1966 by the Syrian regime itself. While Fatah and the Popular Front for the Liberation of Palestine were connected to and received support from the Syrian government, they enjoyed a certain degree of autonomy. As-Sa'iqa, on the other hand, was "100 percent" controlled by the Syrian government. Shay asserts that no terrorist attack could have been conducted in Europe without receiving a "green light" (ibid.) from the authorities in Damascus.

Secondly, the Syrian government was acutely aware of the sensitivity concerning a terrorist attack emanating from the Soviet Bloc. Shay argues that an attack that began in East Germany and Czechoslovakia aiming to hijack Soviet citizens would not be something that Syria would do without careful planning. It would not want to anger its patrons in Moscow. Therefore, Shay reasons this attack could not have been carried out without the explicit approval of the Syrian authorities. "The timing was not accidental," concludes Shay. Allegedly, the attack could have been executed before or after Yom Kippur. Syria eventually chose to act shortly before October 6, 1973, but not too early, to serve Syrian strategic goals. As for the lack of documentation proving the connection, Shay points out that from his experience in researching terrorist attacks, they are mostly undocumented, and when documentation does exist, it remains highly restricted and almost impossible to access (ibid.).

According to Shay, Black, and Morris (1991), the attack could not have been carried out without a "green light" from Damascus. To them, the fact that the terrorists belonged to as-Sa'iqa, a PLO component run by the Syrian government, renders it almost inconceivable that they would have set out on such a politically sensitive mission without official permission. Moreover, only a few days before the attack, the organization's leader, Zuheir Mohsen, had denounced terrorist attacks abroad as "adolescent actions." Perhaps this, too, was a diversionary tactic, which served to rivet Israeli interests for four or five crucial days. Historian Robert Kumamoto (1999) mentions that former secretary of state Henry Kissinger similarly implied that the attack may have been a diversionary move to deflect international attention from the Middle East, if only for a short time.

Finally, the hijackers' testimony must be considered. In November 1973, they gave an exclusive interview to the German magazine *Stern*. There, they employed their pseudonyms: Abu Ali (Khaldi) introduced himself as a twenty-five-year-old lawyer and Abu Salim (Soueidan) as a twenty-two-year-old engineer. They explicitly stated that an attack on a train with Jewish emigrants would divert the attention of Israeli security forces from the Arab preparations for the upcoming war, in general, and the maneuvers of Syrian troops on the border, in particular (Šmok 2018).

KREISKY AND THE YOM KIPPUR WAR: THE SCANDAL OF KNOWLEDGE AND INACTION

On October 3, 1973, one day after the Kreisky-Meir meeting, Egyptian president Anwar Sadat sent his special envoy, Minister of Tourism Ismail Fahmi, to personally thank Kreisky for his choice to "deny services for the Jewish immigration which threatens the Arabs," urging him not to rescind his "courageous decision." This would ensure Austria's "neutral" stance in Middle Eastern affairs (*Yedioth Ahronoth/AFP* 1973, 1). That same day, Kreisky received

Fahmi in his office. While the exact contents of that meeting remain vague, we know that Fahmi hinted that a war with Israel was
coming. Kreisky remembers this meeting in his memoir:

> Following the Schönau affair, Sadat sent Ismael Fahmi,
> one of his later foreign ministers, to Vienna. When he left,
> Fahmi dropped what I regarded as cryptic hints about an
> imminent war. I had to take my leave of him rather hastily,
> because I was due to attend an election meeting at Ried
> im Innkreis. Although we drove at breakneck speed, we
> arrived late. On the way, my colleague Ambassador Thal-
> berg and I discussed Fahmi's visit, and I said that his parting
> remark had struck me as very strange; it sounded as if a
> military confrontation was expected any moment. On the
> very next day war broke out. (Berg 2000, 459)

Contrary to Kreisky's recollections, the war did not break
out the next day but three days later. Political scientist Kathrin
Bachleitner (2018) says that due to the "poisoned atmosphere" between Kreisky and Meir, Kreisky never transmitted the message
to Israel. In his later interviews with the Israeli media, Kreisky
alleged that he had been unsure whether Fahmi had stated that
war would erupt "before Christmas" or "before the end of the
year." He had thought it a "little strange" to hear that from Fahmi,
"even if I was regarded as a friend of Egypt" (Pick 2000). However, in the heated atmosphere generated by the Schönau affair,
Kreisky did not warn the Israelis about the imminent military action against Israel. His longtime personal secretary, the diplomat
Wolfgang Petritsch, critically says, "Kreisky was told about the
war, but he did not talk about it. Once it happened, it naturally
became a much bigger deal than if it would not have happened.
Maybe it was not on his mind. The two prominent Jews, Meir
and Kreisky, were fighting very emotionally. Kreisky, whenever
the Jews tried to solicit him to the Israeli cause, became more
aggressive. Perhaps this explains it" (2014, pers. comm.).

On October 18, 1973, during the war, Israeli ambassador Patish met with Chancellor Kreisky in Vienna. In his secret cable to the Ministry of Foreign Affairs (which was only uncensored in 2006), he references Kreisky's meeting with Fahmi. Apparently, Kreisky stated that the Egyptian envoy had attested that "there is no choice—by the end of 1973," they would go to war with Israel as they could not accept the current situation and their dramatic failure in 1967 (during the Six-Day War).[67]

Kreisky apologized to Patish for not immediately reporting Fahmi's message. He explained that he had not taken it seriously and had needed to continue with his election campaign in Upper Austria.[68] Foreign Ministry officials in Israel were shocked by this report. In his reply to Patish, Deputy General Director Yohanan Meroz writes, "I view these things as very grave. The person allegedly knew about the upcoming Arab attack and did not find it appropriate to warn us. I need not tell you that in these days we are all involved in the military operation and the Prime Minister herself was not informed about this alarming information" (Segev 2006).

On October 4, 1973, prominent Israeli reporter Yesha'yahu Ben Porat was sent to Vienna to interview Kreisky for the newspaper *Yedioth Ahronoth* following the Schönau event. "From the first moment it was as if we were friends," says Ben Porat. "Perhaps it was because I told Kreisky at the beginning that although I was an Israeli journalist, I was born in Vienna." Ben Porat reflects on the "wonderful atmosphere" that ensued after Kreisky's immediate positive reaction, declaring that "now we can speak *Wienerisch!*" Then, sitting in the chancellor's office, Kreisky offered Ben Porat a drink, mentioning sarcastically that he hoped he would not write that he had not received "a glass of water!" Then, after discussing his responsibility as an Austrian chancellor toward the

---

67   Patish to Meroz, telegram, 18 October 1973, (Vienna: September–December 1973), 1.9.1973–31.12.1973, Israel State Archives (Item Reference: 000w3z1/Physical Reference: 7037/15-א), 38, Jerusalem, Israel.
68   Patish to Meroz, 18 Oct. 1973, ISA, 38, Jerusalem, Israel.

Austrian people and following an explanation of his position vis-à-vis the Marchegg event, Kreisky told Ben Porat something that was markedly "off the record and which could not be published" (Petritsch 2011, 21).

"You will soon have war," he shared with Ben Porat. When the latter asked Kreisky to explain the meaning of that surprising statement, Kreisky responded, "A few days ago, I met with a very important Egyptian personality which I cannot name. I understood from this personality that soon there shall be war." Ben Porat says that he did not believe Kreisky at the time as only a couple of days before, he had met Moshe Dayan, Golda Meir, and other senior army officials who had told him that the "Egyptians cannot start a war against us" (ibid.).

Barbara Taufar (2020, pers. comm.), then a journalist in Vienna, provides an interesting perspective of this exchange. Taufar says that immediately after their chat and Kreisky's unexpected warning of a potential war, Ben Porat called his colleague Eitan Haber, the military correspondent at *Yedioth Ahronoth*. After all, Haber had good connections to intelligence agencies in Israel. Ben Porat told Haber about Kreisky's statement that "very soon there will be a war between us and Egypt," and he urged Haber to investigate it. Haber checked the information with his official sources, who replied that they did not know of such preparations.

As a result of these negative official responses, Ben Porat decided not to include Kreisky's quote in the published article to avoid falsely scaring the Israeli public. According to Taufar, Haber trusted his sources and consequently decided with Ben Porat not to publish what could have been the main headline of the article, which was inevitably published on October 5, 1973. "He didn't write it because he believed Eitan Haber, who believed the security forces," says Taufar (ibid.).

Taufar recollects her conversation with Ben Porat, saying, "From this moment on, he told me, the attitude of Israeli journalists toward Israel's security authorities changed as they understood that the internal wars between them caused dangerous disinformation." Before that moment, the political system, the journalists, and the Israeli public had all believed that the intelligence agencies were always right—and after the Yom Kippur War, that changed. Taufar emphasizes that "the journalists were also victims of this internal intelligence war" (ibid.).

When thinking back to the incident, Eitan Haber (2019, pers. comm.) recalls that he and senior editor Dov Judkowski sent Ben Porat to conduct this interview with Kreisky for the newspaper's special Yom Kippur edition. However, he does not remember Ben Porat mentioning Kreisky's ominous line.

Ilich Ramírez Sánchez—also known as Carlos the Jackal, the terrorist integrally involved in various Palestinian operations—highlights the success of this diversionary operation. In a conversation with British journalist David Yallop, Sánchez states, "The plan worked to perfection. It got worldwide publicity. There were protests from Israel's friends and it distracted Golda Meir at just the right time. She first flew into a rage. Then she flew to Vienna. Imagine, the Arabs are about to launch the October War on Israel and they trick the Prime Minister into flying to Austria to rant at Kreisky. Just a few days before the war and two Syrian Palestinians manage singlehandedly to distract the entire Israel nation" (Yallop 1993, 69).

However, Shaul Shay (2018, pers. comm.) is skeptical about the veracity of Fahmi's information and thus the reliability of Kreisky's knowledge of the Egyptian plans. In Shay's estimation, Sadat did not inform his field-army commanders about the war details. "It was, therefore, unlikely that he shared this information with Fahmi," says Shay. Shay also speculates that Kreisky assumed that the Egyptian message was aimed to push Israel to the negotiation table and did not view it as direct information about impending war.

MARCHEGG AS A SIGNIFICANT HISTORICAL EVENT

As it unfolded, there is no doubt that the Marchegg event and its aftermath played a central role in Austrian, Israeli, and Jewish consciousness. In a 1973 protocol, Israeli minister of defense Moshe Dayan goes so far as to state that the event received public attention as no other event had before. "It is the first time that such a matter reached the peak of these [governmental] levels," says Dayan. "It became an international scandal against Austria. If in Austria Kreisky receives letters of support, let him enjoy them! However, the case will come to be regarded as more serious than when the terrorists hijacked the American Jumbo jets and landed them in Zarqa."[69]

While this contemporary reaction is quite clear, the long-term and historical view of the incident is more complex.

Some observers think the event is absent from Austrian, Israeli, and Jewish collective memory. "The Austrians basically erased this chapter because they saw it as a problem that essentially did not concern them directly," Ilan Knapp determines. "For them, this was clearly a Jewish issue" (2019, pers. comm.). As writer Matthias Dahlke (2011) explains, the dramatic events of the Yom Kippur War entirely muffled the Marchegg question. Hans Thalberg, an associate of Kreisky, writes, "The following morning, Schönau was forgotten, and they reported only on the war" (ibid., 221).

Historian Elisabeth Röhrlich (2020, pers. comm.) holds that while the event is not at the forefront of Austrian collective memory, it is remembered when issues concerning refugees and asylum are discussed. In the context of considering Austria's long history of allowing refugees to pass through its territory, vague

---

69 Protocol of Government Meeting, top classified protocol of the Israeli, 3 October 1973, (Protocol of Government Meeting), 3.10.1973, Israel State Archives (Item Reference: N/A as was sent by email directly by the director of the archive, Hagai Tsoref), 25, Jerusalem, Israel.

remarks about Jewish immigration through Vienna and the Marchegg event are mentioned. The event, Röhrlich says, forms part
of a chain of other terrorist events that took place during the
1970s and 1980s in Austria and Europe and is seen in that context.

Located at the juncture of local interests and international
affairs, the events of late September 1973 revealed rifts in the
emerging international community of the 1970s, says historian
Paul Thomas Chamberlin (2012). He notes that the attack and
subsequent hostage crisis set off an international controversy that exposed deep fissures in world opinion regarding the
immigration of Soviet Jews to Israel, the issue of transnational political violence, the extraterritorial privileges of Israeli
immigration agencies, and, ultimately, the meaning of human
rights in the global arena. For the Soviet Jews, their arrival in
Israel represented salvation at the end of a long road to freedom,
states Chamberlin. However, for Palestinians longing for self-determination and sovereignty, it represented another setback in
a decades-long struggle marked by bloodshed, heartbreak, and
shattered hope.

Shaul Shay signals the importance of this event in terms of terrorism history. Most terrorist attacks before and after the Marchegg event were followed by a similar demand, explains Shay:
negotiations to release prisoners. "This attack was unique in the
sense that this was not the case," says Shay. "In Marchegg, the demand was a strategical one vis-à-vis a third party. It is a very rare
example in the history of terrorism" (2018, pers. comm.). Per
his research, this was a unique case that has never been repeated.

As the first transnational terrorist activity in Austria, Dahlke
indicates that Marchegg exposed Austria's intelligence deficits.
He situates the magnitude of the incident in terms of a "global
dynamic" (2011, 215). "I think the event had significance," agrees
Naomi Ben-Ami (2020, pers. comm.), the former head of Nativ.
Kreisky being the first European leader to surrender to terrorism
had a major impact on the international arena, she says. "Kreisky
opened the door on the international level to terrorists," Ilan

Knapp concurs. "He brought them to the negotiation table. All started there" (2019, pers. comm.).

"I strongly agree that this was a completely forgotten event despite being very significant," says Talya Lador-Fresher, the former Israeli ambassador to Vienna. She believes in the possibility that the Marchegg incident was aimed at shifting Israel's focus from the preemptive attack that began the Yom Kippur War, which makes it important enough to be remembered. To Lador-Fresher, the event was "a breakdown point in the relations between Austria and Israel." She speculates that one of the reasons Austria retains its somewhat negative reputation in Israel, even now, is connected to the fact that "the events in Marchegg lie somewhere in the subconscious of Israelis" (2019, pers. comm.). The current Austrian ambassador to Israel, Hannah Liko, agrees that the incident influenced Austria's relations with Israel "dramatically" (2019, pers. comm.).

Hagai Zoref (2019, pers. comm.), researcher and director of the Israel State Archives, similarly emphasizes the importance of this event. As opposed to the 1972 Munich Olympics, the Israeli ambassador was ordered to return to Israel. "That was a serious diplomatic crisis; the Israeli government regarded it very seriously," says Zoref. Apart from the crisis between the two countries, he, too, underscores that it was the first time a leader surrendered to terrorism.

This episode is yet another illustration of the dynamics and ambiguities of Kreisky's political actions and attitudes toward Jewish questions, the State of Israel, and Zionism.

CHAPTER 6: KREISKY, ZIONISM, ISRAEL, AND THE PALESTINIAN ARAB WORLD

IDENTITY AND COMPLEXITY: KREISKY'S RELATIONSHIP TO ZIONISM AND ISRAEL

As already discussed, Kreisky's relationship to Jewish questions was complicated and, if not contradictory, at least highly ambivalent. This applies particularly to Kreisky's relationship with Zionism and Israel. His Austrian identity and loyalty were aspects he considered natural and which remained highly important to him. "Try as I may," he proclaimed, "I cannot see why the land of my real ancestors [Austria-Hungary] should be less dear to me than a strip of desert with which I have no ties" (Berg 2000, 434). In his memoirs, Kreisky makes a fundamental distinction between being a Jew and being an Israeli. For Kreisky, there was a discernable difference between the two identities. Those who lumped them together simply missed something essential. Kreisky insisted that someone who publicly considered himself a non-Zionist Jew had to make the relevant distinctions too. For example, in his interaction with Egyptian president Anwar Sadat, Kreisky explained that "his primary concern was to demonstrate that his position with respect to Israel and his attitude towards Jews in general were two separate matters" (ibid., 478).

Kreisky's criticism of Zionism was radical. He believed that the fundamental idea was problematic. "For a moment I never thought that there is an entitlement to Zionism," Kreisky said in

his interview with Herlinde Koelbl (1989, 146). He even considered Zionism as being in a kind of league with antisemitism.
Zionism welcomed its presence and used it for its own purposes.
"From a very early stage I had the feeling that the Zionists welcomed antisemitism because it bore out their ideas," said Kreisky.
"They have a barely-concealed interest in seeing antisemitism bear
poisonous fruit because this justifies their view. ... The better the
Jews fare, materially and in other ways, the harder it is to attract
them to Israel. ... The Zionists and the antisemites—proceed
from the premise that all the Jews in the world came from Palestine and that essentially they belong to the same ethnic group.
Nothing could be further from the truth" (Berg 2000, 425–34).

Kreisky, moreover, explicitly denied the Jews' right to a des-
ignated homeland. "Jews should not have their own land," he said.
"Their destiny is not having their own land, but their own religion"
(Koelbl 1989, 146). Kreisky argued that the Jewish religion had
"spread all over the world," as the Bible had it, and therefore a
specific land was not relevant. "If there was, or is, a mission for
Judaism, then certainly it was not the one to build their own state
in Israel," he insisted (ibid.). The Libyan Press Association accu-
rately summarizes Kreisky's position by quoting his comments
to Muammar Gaddafi: "Kreisky does not believe that Israel is the
homeland of all the Jews in the world."[70]

Kreisky's negative view of Zionism was closely tied to his
harsh criticism of Israel and its policies. "I do not feel responsible just because I am Jewish for what happens in Israel," said
Kreisky. "I feel responsible as I am representing human rights. My
Jewishness is a completely separate thing: it is a private matter"
(Koelbl 1989, 145). He referred to the establishment of Israel
as an "experiment" to which he "personally does not feel bound."
Furthermore, Kreisky deemed Israel's actions vis-à-vis the Palestinians as no less than the "most rotten methods that we know

---

70   Hacker to Vienna, telegram, 4 November 1973 (Vienna: September–December 1973), 1.9.1973–31.12.1973, Israel State Archives (Item Reference:
000w3z1/Physical Reference: א-7037/15), Jerusalem, Israel.

from modern history." He pondered, "When will the Israelis understand that shooting and breaking legs will damage themselves? There is no justification for what is happening in Israel" (ibid.).

When discussing Israel, Kreisky presented arguments that he would reject when Austrian collective responsibility for Nazi crimes was at issue. While Kreisky often differentiated between "small and big Nazis" and refused to accuse the Austrians of Holocaust crimes, he attributed responsibility to all Israelis for their government's actions. "The guilt does not lie with three or four leading people; all those who participate in the injustice are guilty," said Kreisky. "I see of course that there are people in Israel who don't want this to happen, but as long as they are not able to change the course, they are guilty as well" (ibid.). As racism was "preached in Israel," Kreisky stated, no Jewish ethic existed: "It had been cast out by the Israelis with force" (ibid., 147).

It is evident that the subject was important for Kreisky from the way he raised it on so many private occasions. However, this was surprising given his claim that his Jewishness did not play a significant role in either his private or public life. Nevertheless, quite apart from outside pressure and implied (or explicit) insults, the question of Jewishness weighed on his mind. It was a fraught element of his identity and was informed by conflict, contradictions, ambivalence, and multiple dilemmas.

Consequently, from 1960 to 1973, Kreisky permitted hundreds of thousands of fleeing East European Jews to enter the transit camps in Austria on their way to Israel, despite his opposition to Israeli policies. He was also passionately involved in the Israeli-Palestinian conflict and played an extremely controversial role in mediating several prisoner exchanges between Israel and the PLO.

Kreisky's ambivalence or even hostility towards Israel was related to the fact that in the 1970s, he was vilified almost daily by the Israeli press. "Huge lies about him were written," confirms Taufar (2015, pers. comm.), who was the Austrian press attaché at the Austrian Embassy in Israel from the mid-1970s until the beginning of the 1980s. However, as Menachem Oberbaum in-sists, "I do not think Kreisky was an Israel hater as he was often portrayed" (2020, pers. comm.). Instead, former ambassador Ben-Yaacov claims his public declarations on Israeli affairs were motivated by practical political needs. "I assume that for political reasons and his understanding of the Austrian electorate," says Ben-Yaacov, "he realized that in order to get elected, it would be better to talk against Israel" (2019, pers. comm.).

In his meetings with Israeli officials, Kreisky kept his distance. Ben-Yaacov describes his meetings with the chancellor as "cor-rect." "Even though we both knew we had a similar intellectual background," says Ben-Yaacov, "when we met, it was formal and according to protocol." The former ambassador explains that it was important for Kreisky to keep the image of his relations with Israel as "fair" but never more than that. However, it was equally important for Israeli policymakers and the Ministry of Foreign Affairs to show the world that Israel did not accept Kreisky's at-titude toward Israel. As such, they also did not promote warmer relations, says Ben-Yaacov. Instead, they were ordered to conduct "business as usual" (ibid.). Yossi Ciechanover, director-general of the Foreign Ministry who wanted to maintain Israel's presence in Austria, instructed his staff to limit ministry initiatives. Ben-Yaa-cov claims that diplomatic activity had to proceed on a "low burner" (2012, 231). On a less formal level, Israel's ambassadors maintained close relations with the Austrian Ministry of Foreign Affairs, of which Kreisky was aware. He did not try to tamper with them. "Our differences of opinion with the Austrian govern-ment had no influence on the high-level visits of Israeli Supreme Court justices and the Attorney General and private individuals," says Ben-Yaacov. "They were held in a friendly atmosphere" (ibid., 241).

Once again, contradictions abound—as do personal memo-ries, some of which are much fonder. Ben-Yaacov remembers that "Kreisky came to our Independence Day celebration, and due to my wife Priva's hospitality, I think I won points from him. ... If

Kreisky was still alive, I am nearly certain that if I had traveled to Vienna, I would have met with him" (2019, pers. comm.). He received special permission from the Israeli Ministry of Foreign Affairs to attend Kreisky's funeral in August 1990, even though his term in Vienna had already ended by that time (ibid.).

Ze'ev Shek, the Israeli ambassador to Austria between 1967 and 1971, describes a confidential conversation between himself and the editor in chief of "one of the most important Austrian newspapers." During their chat, the editor shed light on an off-the-record meeting between Kreisky and a German journalist in which they had discussed Middle Eastern affairs. When one of the journalists had praised Israel's pledge for peace, Kreisky had expressed his "appreciation" of Israel's accomplishments while simultaneously insisting that one must "understand the Arabs." He had added that Israel was a "foreign element" in the Middle East and that he understood the stubbornness of Nasser, who aspired to return maximum rights to the Arabs as they had been "robbed of their lands."[71] The editor attributed these harsh verdicts to Kreisky's alleged "Jewish complex." Kreisky, he declared, desperately attempted "to prove his Austrian 'Kosherness' by criticizing Israel." Indeed, the editor asserted that Kreisky's colleagues in the Socialist Party mocked him every time he went out of his way to praise his excellent relations with the Arabs.[72]

Kreisky's contradictions and personal attitudes were often discussed in the Israeli Ministry of Foreign Affairs' reports. In these, it is documented that Kreisky frequently told his counterparts about how proud he was of his brother Paul's son, Yossi, who had served in the Israeli army. Menachem Oberbaum states that Kreisky similarly "admired the Israeli youth" (2020, pers. comm.). Yitzhak Ben-Aharon, a leading member of the left-wing Alignment, met with Kreisky in May 1976. In this meet-

---

71   Shek to Meroz, telegram, 17 June 1970, (Austria: Diplomatic Relations with Austria on a Governmental Level, 1970–71), 1.1.1970–31.12.1971, Israel State Archives (Item Reference: 0002ysm/Physical Reference: 4556/30-חצ), 309, Jerusalem, Israel.

72   Shek to Meroz, 17 June 1970, ISA, 309.

ing, Kreisky described a visit from his young Israeli relative in
Vienna. Kreisky considered him a true "Israeli *sabra*," an officer in
the Israel Defense Forces whose "humanistic figure" had left an
exceedingly positive impression on him and who represented the
"Israeli humanistic creation."[73] Conversely, when talking about
that same nephew with the Israeli ambassador to Vienna Avigdor
Dagan only one week earlier, Kreisky had expressed diametrically
opposite views: "It is extraordinary how these young people do
not believe in any ideal, live a life of constant fear and do not see
a future for Israel."[74]

One possible explanation for this contradiction is that Kreisky
might have viewed left-wing Israeli politicians as allies, and so
showing empathy and appreciation for his nephew was a tool
to strengthen the "humanists." Conversely, he stressed negative
and critical points concerning Israeli policy with the country's
representatives, whom he saw as rivals. There is a chance these
contradictions and deviations were related to his realpolitik,
proving different points to various audiences, and expressing his
own personal conflicts, if not confusion. At any rate, there seems
to be little doubt that Jewish and Israeli concerns were at the
heart of his torn psyche. As Austria's ambassador to Israel, Hannah Liko (2019, pers. comm.) suggests, the two main milestones
in Kreisky's relations to Israel were the Marchegg event and the
Wiesenthal affair.

Kreisky's "contradictions and deviations" did not go unnoticed
by the Israelis. Ambassador Dagan, for one, writes in a telegram,
"The contradictions and deviations in Kreisky's remarks do not
make me angry anymore and I do not get excited by them. They
just become part of the view and there is no need to take them
seriously." Dagan's letter goes on to provide a very harsh personal
and psychological judgment: "We must get used to the fact—I

---

73   Shek to Dagan, telegram, 16 May 1976, (Austria: Diplomatic Relations
with Israel on a Governmental Level, 1976), 1.1.1976–31.12.1976, Israel
State Archives (Item Reference: 000kcf1/Physical Reference: 8488/1-חצ),
243–45, Jerusalem, Israel.

74   Shek to Dagan, 16 May 1976, ISA, 243–45.

personally have already—that in any matter relating, also indirectly, to Israel or to Judaism, we have to deal with a mentally unstable and unbalanced person, who suffers from a harsh case of '*Hassliebe*' [love-hate relationship] which borders on schizophrenia."[75] Beyond a nonqualified psychological judgment, this statement shows the degree of hostility some Israeli officials felt toward Kreisky.

In the 1970s, Otto Schulmeister, the conservative former editor in chief of the influential Austrian newspaper *Die Presse*, described private, off-the-record conversations with senior Israeli diplomats. In these conversations, they discussed Kreisky's policies toward Israel. The diplomats claimed that something irrational motivated the policies.

Schulmeister professed that "it is clear to all in Vienna what the source of his position is, but when someone articulates it, it drives him even crazier. The quiet, balanced, educated, and one could also say mighty man, loses his temper and amazes his audience with his lack of reason and hate without restraint."[76] What is more, according to Schulmeister, Kreisky's policies relating to Israel and the Middle East received neither public support nor did his party support them. "All ask why Austria needs to put a healthy head into a sickbed of mediation or take sides in the Middle Eastern conflict," said Schulmeister. Still, Kreisky's prestige, charisma, and enthusiasm slowly brought him more supporters.[77]

Classified telegrams and thick diplomatic correspondences between the Embassy of Israel in Vienna and the Ministry of Foreign Affairs' headquarters in Jerusalem reveal much about the official,

---

75 Dagan to Shek, telegram, 24 May 1976, (Austria: Diplomatic Relations with Israel on a Governmental Level, 1976), 1.1.1976–31.12.1976, Israel State Archives (Item Reference: 000kcf1/Physical Reference: 8488/1-חצ), 235–36, Jerusalem, Israel.

76 Shek to Dagan, telegram, 9 May 1976, (Austria: Diplomatic Relations with Israel on a Governmental Level, 1976), 1.1.1976–31.12.1976, Israel State Archives (Item Reference: 000kcf1/Physical Reference: 8488/1-חצ), 257–59, Jerusalem, Israel.

77 Shek to Dagan, 9 May 1976, ISA, 257–59.

yet confidential, Israeli policy regarding Kreisky. In a myriad of diplomatic correspondences, the advisable policy concerning Kreisky is discussed.

From one perspective, realpolitik considerations were of importance. In a telegram sent to Jerusalem, Ambassador Dagan explains that the Israeli dependence on Kreisky was due to his absolute power in Austrian decision-making. "We are dependent on Kreisky in matters of immigration and emigration, the Kfir fighter plane, compensation from Austria, the opening of the PLO offices in Vienna and in fact, all other topics," says Dagan, "as there is nothing in Austria that one can achieve without his personal consent."[78]

Dagan refers to the tension between Chancellor Kreisky and Prime Minister Yitzhak Rabin and emphasizes the need to continue with the previous "method of handling the relations with Kreisky" (see the next section for the causes and background of this tension). In one short and cynical sentence, he reveals the prevailing Israeli thinking at the time. "We need to continue with the game," Dagan says, "in which we leave the Chancellor with the impression that we accept his opinion that he can play a role in the Middle East, even if we know that it is fiction."[79] In another telegram, Deputy Director-General Shek references Rabin's recent meeting with Kreisky in Geneva, saying that the prime minister "went according to the rule—preventing the rift with Kreisky without authorizing him to be a mediator."[80]

---

78   Dagan to Shek, telegram, 22 November 1976, (Austria: Diplomatic Relations with Israel on a Governmental Level, 1976), 1.1.1976–31.12.1976, Israel State Archives (Item Reference: 000kcf1/Physical Reference: 8488/1-חצ), 41–43, Jerusalem, Israel.

79   Dagan to Shek, 22 Nov. 1976, ISA, 41–43.

80   Shek to Dagan, 9 May 1976, ISA, 257–59.

KREISKY AND ISRAELI LEADERS

Kreisky's relationships with Israeli leaders were particularly charged and, unlike other diplomatic relationships, were often very personal and went to the heart of his complicated identity (Embacher and Reiter 1998). This especially concerned the tension between Diaspora and Zionist Jews. Kreisky stated that Israeli politicians could not stand that successful non-Zionist Jews like Henry Kissinger and himself had become leaders in their home countries; that Jewish national sovereignty was not the only road to power and influence.

However, mainly attitudes towards Kreisky were ambiguous. "On the one hand," says former Israeli prime minister and president Shimon Peres, "we were proud that here was a Jewish person who became Chancellor. On the other hand, we felt the cold wind that was blowing from him towards Zionism and to all the other attitudes of life, our way of life" (1997).

Whenever Kreisky was accused of being a self-denying Jew by Israeli politicians, he would say, "Everybody that looks at me could see that I am a Jew'" (Taufar 2015, pers. comm.). Despite his complicated relation to Jewish identity, Kreisky apparently thought that there was such a thing as a Jewish physiognomy. Shimon Peres, who had criticized Kreisky on many occasions, observed Kreisky's conflicted Jewishness, saying, "He was very warm on Jewish issues and even referred to his sense that he was surrounded by antisemitism. But on the other hand, being Jewish, in his eyes, I believe, limited his capacity to move around politically in the world." Peres alleges that Kreisky's "attacks" on Israel were motivated by practical concerns tied to his foreign policy and willingness to tighten Austrian connections with Arab countries. "Kreisky thought that by attacking Israel he would gain more attention and a hearing in the Arab world," says Peres (1997).

Petritsch, however, disagrees with this assertion. "He was so emotional toward Israel because he felt part of it," says Petritsch.

"His emotional tie, especially toward the end of his life, played an important role in his policies vis-à-vis Israel" (2014, pers. comm.).

There are significant differences in Kreisky's relationship with and opinions of high-ranking Israeli politicians. During the 1970s, Kreisky was very impressed by Peres, at least in Barbara Taufar's estimation. However, Kreisky quickly understood that Peres spoke differently about the Palestinians to his own Labor Party and the Israeli media than to the Socialist International and its leaders in Europe. "Kreisky truly believed Peres, who pretended to be the only left-wing Socialist in Israel," says Taufar. "Nevertheless, he opposed Kreisky's stance on the Palestinians" (2015, pers. comm.). In retrospect, it is hard to say what Kreisky and Peres truly thought of each other. While expressing his admiration for Peres, in his memoirs, Kreisky writes that "I am reluctant to mention Peres in this context [people of peace], since I have found him a very ambiguous figure" (Berg 2000, 441). Overall, it seems safe to say that the two politicians had an ambiguous opinion of each other.

Kreisky's relationship with Golda Meir was much more complicated and emotional, as discussed in the Marchegg chapter. However, Kreisky could still find consensus with Meir because she was nominally on the left. In contrast, Kreisky's opinion of former prime minister and foreign minister Yitzhak Shamir was purely negative. Kreisky referred to him as a "Fascist" and politician who "worked together with the Nazis" (Koelbl 1989, 145). "It is a historical fact that I do not understand [how] this is not well-known yet," said Kreisky and added that "the sad truth is that Fascist Jews like Shamir wished for the victory of Hitler. They wanted the victory of Hitler over England in order to win Israel for themselves" (ibid.).

Kreisky's relationship with Prime Minister Yitzhak Rabin was complicated as well. "Kreisky had a big mouth and always said what was on his mind," Uri Avnery states. Avnery reports that Kreisky once "told me about Rabin—'Der Mann hat es nicht endlich' [This man is worthless]" (2015, pers. comm.). In November 1976, three years after his confrontations with Gold Meir, a clash between Kreisky and Rabin received wide attention in the Austrian and Israeli media. On its front page, the Israeli newspaper *Maariv* published an article in which Kreisky accused Rabin of attempting to hamper a meeting that he had convened between Egyptian president Sadat and Diasporic Jewish leaders. Rabin hurriedly dismissed these accusations and criticized Kreisky, saying, "In the eyes of some statesman their countries are too small, and therefore they interfere in problems of other countries, although they have many problems of their own." It was also reported that Rabin had called Kreisky "one of those naïve European statesmen."[81]

Kreisky vehemently denied that he had accused Rabin of hampering the meeting and denounced Rabin's "harsh response which was unclear to me." He complained that Rabin's "grumbling" comments were "astonishing."[82] The popular Austrian newspaper *Kronen Zeitung* linked Kreisky's mishandling of his meeting with Meir to the current conflict with Rabin. "As in the reaction to Meir's claims about the 'glass of water' in their meeting," reported the newspaper, "Kreisky was angry at Rabin's reactions."[83]

Forever the mediator, Ambassador Dagan appealed for a "lowering of the unnecessary tensions and clarify[ing] misunderstandings." However, a classified telegram written by Dagan to his headquarters reveals that Kreisky most likely did believe that Rabin had sought to interfere with the meeting. Per Dagan, about one month before the article was published, Karl Kahane, Kreisky's close friend, had told him that Kreisky had been furious

---

81   Shek to Dagan, telegram, 21 November 1976, (Austria: Diplomatic Relations with Israel on a Governmental Level, 1976), 1.1.1976–31.12.1976, Israel State Archives (Item Reference: 000kcf1/Physical Reference: 8488/1-חצ), 56, Jerusalem, Israel.

82   Shek to Dagan, 21 Nov. 1976, ISA, 56.

83   Israeli Embassy Vienna Press Brief, 19 November 1976, (Austria: Diplomatic Relations with Israel on a Governmental Level, 1976), 1.1.1976–31.12.1976, Israel State Archives (Item Reference: 000kcf1/Physical Reference: 8488/1-חצ), 51, Jerusalem, Israel.

with Rabin, although Kreisky had not been willing to explain why.
Dagan then reports that an examination Kreisky had conducted
concluded that the leak had probably come from the president of
the WJC, Nahum Goldmann.[84]

A meeting between Kreisky and Rabin had been scheduled
to take place in Geneva on November 25—independent of the
dispute between them. The meeting presented an opportunity
to settle the controversy. The meeting was private, and thus no
protocol was published. However, Shek states that although the
meeting began coldly, Rabin managed to "break the ice" and discuss Israel's desire for peace.[85] The Austrian press published various accounts of the meeting. The Socialist *Arbeiter-Zeitung* wrote
that "Rabin invited Kreisky to the Labor Party Convention;" the
independent *Die Presse* reported that "Israel is for a Middle East
Peace Convention;" the *Kronen Zeitung* warned that "new explo-
sives are awaiting" the two leaders. Regardless of other matters
dealt with in this meeting, it ended the mini-crisis.[86]

Kreisky's encounters with other "colorful" Israeli leaders
were inevitably charged. For example, his relationship with
Menachem Begin was both emotional and noteworthy. As Menachem Oberbaum muses, "I do not know who Kreisky hated
more—Golda Meir or Menachem Begin" (2020, pers. comm.).
For one thing, on several occasions, Kreisky described Begin
as an *Ostjude*. In an interview with a British journalist in 1978,
Kreisky—enraged over Prime Minister Begin's dilatory tactics

---

84   Dagan to Shek, telegram, 30 August 1976, (Austria: Diplomatic Relations
with Israel on a Governmental Level, 1976), 1.1.1976–31.12.1976, Israel
State Archives (Item Reference: 000kcf1/Physical Reference: 8488/1-חצ),
135, Jerusalem, Israel.

85   Shek to Dagan, telegram, 19 December 1976, (Austria: Diplomatic Relations with Israel on a Governmental Level, 1976), 1.1.1976–31.12.1976,
Israel State Archives (Item Reference: 000kcf1/Physical Reference: 8488/1-
חצ), 10, Jerusalem, Israel.

86   Peled to Shek, telegram, 30 November 1976, (Austria: Diplomatic Relations with Israel on a Governmental Level, 1976), 1.1.1976–31.12.1976,
Israel State Archives (Item Reference: 000kcf1/Physical Reference: 8488/1-
חצ), 27, Jerusalem, Israel.

in his negotiations with Sadat—characterized the Israeli leader as "a little lawyer from Warsaw with the soul of a narrow-minded shopkeeper." Later, Kreisky expanded on that remark by calling Israel a "police state that was run by men with a Fascist mentality" (Secher 1994, 25).

In 1974 during Kreisky's visit to Israel, as part of a fact-finding mission, he was invited by Begin, then the opposition leader, to appear in front of the committee of the right-wing political party Herut (later Likud). Some prominent members of the committee threatened to boycott the event. Kreisky, they determined, was not deserving of such an honor. Despite these objections, Begin insisted on honoring the invitation "because he wanted to listen" to what the Austrian leader had to say, recalls Begin's secretary, Yona Klimowitzky (1997).

Begin justified his position by saying, "Kreisky was a Jew after all." Begin was critical of Kreisky, but he still wanted to hear him out, Klimowitzky explains. Kreisky remarked that Begin, "with all this façade of being extremist, was a great democrat at heart, and always respected the other side's opinion and it did not matter what they were." In the end, Kreisky spent almost three hours at the meeting. Klimowitzky remembers intense but fruitful discussions.

Despite his tolerance towards Kreisky, Begin's opinion was still highly ambivalent. He took Kreisky and Kissinger to be "self-hating Jews" and said they were more dangerous to Israel than critical non-Jewish leaders precisely for that reason. At the same time, however, he shared a similarity to Kreisky since all Jewish leaders contained some degree of ambivalence regarding such questions. Begin even respected Kreisky's intelligence and achievements, noting that "it wasn't easy for somebody like Kreisky to become Chancellor of Austria" (Klimowitzky 1997).

Klimowitzky states that, ironically, Begin was proud that a Jew could become the chancellor of Austria "of all places." Zionism or no Zionism, Begin perceived Kreisky's personal political achievements as a collective Jewish success. "We made it," Begin said, "The Jew is the Chancellor of Austria." A sentiment that would have appalled Kreisky. Although they had engaged in bitter debates, as Klimowitzky herself observed, this did not matter for Begin. "Amid all this love-hate there was great admiration," says Klimowitzky, "because Kreisky was a person you could not help but admire." Nevertheless, the relationship was complicated. Because both personalities were very stubborn and very ideological, "it could not work even if they wanted to," explains Klimowitzky (ibid.).

Begin's attitudes to Kreisky were as mixed and contradictory as Kreisky's own. Perhaps that is why the meeting between these two titans is so fascinating. As Klimowitzky says, "Begin never hesitated to mention Kreisky as a person to go to, whether there was trouble or Israel wanted peace. He always referred to him." Simultaneously, there was something in Begin's emotional make-up that could not make sense of Kreisky's person and actions. Possibly because he had been traumatized by the Holocaust, he could not imagine a Jew who did not place "the interest of the existence of the Jewish people as his first priority." To Klimowitzky, this constituted the main divide between the two. Begin wanted Kreisky to identify himself as a Jew, and he could not conceive of the idea that Kreisky considered himself an Austrian above all. Given these extreme positions, Begin labeled Kreisky's dialogue with the PLO literally as a dialogue with Adolf Hitler. How, Begin asked, could a Holocaust survivor such as Kreisky legitimize a person who wanted to "destroy the people of Israel"? This obviously infuriated Kreisky (ibid.).

On November 22, 1981, Prime Minister Begin sent Minister of the Interior Yosef Burg to meet with Kreisky in Vienna. This meeting took place despite the opposition of Foreign Minister Yitzhak Shamir and the Israeli ambassador to Vienna Yissakhar Ben-Yaacov, who had said that meeting Kreisky after his recent "anti-Jewish and anti-Israeli statements" was wrong.[87] (It is not clear what specific

---

87   Europe 1 Department to Israeli Embassy in Vienna, telegram, 12 November 1981, (Austria: Diplomatic Relations with Israel on a Governmental Level, 1981), 16.4.1981–28.12.1981, Israel State Archives (Item Reference: 000bftp/Physical Reference: 8895/16-חצ), 155, Jerusalem, Israel.

incident Ben-Yaacov was referencing. Maybe it was Kreisky's refusal to back down from his harsh, continued statements about Prime Minister Begin.) This was the first meeting in years between Kreisky and an Israeli minister and the first with a member of Begin's cabinet. Per a *Maariv* report, the first question Kreisky asked his guest concerned "coffee or tea," unmistakably referring to the "glass of water" incident with Golda Meir a few years earlier. According to the Israeli protocol, the meeting took two hours longer than initially planned, and the two sides decided to lower the "decibels" between their governments and further discuss the issues at stake. Kreisky described the bilateral relations between Israel and Austria as "good and with no problems."[88]

The Austrian press described the meeting positively, in contrast to the antagonistic atmosphere during the Kreisky-Meir clash. The meeting was depicted as a fruitful dialogue between two parties who had agreed to disagree.[89] As mentioned before, Ben-Yaacov was present at the meeting and served as a "watchdog" on behalf of Minister Shamir, who had objected to the meeting. Reporting back to the ministry, Georg Lennkh, Kreisky's diplomatic secretary at the time, told Ben-Yaacov that regardless of their differences, he considered the meeting a crucial one and one that would improve the dialogue between the two countries, with which Ben-Yaacov agreed.[90]

However, this viewpoint was not shared by Minister Shamir. In a handwritten note, he wrote, "I disagree with the assessment of

---

88   Europe 1 Department to Israeli Embassy in Vienna, telegram. 23 November 1981, (Austria: Diplomatic Relations with Israel on a Governmental Level, 1981), 16.4.1981–28.12.1981, Israel State Archives (Item Reference: 000bftp/Physical Reference: 8895/16-חצ), 127, Jerusalem, Israel.

89   Israeli Embassy Vienna Press Brief, 24 November 1981, (Austria: Diplomatic Relations with Israel on a Governmental Level, 1981), 16.4.1981–28.12.1981, Israel State Archives (Item Reference: 000bftp/Physical Reference: 8895/16-חצ), 105–117, Jerusalem, Israel.

90   Ben-Yaacov to Ministry of Foreign Affairs, telegram, 30 November 1981, (Austria: Diplomatic Relations with Israel on a Governmental Level, 1981), 16.4.1981–28.12.1981, Israel State Archives (Item Reference: 000bftp/Physical Reference: 8895/16-חצ), 103, Jerusalem, Israel.

the Ambassador. Did he not know that the Minister opposed the meeting? Dialogue with us is the aim of Kreisky who wants to show that he is bipartisan and to get a 'Kosher Certificate' for his support of the PLO."[91] Despite the relations being alternatingly more and less sympathetic, one thing remained: Kreisky sought to be seen as an "objective" participant in Middle Eastern affairs. In contrast, the Israelis sought to keep him from supporting the PLO.

At the beginning of the 1982 Lebanon War, Kreisky tried to form an international coalition to stop what he viewed as Israel's aggressions. According to Uri Avnery, Kreisky attempted to recruit François Mitterrand and Willy Brandt to stop Begin and Sharon. Both leaders refused to take part in such efforts. Avnery recalls Kreisky harshly describing Mitterrand as a "Fascist." "I decided to publish it, and Kreisky was very mad at me," says Avnery (2015, pers. comm.). During that war, every Israeli diplomat was faced with the challenge of publicly explaining and justifying Israeli policy. Consequently, the Embassy of Israel in Vienna went on "war status," Ben-Yaacov (2012) writes. In Vienna, another problem developed. "The war gave Chancellor Kreisky an excuse to renew his efforts at strengthening the PLO position and to paint Israel as the aggressor," says Ben-Yaacov. He includes that most of Kreisky's statements were unacceptable, such as his interview with the Parisian weekly magazine *Le Nouvel Observateur*, where he had described the Jewish people as "a joke in the history of the world" (ibid., 251).

However, as always, there was another side to Kreisky's actions during the Lebanon War. He played an important role in negotiating the release of twenty Israeli soldiers taken as prisoners by Palestinian militants. Israel found itself in a precarious position. Neither the Syrian government nor the PLO permitted the Red Cross to meet them, and the Israeli intelligence agen-

---

91   Shamir to Meroz, 1 December 1981, (Austria: Diplomatic Relations with Israel on a Governmental Level, 1981), 16.4.1981–28.12.1981, Israel State Archives (Item Reference: 000bftp/Physical Reference: 8895/16-חצ), 102, Jerusalem, Israel.

cies did not have any information about their whereabouts. The imprisonment was not reported on in the Israeli press due to strict censorship. However, the Israeli government and security forces searched for nonpublic solutions through various methods. One of these attempts was related to the retired Israeli left-wing politician Lowa Eliav. Eliav explains the surprising phone call he received on September 21, 1982, from an Israeli army general asking to meet him immediately.

In this meeting, the general asked him, on behalf of Prime Minister Begin, to use his connections to bring the prisoners back to Israel, employing any method he could. Eliav accepted the mission and immediately contacted his friend Kreisky, who he assumed could help. He notified Begin of this plan and received his approval. "I don't care if you go and see the devil," said Begin, "as long as you know something. Bring the bodies; bring us a signal, that they are alive. I don't care, and we will give you all the help that we can." The following day, Eliav flew to Vienna to meet Kreisky. The chancellor joined him that same afternoon in his home on Armbrustergasse, in the eighteenth district. Kreisky's resentment toward Israeli policies and his harsh public criticism of Israel's role in the Lebanon War notwithstanding, he agreed to help. As Eliav describes the encounter, "First of all, I will help you, Kreisky told me, because you are on a humanitarian mission and you say you act on behalf of the families. I will help you, as much as I can" (1997).

Kreisky then appointed Dr. Herbert Amry, the Austrian ambassador in Beirut, as his special envoy and made unprecedented efforts to resolve this matter, says Eliav (ibid.). Next, Kreisky contacted the people he knew in the PLO and sent a personal, touching letter to Syrian president Hafez al-Assad, requesting permission to send his special envoy through diplomatic channels. The Syrians quickly agreed, and Amry was sent from Vienna to Damascus. From that moment, the situation changed, and uncertainty was replaced with hope. During the process, Kreisky longed for a "two-way road." Amry would see what was happen-

ing with the Israelis while also observing what was happening to
Arab, Syrian, or Palestinian prisoners of war in Israel.

After continuous and arduous mediation efforts, the Popular
Front for the Liberation of Palestine, led by Ahmed Jibril, returned six Israeli soldiers alive. In exchange, Israel released four
thousand prisoners. Eliav emphasizes that Kreisky told him repeatedly that his help was on a "purely humanitarian basis" (ibid.).
That was his motivation for this undertaking. Although there was
an ongoing effort by Kreisky to bring back the Israeli soldiers, the
Israeli press portrayed Kreisky as the one who had agreed to the
release of four thousand Arab prisoners and was thus responsible
for an unfair deal. Per Taufar, the Israeli government was embar-
rassed by the respective numbers in the prisoner exchange; they
required a "black sheep" and therefore blamed Kreisky. There was
something cruel in this. Klimowitzky describes the situation like
this: "There was now an old man [Kreisky], very sick, he even
traveled on a wheelchair to Damascus to Jibril to get the boys out
and then at the end they lie to the public through the media telling them that it was Kreisky who demanded these people" (1997).

These were all stubborn men. Eliav (1997) recounts that Begin
could not bear to write a letter of appreciation to Kreisky for his
efforts during the Lebanon War. Instead, he asked Simcha Ehrlich,
the acting prime minister during Begin's trip to the United States,
to thank him. Kreisky understood that Begin had not wanted to
write such a letter himself and was disappointed. Begin mostly
needed Kreisky to assist in matters concerning Israel and the Arab
world. As reflected in the prisoner-exchange episode, Begin did
not hesitate to contact Kreisky when necessary. "When he was in
trouble," says Klimowitzky, "he always turned to Kreisky" (1997).
However, at better times, he found approaching him more difficult.

Both men were mercurial in their moods and statements. In his
infamous interview with James Dorsey for the Dutch newspaper
Trouw in 1978, Kreisky took a sweeping swipe. He harshly criticized and insulted Israeli leaders, especially Begin, and portrayed
Israeli society in wildly negative ways. Begin, in response, resort-

ed to a bit of amateur Freudian psychology and labeled Kreisky "a person who hates his father and his mother." However, Kreisky's polemic was not limited to Begin. As a result, the German-born Israeli interior minister Yosef Burg, who had read Dorsey's interview in German, thought that Kreisky's choice of terminology resembled that of Joseph Goebbels. (Ironically, many of the claims that Burg opposed so harshly closely resembled ideas in the book *Defeating Hitler* [2007], written by the former head of The Jewish Agency, Avraham Burg, Yosef's son.)

BRUNO AND PAUL KREISKY: A SURPRISING FRATERNAL INTERLUDE

While Kreisky had a strained relationship with Israeli leaders and the state of Israel, other members of his family did not share his antipathy. As previously mentioned, Kreisky's nephew, Yossi, had served in a paratrooper unit in the Israeli army, of which Kreisky was immensely proud, despite his harsh criticism of Israeli militarism (Embacher and Reiter 1998). However, what is even more surprising, is that Kreisky's brother Paul actually lived in Israel. Paul was born in Vienna in 1909 and fought against the Austrofascist state. Later, he became a Zionist and a religious Jew and moved to Jerusalem in 1938. During one of Kreisky's visits to the country, he met with his brother. Apparently, he had not seen him for thirty-six years, and for a long time, little was known about Paul in general—and even less about his relationship to his famous brother, Bruno (ibid.). However, the interviews conducted for this book fill in some of the blanks and paint a sharper, more unique picture of the complex relationship between the Kreisky brothers.

First, it is essential to delve into Paul's history. Taufar (2015, pers. comm.) relates that when Paul was sixteen, he climbed a tree and fell on his head. This accident caused severe brain damage and, to some extent, rendered Paul mentally disabled. From an early age, Paul underwent psychiatric therapy. In addition to

mental plight, Paul also faced family tragedy. Although the details
are unclear, it is known that his wife committed suicide after giving birth to their son, Yossi.

Nevertheless, Paul was a well-known personality in Jerusalem, Taufar indicates. The brother of Austria's chancellor became
notorious as a kind of panhandler, begging for money, wandering
Jerusalem's streets and coffee shops, and immediately spending
what he had collected. Unable to find a job, he would constantly
inform people that he was "Bruno Kreisky's brother" (ibid.). This
strange connection naturally attracted the attention of Israeli
journalists as ideal gossip material.

They would have found a point that hardly fit Kreisky's negative image in Israel, Taufar says, had they known that Bruno had
supported Paul financially throughout the postwar years. At first,
he had done so with the help of Dr. Jacob Brenner, who became
the Austrian honorary consul general in Tel Aviv after the establishment of relations between Austria and Israel. Later, this task
fell to the prominent Israeli lawyer Yehezkel Beinisch.

Beinisch describes his first meeting with Chancellor Kreisky
in Vienna, where Kreisky requested he take care of his brother.
"I met Kreisky in his Vienna office in 1983," says Beinisch. "He
asked me to open an Israeli bank account in Jerusalem, which I
did. He told me to take care of everything that Paul needed but
to also take care of his expenses—to see that he did not spend it
on unimportant things" (2015, pers. comm.). Beinisch highlights
Kreisky's profound sense of responsibility for his brother, saying
he had never seen anything like it before.

This explains Kreisky's strong reaction to an interview with an
Israeli newspaper in which both his former friend Karl Kahane
and the Viennese-born mayor of Jerusalem Teddy Kollek accused
Kreisky of "abandoning his brother, Paul." Taufar says that this
was one of the few times she saw Kreisky truly angry. Oberbaum
confirms this, saying, "He personally showed me his wire transfers, sending funds to his brother in order to support him" (2020,
pers. comm.).

However, there is still a more intriguing aspect to this story. Besides the touching way the powerful Austrian chancellor cared for his hapless brother, there was also Kreisky's determination to have a personal connection to Israel. As Beinisch relates, "I felt it. During our telephone calls and our meetings, it was clear that Kreisky wanted to have a deep, personal connection to Israel. While he was always attacking Israel for its policies vis-à-vis the Palestinian issue, he believed that he had been incorrectly understood. Margit Schmidt and Barbara Taufar told me that the reason he took me for this job was my connection to high officials in Israel" (ibid.).

At the same time, Kreisky's wish for a personal connection to Israel and Israeli officials through his brother and the person tasked to watch out for his brother led to some absurd situations. Prime Minister Begin's advisor, Yehuda Avner (2009), recollects that one day—as he was about to walk into the room of Begin's bureau chief, Yehiel Kadishai—he noticed "a bedraggled-looking fellow in a battered trilby hat and a tattered raincoat, whom I recognized as a peddler of matches in downtown Jerusalem."

"His name is Kreisky," said Kadishai to Avner.

"Kreisky who?" he asked.

"Paul Kreisky, brother of the chancellor of Austria, Bruno Kreisky."

Avner reports that his "mouth dropped open" when told that Paul had been living in Israel for years and that he was "a great fan of Begin." Begin had even "occasionally helped him out," said Kadishai (ibid.).

However, there is an even more outlandish story about Paul and Bruno Kreisky's relationship revealed in a strictly confidential telegram by Ze'ev Shek to the Ministry of Foreign Affairs' director-general's office on October 22, 1976. In this unusual telegram, Shek enumerates Bruno Kreisky's accusations and charges against Israeli security services' alleged actions towards Paul Kreisky. The report states that in various talks with Israelis and other Jews, Bruno Kreisky claimed that the "Israeli security forces" had aided Wiesenthal in an operation to kidnap Paul, bring him to the Netherlands for interrogation, and exploit him against his brother, the chancellor. Supposedly, the goal had been to extort concessions from the chancellor in his struggle against Wiesenthal. Shek reports that he personally heard this version from WJC president Nahum Goldmann and his team and Avigdor Dagan, the Israeli ambassador in Vienna. In his telegram, Shek requests all details related to Paul Kreisky's voyage, just in case the chancellor would raise the matter in his upcoming meeting with the Israeli foreign minister.[92]

"Kreisky suddenly added that horrible things were being done to Paul," says Ambassador Dagan. "His retarded brother disappeared from Israel and after one month no one knew anything about him or his whereabouts. He suspected that he was forced to leave the country—probably to Holland, where Wiesenthal had many friends and was being held in order to use Paul in the right moment against him."[93]

Menachem Oberbaum (2020, pers. comm.) recalls further details that Kreisky shared with him: After being unable to get ahold of his brother, he suddenly received a phone call from him. Still unaware of Paul's whereabouts, Kreisky used his connections—asking the German secret service to help—and was informed that the phone call had originated from Germany. Eventually, Paul was found at a local brothel. Oberbaum says Kreisky accused Begin of sending Paul there to embarrass and harm him politically. Soon after that, Paul was sent back to Israel.

---

92   Shek to Dagan, telegram, 22 October 1976, (Austria: Diplomatic Relations with Israel on a Governmental Level, 1976), 1.1.1976–31.12.1976, Israel State Archives (Item Reference: 000kcf1/Physical Reference: 8488/1-חצ), 97, Jerusalem, Israel.
93   Shek to Dagan, 23 Oct. 1975, ISA, 138–39.

KREISKY, ISRAEL, THE MIDDLE EAST, AND THE ISRAELI-PALESTINIAN CONFLICT[94]

Kreisky was involved with and often played a crucial role in many critical aspects of Middle Eastern affairs, developments in the Arab World, Israeli politics, and, above all, the Israeli-Palestinian conflict. There are probably many reasons for his deep commitment to these issues, including his Socialist worldview, his desire to render Austria a significant power, and—somewhere in the mix (and always in complicated ways)—his own Jewishness. However, to better contextualize Kreisky's intricate role, it is first necessary to examine his relations and attitudes toward questions relating more broadly to the Middle East.

During the first half of the 1970s, the Socialist International leaders—Willy Brandt, chancellor of the Federal Republic of Germany, Bruno Kreisky, Austria's federal chancellor, and Olof Palme, prime minister of Sweden—forged a unique Social Democratic network for Europe's policy toward the Middle East. This "Top Trio" had already become close friends during World War II in Swedish exile. B. Vivekanandan describes their connection in his book *Global Visions of Olof Palme, Bruno Kreisky and Willy Brandt* (2016). "There are times in the course of history when great personalities make enlightened interventions and point the way for changes which would be beneficial to humanity as a whole," says Vivekanandan. "The greatness of Palme, Kreisky and Brandt rests on the fact that together they made a spectacular intervention in the second half of the twentieth century by pointing the way towards building a world society wedded to peace, equality, freedom, justice and solidarity" (Vivekanandan 2016, 2).

Brandt and Kreisky divided their international efforts by geographical areas. Kreisky focused on the Middle East, while Brandt

---

94   This chapter is based on my master's thesis: Daniel Aschheim, "Bruno Kreisky's Premature Role as a Peacemaker in the Middle East: The Paradoxes of Jewishness, Socialism and the Middle Eastern Conflict" (master's thesis, Hebrew University in Jerusalem, 2015).

invested his time in East-West politics, leading to his famous Ost-politik (Eastern policy). Kreisky's growing involvement in the Is-raeli-Palestinian conflict was, perhaps, also a result of a particular interest in minorities in general. He had always been interested in the South Tyrol dispute, supporting South Tyroleans' claims for self-determination while denouncing their terrorist acts against Italy. Kreisky had negotiated with the terrorists as he had been convinced that talking to them would resolve the conflict peacefully. Georg Lennkh discloses that Kreisky saw the South Tyrol issue as similar to the Israeli-Palestinian question. "Kreisky always tried the 'double track policy,'" says Lennkh. "He tried to convince the PLO to cease their use of violence, similarly to the way he convinced the South Tyrol population to cease employing terror as a means of protest" (2015, pers. comm.).

His commitment was both pioneering and substantial. Kreisky had already begun his peacemaking efforts in the early 1970s. A significant milestone came in 1973 when he addressed a confer-ence of Socialist International party leaders in London with a pro-posal to send a fact-finding mission to the Middle East under his leadership. This idea engendered much opposition. Responding to accusations that the mission would not be balanced due to his pro-Arab stance, Kreisky cynically said that there was no need to hear the Israeli side as "representatives of other countries were more than willing to argue their case for them" (Berg 2000, 451). Kreisky made three trips to the Middle East after that: in 1974, 1975, and 1976—two of which involved a visit to Israel.

The results of all three fact-finding missions are detailed in a final report to the Socialist International in 1977, to which the Austrian chancellor wrote the introduction. The whole final recommendations also bear the imprint of Kreisky's thoughts. Kreisky favored the creation of a Palestinian state, though he was aware of the tenuous economic condition of that state unless it received financial support from its oil-rich Arab neighbors initial-ly. He also recognized that the existence of a Palestinian state was bound to diminish the "messianic" character of Israel, no longer distinguishing it greatly from its Middle Eastern neighbors (Secher 1994, 23).

In March 1974, Kreisky made a trip to Israel for the first time as part of an official visit. During his three-day tour, Kreisky feared that he would face hostile mass demonstrations. Some journalists described him as "nervous" upon his arrival. However, the pressure was somehow relieved as a few days beforehand, the Histadrut (Israel's labor association) Congress had already aired their grievances towards the two Austrian representatives. Kreisky's visit turned out to be relatively calm (Embacher and Reiter 1998). He deemed his trip to Yad Vashem (The World Holocaust Remembrance Center) a meaningful, emotional experience. When he saw his cousin's name on the victims' list, he was touched (ibid.). His second trip to Israel took place in 1976, where he participated in the Israeli Labor Party's convention as the representative of the Socialist International.

Kreisky was always at the controversial center of debate and inevitably critical of Israeli policies, yet at no stage did Kreisky undermine the legitimacy of the State of Israel. He stressed this point on several occasions. He also sincerely cared for people's safety in a country that "is in its building stages" (ibid., 182). However, his concern for Israel's survival was sometimes expressed in somewhat-unconventional ways. What was seen as paradoxical at the time was his conviction that only consideration for the Palestinians would be a safeguard for Israel's continued existence. "I believe that an autonomous Palestinian State would be the best solution for Israel, too," said Kreisky. "How long Israel as we know it today will survive I cannot venture to say, given the unbounded intolerance it shows towards its Palestinian co-inhabitants and its refusal to create the conditions for peaceful coexistence with the Arab States" (Berg 2000, 439–42).

When Kreisky was later asked why he had been so involved in the Israeli-Palestinian conflict, he responded that he had done it because, as a Jew, he did not "need to fear being called an anti-Semite" (Koelbl 1989, 145). Moreover, he regarded the

Israeli-Palestinian conflict as fatal. "If it's not resolved," warned Kreisky, "then one day 50,000 young Muslims will stand in front of the Al-Aqsa Mosque in Jerusalem" (Berg 2000, 440). Perhaps most poignantly, Kreisky saw the Israeli-Palestinian question as a matter of global Jewish responsibility, saying, "I think it is the duty of every person of Jewish descent to be involved in the Palestinian matter" (Koelbl 1989, 145).

At times, Kreisky even criticized Israelis for moral failings linked to Jewish history. The Israelis, he complained, had not learned from their tragic Jewish past in their dealing with the Palestinians. "Jews were expelled from their countries and murdered; they should know better what it means to be expelled and robbed of their belongings," said Kreisky. "But the Israelis and their followers obviously don't know it—the fact that people don't learn from their own history is especially saddening to me" (ibid.).

While Kreisky was critical of Zionism and the Israeli leadership publicly, Barbara Taufar notes that Kreisky underscored the need to protect Israel as a sanctuary in private conversations. She recalls Kreisky telling her that "Israel must have a future so that any Jews in the world could have refuge if ever a situation like the Holocaust should appear again" (2015, pers. comm.). Because another Holocaust was not inconceivable, Israel's continued existence was vital. Simultaneously, the memory of the Holocaust was the moral standard by which Kreisky judged Israel's actions— actions that he presumed jeopardized its existence (ibid.). In a similar vein, former Israeli prime minister Shimon Peres (1997) quotes Kreisky's dialectically ironic response to Peres's accusations that he was "so much against Israel." Kreisky retorted, asking, "If I was not against you, how could I help you?" Lennkh, who Kreisky often sent to the Middle East for missions, reaffirms this point. By Lennkh's account, even with his criticism of Zionism and the State of Israel, Kreisky looked at the situation in a pragmatic and realistic way. "He understood that its existence was a fact," says Lennkh. "He knew that it would be a catastrophe if it

would be wiped off the map. 'Jews are still threatened in Europe,'
Kreisky told me. 'We have to do everything to ensure that Israel
is safe for the Jews'" (2015, pers. comm.).

Nevertheless, there are reports of private conversations in
which Kreisky was exceedingly critical. A telegram to the Ministry of Foreign Affairs containing the report of Dov Taborsky,
an Israeli-worker union representative to North Europe, is one
example of this. Taborsky details his conversation with B. Carlson, the secretary responsible for foreign relations at the Swedish
Socialist Party. Carlson was a member of Kreisky's fact-finding
mission of the Socialist International to the Middle East in February 1976. From Carlson's point of view, "Kreisky, in his talks
with the Arab leaders, was extreme in his condemnation of Israel,
more extreme than in the interviews he had given to the press on
his return to Vienna."[95]

Nevertheless, even in these hyper-critical moments, the positive side remained. "Kreisky's attitude contained an internal contradiction," says Israeli peace activist Uri Avnery. On the one hand, he
wanted to treat Israel no different than any other country and not
pay special attention to it. He was the Austrian chancellor, and he
did not want his Jewishness to play a role in his agenda. However,
on the other hand, Israel was incredibly important to him after all,
and it truly hurt him that the Israelis hated him and refused to heed
his advice. "I think that all that he had done and the advice he had
given were for the sake of Israel's future," says Avnery. "However,
the Israelis responded with hatred toward him." Avnery also mentions that it bothered Kreisky that the Israelis were willing to accept
criticism from any other statesman in the world—on the condition
that they were *not* Jewish. This was how a "magic circle" began. "He
was very dedicated to Israeli matters and had definite opinions
about them," says Avnery, "but on the other hand, he pretended

---

95 Eldar to Israeli Embassy in Vienna, telegram, 3 June 1976 (Austria: Diplomatic Relations with Israel on a Governmental Level, 1976), 1.1.1976–
31.12.1976, Israel State Archives (Item Reference: 000kcf1/Physical Reference: 8488/1-חצ), Jerusalem, Israel.

that Israel doesn't interest him." In a roundabout way, Kreisky's attentiveness to the Palestinian cause reflected his great love for Israel, reasons Avnery. "I consider Kreisky's relations to Israel as a man who has an unrequited love to a woman that doesn't want to accept him" (2015, pers. comm.).

Even though he was usually very critical of Israel publicly, Kreisky responded in a markedly different way, following Israel's 1976 rescue operation in Entebbe. In an official response to the *Arbeiter-Zeitung*, Kreisky voiced support for and understanding of Israel's actions. In Entebbe specifically, Kreisky explained, the act of terrorism had not been in line with international law (on June 27, 1976, two members of the Popular Front for the Liberation of Palestine and two members of the German Revolutionary Cells hijacked a plane, including 248 passengers, trying to free 53 Palestinian and pro-Palestinian prisoners). Kreisky referred to the hijacking of the plane and its passengers as an "unjust and outrageous action" and called for new "judicial norms," which would first and foremost provide an answer to protect innocent human lives.[96]

Nevertheless, he insisted that one could not compare the terrorist actions in Entebbe with those in Marchegg and OPEC. The differences, he avowed, were "extreme." Three main reasons accounted for such differences: First, the terrorists in Marchegg had not asked the Austrian government to release criminals but, instead, had asked for criminals to be released in other countries. Second, during the attack on the OPEC's center, the countries whose citizens were taken hostage had asked Austria to save their lives, and Austria had done so. Ugandan president Idi Amin had instead sided with the terrorists. Third, Austria had openly communicated with the countries involved to coordinate steps. Conversely, no direct communication had been possible between

---

96   Peled to Director General of Ministry, telegram, 6 July 1976, (Austria: Diplomatic Relations with Israel on a Governmental Level, 1976), 1.1.1976–31.12.1976, Israel State Archives (Item Reference: 000kcf1/Physical Reference: 8488/1-חצ), 154–56, Jerusalem, Israel.

Israel and Amin, and Uganda as a country had been actively involved in the operation. As the event had taken place at an isolated airport, it had been possible for Israel to send its forces to a country that had been aiding the terrorists. In these conditions, concluded Kreisky, it had been legitimate to use terror against terror.[97]

Israeli archival material reflects the seriousness and persistence of Kreisky's attempts to act as a mediator in the Middle East. In August 1976, General Hannes Philipp, the Austrian commander in charge of the United Nations Disengagement Observer Force, met with Chancellor Kreisky in Vienna. Philipp, in turn, described Kreisky's views to the Israeli liaison officer to the United Nations, Colonel Shimon Levinson. Per Philipp's account, Kreisky intended to become the middleman between Israel and its neighbors. He specifically mentioned the opportunity to reach an interim agreement between Israel and Syria, which Kreisky saw as a primary goal. Kreisky suggested concrete tactical and geostrategic principles for such an agreement. When reviewing these principles, it became evident that Israel's security needs and its lack of willingness to evacuate settlements had been considered.[98] Ambassador Dagan doubted the report in a telegram, claiming that these were not Kreisky's genuine propositions. Kreisky, he believed, did not have sufficient topographic and military knowledge to propose such tactical moves. Ambassador Dagan estimated that these were General Philipp's ideas, passed off as Kreisky's, because of his desire to become a relevant actor in the Middle Eastern conflict.[99]

---

97 Peled to Director General of Ministry, 6 July 1976, ISA, 154–56.

98 Levinson to Israeli Minister of Defense, telegram, 3 August 1976, (Austria: Diplomatic Relations with Israel on a Governmental Level, 1976), 1.1.1976–31.12.1976, Israel State Archives (Item Reference: 000kcf1/Physical Reference: 8488/1-חצ), 145, Jerusalem, Israel.

99 Dagan to Prat, telegram, 10 August 1976, (Austria: Diplomatic Relations with Israel on a Governmental Level, 1976), 1.1.1976–31.12.1976, Israel State Archives (Item Reference: 000kcf1/Physical Reference: 8488/1-חצ), 142, Jerusalem, Israel.

Sometimes this desire to be involved in the conflict led to fascinating situations. One of these occurred in October 1976. The Israeli Foreign Ministry's telegrams refer to this episode simply as the "Oberbaum Paper."

To proceed with his peace-making plans, Kreisky wanted to deepen his understanding of the historical relations between Arabs and Jews from the beginning of the Zionist movement through to the present. Kreisky, whose intellectual skills were acknowledged by his rivals and his supporters, decided to go about this in an unorthodox manner. He turned to Emil Sharap, a Palestinian student who had received Austrian citizenship shortly before, and asked him to write a thirty-page paper that would describe the "Arab Perspective." Soon after, he requested the same from Menachem Oberbaum, who was to outline the Israeli perspective. Kreisky told him that it was important that these papers were written by young students and not by any official institution. He made it quite unequivocal that he did not want any involvement from the Israeli embassy. Oberbaum, then a medical student and a journalist, duplicitously turned to the Israeli deputy ambassador, Michael Peled, and suggested that the paper be prepared by an Israeli research institution. Oberbaum, however, would hand it in as his own work. "One day, Kreisky came to me and said that he would like to receive the Palestinian and Israeli version of the conflict and that he wanted me to write a position paper," says Oberbaum. "I quickly reached out to the embassy and said that I would do it but that I needed a 'ghostwriter'" (2020, pers. comm.).

In Deputy Ambassador Peled's report to the Foreign Ministry, he recommends a positive response to Kreisky's request and that such a paper be completed within three months. Peled adds, "We know that this whole matter is weird, however, it is typical of Kreisky's working methods."[100] Despite Kreisky's explicit demand that no

---

100   Peled to Shek, telegram, 5 October 1976, (Austria: Diplomatic Relations with Israel on a Governmental Level, 1976), 1.1.1976–31.12.1976, Israel State Archives (Item Reference: 000kcf1/Physical Reference: 8488/1-חצ), 110, Jerusalem, Israel.

official body be involved, the Israeli Foreign Ministry decided to deliver such a paper in Oberbaum's name. On December 26, 1976, Shek sent a telegram to Dagan in which he summarized the events. The Shiloach Research Institute, headed by Israeli diplomat Alouph Hareven, prepared a detailed document in Hebrew for this purpose. Shek, who had read the document with other senior officials at the ministry, concluded that Oberbaum could not sign the document as "no person would believe that a person who can compose such a paper continues to study medicine." Shek suggested that the document be sent to Vienna and that the embassy staff would sit with Oberbaum and compose a document based on "his style and spirit, but with content that we would like." This document, writes Shek, would then be handed to Kreisky. Before handing him the Shiloach Research Institute report, Oberbaum was to say to the chancellor, "I have done what you told me to do, however, you must know that I am no expert on these topics. In the material I reviewed, I found a comprehensive overview which I suggest that you fully read as it faithfully represents the Israeli perspective."[101]

The Palestinian student's report was handed to Kreisky in January. The chancellor then gave a copy to Oberbaum, who gave it to the Israeli embassy. The Israeli diplomats deemed the Palestinian paper important, for it reflected the low quality and dubious sourcing of information from which Kreisky derived his views toward the conflict. Peled determines via telegram that "if these are Kreisky's prime sources on which he bases his assertion that the PLO is moderate, then we can doubt his seriousness, as it is unclear who the writer is and on whose behalf he speaks. He is definitely not an official spokesperson of the PLO."[102]

---

101   Shek to Dagan, telegram, 26 December 1976, (Austria: Diplomatic Relations with Israel on a Governmental Level, 1976), 1.1.1976–31.12.1976, Israel State Archives (Item Reference: 000kcf1/Physical Reference: 8488/1-חצ), 4, Jerusalem, Israel.
102   Peled to Shek, telegram, 29 December 1976, (Austria: Diplomatic Relations with Israel on a Governmental Level, 1976), 1.1.1976–31.12.1976, Israel State Archives (Item Reference: 000kcf1/Physical Reference: 8488/1-חצ), 2, Jerusalem, Israel.

There is no further information as to the fate of the Israeli document. However, Oberbaum claims that he never provided Kreisky with a report. "I never received the document from Hareven, whom I met in Israel," he says. "I do not know why" (2020, pers. comm.). However, he does remember the shame he felt by not fulfilling Kreisky's request. "It was extremely embarrassing—after I confirmed to Kreisky that I will do it, I did not," states Oberbaum. "I said I was busy with my medical studies and that was it."[103]

Kreisky's request for information was not a casual affair. He invested much of his time, energy, and effort trying to solve the Israeli-Palestinian conflict. Observers agree that Kreisky had a deep personal connection and commitment to these matters. His involvement went beyond diplomacy. He saw this as his life's mission and was highly emotional about these activities. He never hesitated to express his vision and his desire to implement it. At times, he was even prepared to risk his reputation on this issue.

In this respect, Kreisky was well ahead of his time. Early on, he realized that recognizing the PLO was essential, as was establishing a Palestinian state in the West Bank and Gaza to exist side by side with Israel (Bunzl 1997). He was the first European politician to suggest this solution (Embacher and Reiter 1998). At the same time, he was an early and severe critic of the Israeli occupation of the territories captured during the 1967 Six-Day War while also opposing Palestinian terrorism as a means of resistance.

By 1965, he had already acknowledged the "rights of the Arab people of Palestine, including their inalienable right to self-determination" (Timm 1993). Kreisky knew it was necessary to forge a relationship with Yasser Arafat, the leader of the PLO, if he wanted to further his peace plans. In 1974, as part of the fact-finding mission to Cairo, which Kreisky headed, Sadat organized a secret meeting between Kreisky and Arafat (Kriechbaumer 2004). Arafat was—and remains—a highly controversial figure whose leg-

---

103 Peled to Shek, 29 Dec. 1976, ISA, 2.

acy has been widely disputed. Many Palestinians—regardless of political ideology or faction—still view him as a heroic freedom fighter and martyr who symbolized the national aspirations of his people, while many others have described him as an unrepentant terrorist.

While Arafat was of central importance, Kreisky had started meeting Palestinian intellectuals from the early stages of his political career. In 1960, he had already met with the Algerian delegation during the United Nations General Assembly meeting. Later, he would meet the Tunisian and Moroccan delegations. Kreisky's efforts on behalf of the Palestinians were well known to Sadat and Arafat. Despite major opposition, Kreisky used his international influence as the vice president of the Socialist International to introduce the Palestinian position to the international community (ibid.).

Above all, Kreisky was intent on demonstrating that the PLO did not reject the existence of Israel. He invited Arafat to visit Vienna on July 7, 1979. This was, undoubtedly, a pioneering act and event. Vienna became the first Western capital to host the PLO as an official delegation. At the same time, there was the implicit recognition that Vienna was the first European capital to recognize the PLO leader as the future prime minister of a Palestinian state. "Due to the fact that Kreisky was the first Western European head of state to meet Arafat, the Israeli MFA decided to recall its ambassador for consultations," states Yissakhar Ben-Yaacov, the Israeli ambassador to Austria at the time (2012, 231). While Austria was the first *Western* State to recognize Arafat and the PLO, it is important to acknowledge that the German Democratic Republic had cooperated with the PLO since the early 1970s. In this respect, Kreisky was only a pioneer in the Western world. In March 1980, under his Premiership, the Austrian government officially recognized the PLO. Kreisky hoped that after the Venice Declaration of June 1980 (in which the European Community had approved the right to self-determination for the Palestinian people for the first time and had allowed the PLO to

take part in the negotiations), other European countries would
follow suit (Bunzl 1997). As Crown Prince Hassan of Jordan puts
it: "Kreisky was offering [Arafat and the PLO] an entrée into European strategic conversations, in the spirit of the Venice declaration and the spirit of broader Euro-Atlantic exchanges" (1997). In
1979, Kreisky delivered a speech at the General Assembly of the
United Nations, announcing Austria's forthcoming recognition
of the PLO. The following year, Arafat assigned an official PLO
representative, Ghazi Hussein, to represent the PLO in Austria.
This was the final step in ushering in Austrian recognition of the
PLO (Bunzl 1997).

When asked why Austria should lead the charge on this issue,
Kreisky's answer prompted widespread criticism. "Had there
been united Austrian representation after 1938," said Kreisky,
"the country could have been greatly spared, including perhaps
the ten years of Allied occupation after the liberation in 1945"
(ibid., 58). Some regarded the analogy between the Anschluss of
1938 and the Israeli occupation of Palestinian territories as highly
problematic. However, Barbara Taufar (2015, pers. comm.) says
Kreisky's analogy was misunderstood. He meant to refer to the
two underground Austrian Socialist movements that had worked
separately, and therefore ineffectively, in Moscow and London
during World War II (ibid.). Had they worked together, she explains, they could have been officially recognized by the international community and could have potentially prevented many
problems for Austria after the war.

Another mission that Kreisky took upon himself was bringing Israel and Egypt together to sign a peace agreement. Kreisky
foresaw the many benefits of such a deal even before most Israeli
politicians registered it. He worked with his friend Hassan Mohammed el-Tohami to unite the two sides. "I think that Kreisky
played an important role in bringing Egypt and Israel together,"
says Peres (1997). Peres also explains that the main difference
between him and Kreisky was that Kreisky believed peace was a
matter of courage, while it was a function of time for Peres.

The men who most influenced Kreisky when it came to relations with Egypt were Mahmoud Fawzi, Egypt's undersecretary
in the Ministry of Foreign Affairs, and later Hassan Mohammed
El-Tohami, the Egyptian ambassador in Vienna who was close
to President Gamal Abdel Nasser. Kreisky viewed Fawzi as a
moderate, peace-seeking figure compared to the "high rhetoric"
from official Egyptian governmental sources. Taufar (2015, pers.
comm.) also remembers arranging meetings between Kreisky
and many Arab intellectuals, whom she had met in Palestinian
cities before. Most importantly, these included the mayors of
West Bank cities. In the 1970s, after a Jewish terrorist attack in
the West Bank, Kreisky immediately had the injured brought to
the Vienna University Hospital for treatment.

While the Arab countries welcomed his role as mediator, the
Israeli government condemned it (Bunzl 1997). Israel accused the
Austrian government of forgetting "the sufferings of the Jewish
People during World War II" and expressed its fury that Austria,
of all countries, should act in a way that was seen as threatening
to Israel. When a journalist from the German newspaper *Die Zeit*
asked Kreisky about his policy, he answered that the Germans
had to be more cautious than him, for they were unable to "jump
over the shadow of their guilt vis a vis the Jews" (ibid., 59). Inside
the PLO, Kreisky was seen as favoring a more "moderate" policy,
aimed at providing the PLO leadership with greater credibility
and legitimacy in the West and encouraging a willingness to negotiate with Israel. However, the more radical wing, Abu Nidal,
tried to sabotage these efforts and opposed any cooperation and
negotiations with Israel.

The Israelis officially objected to Kreisky's recommendation
to recognize the PLO. Despite these objections, Ambassador
Ben-Yaacov was not called back to Israel for consultation, which
left room to presume that Israel had decided to accept Austria's
recognition of the PLO, for better or for worse (Ben-Yaacov 2012,
245). Nevertheless, despite his criticism, Kreisky's principal concern was Israel's survival. In the absence of a solution, he feared

that Israel would be in a state of constant battle against its neighbors. "It is only a matter of time before Israel is destroyed in one of these conflicts," Kreisky declared (Berg 2000, 444). For Wolfgang Petritsch, another factor was involved. Kreisky frequently expressed his fear that Israel would cease being a democratic state should the conflict continue. "He considered Israel a democratic state, which needs to resolve its problems—if not, he used to say, it would turn into a 'crusader state,'" says Petritsch. "He was concerned about Israel becoming an apartheid state" (2014, pers. comm.).

Kreisky's concern for the Arab world was also unusual for the time. Unlike many other European leaders, Kreisky insisted that "we cannot afford to remain indifferent to the Arab world. We cannot ignore the political consequences of our clear dependence upon essential reserves vital to Europe's energy economy situated in these countries" (Berg 2000, 444). It was Kreisky who, above all, brought the Middle Eastern conflict to the attention of Europeans. "No one in Europe today," he proclaimed, "seriously doubts that [the] Middle Eastern conflict is currently a problem of central importance" (ibid., 445).

The US and Soviet Union did not look too kindly upon Kreisky's involvement in the Middle Eastern conflict. There was a blatant disproportion between Austria's international status and its role in the Middle East. The Soviets and Americans had their own problems with the PLO and, for various reasons, did not want to change its status. Moreover, some of Kreisky's ideas appeared threatening at times. As Taufar explains, "Under Kreisky, the Socialist International became an important player in Third World countries. From a tiny, insignificant European country, suddenly Kreisky's Austria acted like a new world power" (2015, pers. comm.). Shimon Peres also speaks of Austrian megalomania cynically. "In one worldwide operation you have to be a world-class power," he says. "It's not enough to have a world-class intellect. Kreisky didn't have the power" (1997). According to social scientist Otmar Höll (1994), Austria's disproportionate role in the Middle Eastern conflict was solely due to Kreisky's personal ambitions and actions.

That this personal concern was crucial in Kreisky's political and diplomatic career cannot be doubted. "Many of my compatriots regarded my involvement in the Middle Eastern problem, as excessive," said Kreisky. "But without this 'excessive cosmopolitanism,' I would have felt the entirety of my political engagement to be largely void of any meaningful content" (Embacher and Reiter 1998, 446).

Political scientist John Bunzl (1997) thinks Kreisky risked his Austrian political career because of this intense focus on Middle Eastern affairs. Confident in his advocacy for the Palestinian people, Israel, and especially the Labor Party, Kreisky found himself constantly frustrated. However, while accepting that Kreisky might have been frustrated, Barbara Taufar (2015, pers. comm.) disagrees with the claim that he risked his political career in Austria. She insists that every action of his was based on clear and rational political strategies. Therefore, he would not have done anything that jeopardized his political power in Austria.

Another sign of Kreisky's commitment to the Middle Eastern conflict is that even after his 1983 resignation, he continued to advocate for Middle Eastern peace and helped negotiate an exchange of Israeli and Palestinian prisoners of war in 1983 and 1985. Bunzl (1997) analyzes how Kreisky's activities—both in the Socialist International and as the Austrian chancellor—affected the Middle East. He finds that Kreisky did the following:

- Assisted in spreading the understanding that the Palestinian dimension was central to the conflict

- Promoted the cause of the Palestinians in the West

- Influenced Palestinian and Arab leaders in favor of co-existence with Israel

- Encouraged Israeli-Palestinian dialogue

- Aided Jewish emigration from the former Soviet Union

- Created tensions with Israel and her friends in the West by polemics about Middle Eastern policies

Kreisky's idiosyncratic views of Arab and Israeli political leaders often proved contradictory. There is a disjunction between his ideological position as a democratic Socialist committed to liberal, universal norms who constantly preached justice and liberty for all and his positive portrayals of some of the most brutal Arab dictators like Anwar Sadat, Hafez al-Assad, and Muammar Gaddafi. Moreover, his descriptions of and interactions with these controversial leaders were at odds with the stark contrast in their respective humanitarian policies.

His idealized and romanticized descriptions of these men reveal a kind of wishful, selective thinking and perception (Even though it must be noted that Kreisky was neither the first nor the only politician in the twentieth century to show these skewed views). For example, he considered Syrian president Hafez al-Assad no less than a leader with "an outstanding personality" (Berg 2000, 468). His assessment of Sadat was even more positive: "From the standpoint of firmness and excellence of character," said Kreisky, "his was the most significant personality I have encountered in the second half of this century" (ibid., 476). Crown Prince Hassan of Jordan is very critical of these relationships. "Kreisky was in a sense ruled by the Arab interlocutors, including Ghaddafi [sic], whom he, of course, received in Vienna," says Hassan. "I think frankly his contact with the Arab world began to become a little controversial, both subjectively and objectively, and under the pressure put on us by others who criticized this somewhat unexpected move" (1997).

Besides his overly optimistic view of controversial Arab leaders, Uri Avnery—considered by many to be an incurable dreamer because of his visions of a peaceful Middle East—adds another point of criticism against Kreisky's treatment of the Middle East (2015, pers. comm.). Avnery attests that Kreisky lacked an understanding of the area's unique culture. "Kreisky was never as well acquainted as he himself thought he was with Middle Eastern affairs," says Avnery (2015, pers. comm.). "He was very informed as a politician and statesman. However, he was not engaged in Arab culture. As far as his outlook on the Middle East went, I would argue that he saw it as a European, peering the mystic and fascinating 'Orient'" (ibid.). This charge by Avnery is in line with Edward Said's (1979) critique of general Western perceptions of the "Orient." Furthermore, Avnery thinks that Kreisky "was naïve at times" (2015, pers. comm.). However, the Israeli writer and politician Elazar Granot, who knew Kreisky well, counters this statement. "He wasn't naïve," says Granot, "but he judged us in European terms and international European terms. He didn't go deep enough into the fear and the hatred. This is a conflict of more than one hundred years" (1997). Shimon Peres adds to this line of criticism, simply saying that "Kreisky surely was not a great expert on the Arabs" (1997).

KREISKY THE VISIONARY

Despite criticism regarding Kreisky's relationships to Middle Eastern leaders or his lack of cultural sensitivity, it bears repeating that Kreisky was ahead of his time in many respects when it came to his vision regarding the Middle East—and especially in his efforts to bring the Palestinian cause to the world's attention. At the time, most observers considered the PLO to be a terror organization, banned by all Western governments. Kreisky understood that the terrorists of today are the peace partners of tomorrow and worked accordingly. He did not live to see the Madrid Conference of 1991, nor did he witness the Oslo Accords of 1993–95, but these were goals and ideals that he had laid the foundation for years before.

One can imagine Kreisky's reaction when Shimon Peres and Yitzhak Rabin shared the Nobel Peace Prize with Arafat and warmly shook hands. For most people but Kreisky, this would have been an unimaginable event. However, what previously had seemed entirely utopian had become a distinct actuality. Today, the same PLO that Kreisky had promoted in the international arena is Israel's official peace partner. It seems ironic that his pioneering efforts have been more or less ignored in the history of the Israeli-Palestinian peace process—his role as a crucial forerunner and visionary almost forgotten.

Still, there has been some recognition of his visionary capacity. "No doubt," says former Israeli minister Micha Harish, "the time was too early to play a role" (1997). Shimon Peres professes, "While his efforts were early and for that reason seen on most occasions as irrelevant, they also prepared the ground for what was to come later. He—I admit it—had a better idea of what the PLO was and what could be done, after the Jordanian option had failed. At that stage, I came to the conclusion that this is the way to go and to move" (1997). Kreisky's personal assistant, Margit Schmidt, adds, "Kreisky was ahead of his time. When the Oslo Accords were signed, no one talked about Kreisky's attempt to bring people together. ... Every person who thinks ahead of his time has problems, and people misunderstand him" (2014, pers. comm.).

Menachem Oberbaum recalls an "off-the-record" interview with Kreisky in 1970. In this interview, Kreisky said that "if you offer Egypt today half of Sinai, the Syrians half of the Golan Heights, and the Jordanians half of the West Bank, they will say yes." He went on to add, "Within ten years, because of your hubris, you will get many casualties and suffer." "Kreisky was a man of vision," remarks Oberbaum. "He said then things that the moderate Left and mainstream say today" (2020, pers. comm.).

However, as a visionary, Kreisky also had some dark premonitions concerning the Middle East's military future. "If nothing changes, the Palestinians will become Islamic fundamentalists," he warned (Koelbl 1989, 146). In 1989, almost prophetically, Kreisky shared the insight that "there are so many Palestinians who have nothing to lose and as fundamentalism comes together with a wish to die, this is the most deadly thing for Israel" (ibid.). A few months after this interview, Israel experienced its first Palestinian suicide attack.

Even more foreboding, Kreisky was among the first to predict a situation in which certain groups might acquire atomic weapons and plunge entire areas into chaos. He feared that it would not be governments acquiring these weapons but out-of-control terrorist groups. While he only voiced these fears in private conversations, both Taufar (2015, pers. comm.) and Granot (1997) mention hearing such warnings from Kreisky. In the age of ISIS, there is hardly a need to exaggerate Kreisky's prescience. Today, it might seem commonplace to discuss threats of nuclear proliferation, and intelligence agencies worldwide are trying to cope with the tumultuous situation in the Middle East. In the 1970s, however, such a nuclear scenario seemed unimaginable. During the Cold War, it appeared that only two superpowers with nuclear capabilities existed (Taufar 2015, pers. comm.).

KREISKY AND OTHER JEWISH POLITICIANS

Kreisky was not just unique because of his foresight on certain issues. He was also exceptional when it came to his political career. It is a testament to his unique appeal that postwar Austria, despite its glaring—though long-repressed—complicity in the Third Reich, should elevate a Jewish politician to the highest pinnacles of power. (Regardless of how narrowly Kreisky defined his Jewishness, his identity was well known.) Kreisky was foreign minister between 1959 and 1966 and chancellor between 1970 and 1983, still the longest tenure in republican Austrian history. Ambitious, intelligent, sometimes ruthless, controversial, forward-thinking, high tempered, and—at times—irrational, he was undoubtedly one of the most gifted, intriguing, and successful European Jewish statesmen and politicians of the twentieth century.

A short historical comparison of such figures with Kreisky and the politics of their identity may be illustrative. The most prominent names for such a comparison are Walter Rathenau, Léon Blum, and Pierre Mendès-France. For all three, the question of Jewishness is inescapable—for their self-definition and how they were perceived publicly, both. An important distinction for Rathenau is that he was part of pre-World War II politics. An organizer of the German-militarized World War I economy, he was Germany's foreign minister during the Weimar Republic. In some ways, Rathenau's Jewishness was even more conflicted than Kreisky's. He was not only a proud "Prussian" (just as Kreisky insisted upon his "Austrianness"), but as a young man, he even published an anonymous vituperative attack ("Höre Israel") on the pushy, coarse public behavior of his fellow Jewish citizens and their easily recognized Jewish physiognomy (a piece he later rescinded). Nevertheless, just as Kreisky, he exhibited an ambivalence of identity and, at one stage, took an enthusiastic interest in Martin Buber's Hasidic stories. However, the most tragic difference between Rathenau and Kreisky is that while Kreisky was sometimes attacked because of his Jewishness, Rathenau's story had a more tragic end. On June 24, 1922, when the wealthy Rathenau was assassinated by the right-wing Organisation Consul (a paramilitary terrorist organization in the Weimar Republic), it was evident that his Jewishness had been a central motivating factor in the killing of this "interloping" "stabber in the back of the German people" (Volkov 2012; Aschheim 1982).

In France, Léon Blum, a progressive Socialist comparable to Kreisky, was elected prime minister three times (twice during the pre-World War II Popular Front between 1936 and 1940 and then briefly between December and January 1947). Like Kreisky, he stood out as a reformer and Socialist modernizer. Unlike Kreisky, however, Blum was a proud and publicly visible Jew and a proclaimed Zionist. Zionism, Frenchness, and Socialism, he pointed out, were compatible as all were "just, humane and of the people" (Birnbaum 2015, 147). During the Vichy regime, this great man and French patriot was imprisoned in Buchenwald and later transferred to Dachau. After the war, Blum was prime minister for under five weeks and helped pave the way for the French Fourth Republic.

An associate of Blum's, progressive Socialist Pierre Mendès-France, became president of the Council of Ministers (equivalent to prime minister) in the French Fourth Republic from 1954 to 1955, despite being more of an intellectual than a politician. Unlike Kreisky, who was not radically attacked by antisemites in Austria (but, instead, labeled as one himself by various Jewish and Israeli circles), Mendès-France was subject to vicious antisemitic aggressions given his policy of withdrawing France from the Indochina War. However, like Kreisky, while never denying his Jewish (Portuguese) origins, he insisted upon not categorizing Jews as a separate group. Consequently, when he was asked as part of the Free French Forces in 1944 to provide funds for Jewish children freed from France, he agreed but stated, "They are French children to be saved and I do not know of any special category called French Jews" (Aberbac 2017, 35). Nevertheless, like Kreisky, he ultimately did feel a kind of Jewish responsibility and kept close ties to the Arab world toward the end of his career and brought representatives of the Israeli Left to conferences with moderates in the PLO (Holoch 1986).

For all these prominent Jewish statesmen, Jewish identity politics entered into their biographical and political equation, whether they experienced them positively or negatively. In truth, since the era of emancipation conflicts, dilemmas, negations, and affirmations of their identity have been the fate of modern Jewry as it sought to negotiate its presence within modern culture and the nation-state. Kreisky fits into this overall mold, but his was a unique case at a particular historical moment. Thus, his actions, policies, and attitudes—his achievements, peculiarities, and failings alike—must be judged within that context.

In contrast to the other Jewish politicians discussed, Bruno Kreisky cannot be understood outside the traditional Habsburg and postwar, republican, Austrian circumstances. In many ways, his confused and often-contradictory conception of Jewishness, as well as his profound commitment to the Austrian state, were aligned with much of Austria's fin-de-siècle Jewish achievements and dilemmas. As stated earlier in Chapter Two, Vienna's late-nineteenth- and early-twentieth-century Jews were characterized both by astonishing creativity and achievement and identity confusion and the search for new intellectual, political, and psychological solutions to their predicament. The famous and highly diversified names of that time and a slightly later era—including Ludwig Wittgenstein, Theodor Herzl, Sigmund Freud, Karl Kraus, Gustav Mahler, and Stefan Zweig—all had to deal with questions and dilemmas of their Jewish identity. Identity confusion was ubiquitous—whether of the religious, ethnic, sexual, or political kind. The modes of resolving this were, naturally, varied. As previously noted, Vienna even produced two of the most famous "self-hating" Jews: Otto Weininger and Arthur Trebitsch, both of whom produced pseudophilosophical, ideological tomes "explaining" their contempt for Jews and Judaism. Nevertheless, even though Kreisky fits into this complex image of Viennese Jewishness for a large part, he still had to operate within a post–World War II context (rather than at the fin de siècle or in the interwar period), which presented an entirely different set of problems.

CHAPTER 7: CONCLUSION

This book is not a comprehensive biography of Kreisky. Many others have already undertaken that task, as evidenced in the Literature Review section of this book. Instead, it attempts to document and place Kreisky's fraught engagement with his Jewishness and the related sensitive issues that touched upon it in a historical, political, ideological, and personal context. These issues include his role in Austrian politics and his attitude to its contested World War II past; his often-tense connections with the Austrian Jewish community; his actions regarding Palestinian, anti-Israeli actions within Austria (particularly the Marchegg incident); his attitudes toward and policies concerning Zionism, as well as the State of Israel and its leaders; his controversial role and involvement in Middle Eastern affairs; and his pioneering, peace-seeking role in the Israeli-Palestinian conflict.

Kreisky's reasoning and reactions in many events discussed in this book can be traced back to the entangled and always-ambiguous politics of identity, especially his understanding of his Jewishness. While acknowledging descent and never denying his origins (at times, he would even rhetorically exploit it for political advantage), Kreisky most definitively rejected "national" definitions and affiliations of Jewishness. He was an overt opponent of Zionism and viewed himself as exclusively Austrian. While there was such a thing as the "Israeli" people for Kreisky, the "Jewish" people as such did not exist. However, as evidenced in his actual dealings and handling of crises, things were never that clean-cut or consistent. Obscurities and conflicts of identity and identification made themselves apparent throughout this his life and this book.

The archival files, documents, memoirs, and interviews presented in this book all bear witness to the fact that contradictions and ambiguities abound in Kreisky's case. On the one hand, there are repeated Jewish and Israeli accusations as to his "antisemitism" and his alleged "self-hate," including his oft-repeated insistence that there is no such thing as "the Jewish people." Like many "assimilated" Jews, he detested what he presumed to be Jewish conspicuousness and a certain Jewish sense of superiority. He even argued that there were similarities between Nazi race theory and Jewish ideas of "chosenness." Furthermore, he displayed an apparent insensitivity to the horrors of the Holocaust and the patent historical failures of Jewish integration. Petritsch says that "Kreisky remained throughout his life a pre-Holocaust Jew. He would simply not deal with it although twenty-one of his family members were killed" (2014, pers. comm.). Whatever his motivation—genuine Austrian patriotism or cynical political opportunism—he was a key proponent of the Austrian victim's doctrine and Austria's denial of its complicity in the Third Reich. He included ex-Nazis in his administration, even befriended some while in prison, championed Kurt Waldheim, and mercilessly attacked Simon Wiesenthal.

However, these attitudes were not harmful to his ascent to become Austria's most influential and popular politician. Unlike Rathenau, Blum, or Mendès-France, Kreisky was mostly spared vicious anti-Jewish attacks (although he was exceedingly sensitive to the dangers of antisemitism in Austria). Instead, potentially because of his constant insistence of being an Austrian above all else, upon his return from Swedish exile, he was received by most of the Austrian public not as a returning Jew but as an anti-Fascist Austrian Social Democrat (Wistrich 2007)—a perception he was very interested in perpetuating.

These perceptions were complemented by many of Kreisky's actions, including:

• His explicit rejection of Zionism, claiming that its aims were in a kind of alliance with antisemitism

- His—at times extreme—criticism of Israel and its policies while dismissing notions of collective Austrian guilt

- His fraught and almost-archetypical confrontations with Israeli officials (which in retrospect look like a symbolic clash between "Zionist" and "assimilationist" Jews)

- His alleged "softness" on terrorism, including his belief that it could be justified in some cases

- His apparent pro-Arab stance

- His closure of the Schönau transit center

- His very early insistence on recognizing the purported terrorist PLO

Any fair assessment of Kreisky is complicated by his many moments of extremity, motivated by what some observers have dubbed his "Jewish identity complex" and his desperate attempt to prove his Austrianness (Embacher and Reiter 1998). Some of Kreisky's acquaintances have reported that he occasionally appeared irrational, even paranoid. For instance, he accused Wiesenthal not only of being a member of the "Conservative Jewish Mafia" (in which Israel also allegedly played a role) but a Nazi collaborator. In addition, he claimed that Wiesenthal and the Israelis had kidnapped his brother, Paul, as a form of extortion. Kreisky's temper could be so extreme that one Israeli ambassador describes it as being "on the edge of insanity" (Segev 2020, pers. comm.). Consequently, historian Tom Segev (ibid.) somewhat jokingly suggests that Kreisky should be the subject of psychological, rather than historical, analysis.

Nevertheless, this is only half the picture. Kreisky was a complicated individual, and any balance sheet would have to include many positive aspects. For example, despite closing Schönau,

Kreisky still went out of his way to insist that Austria remain open to immigrants in transition. Even though he justified this policy on humanitarian (and not Jewish) grounds, some argue that he did so as a result of his "Jewish conscience" (Knapp 2019, pers. comm.).

Likewise, despite many claims that he was insensitive to the Holocaust, his visit to Yad Vashem was obviously a meaningful experience. Even if he did not invoke it as part of his daily political rhetoric, he did privately link it to a recognition of Israel's enormous post-Holocaust importance as a place of Jewish refuge and a site preventing the possibility of any future Jewish genocide. Moreover, his pioneering recognition of the PLO, which Israel reckoned to be dangerously hostile to its interests, is seen by many as a function of his commitment to Israel and the realization that in the absence of a peace arrangement, there would be no future for the state. Kreiskey was even aware of a certain paradoxical duality in his policy. As he told Shimon Peres (1997), "If I wouldn't be against you, how could I help you?"

It was in a private capacity that many of Kreisky's most intimate—and contradictory—sentiments regarding his Jewishness and Israel were revealed. For example, his extreme criticism of Israeli militarism notwithstanding, he was incredibly proud of his twenty-year-old nephew, Yossi, who had served in a paratrooper unit in the Israeli army. Additionally, many Israeli acquaintances were convinced that his caring friendships were based upon a bond between Jews, even if only implicitly.

To accusations that he was a self-denying Jew, he commented, "Everybody that looks at me could see that I am a Jew" (Taufar 2015, pers. comm.). Even with all his denials about "blood ties," Kreisky apparently believed that there was such a thing as a Jewish physiognomy. Furthermore, a brief look at Kreisky's sociological profile reveals how his upbringing and background conformed to the pattern of other acculturated Jews.

To begin with, Kreisky and his family never denied their Jewish background or descent (although they had no ties to official

Jewish religious observance). In many respects, he resembled other middle- and upper-class Western Jews. In this, paradoxically, he was "typical." His occupational preference, matrimonial choice, friendships, cultural predilections, and patterns of sociability very much resembled the group with which he stood in permanent dialectical tension—and identification.

For all that, Kreisky was no ordinary Jew. He was the chancellor of a European nation, a state modernizer, a visionary of peace—Kreisky was, overall, unique. While they may account for his weaknesses, it were possibly the contradictions, ambivalences, and conflicts outlined in this book that were also responsible for his not-insignificant achievements.

REFERENCES

ARCHIVAL SOURCES

אוסטריה – יחסים מדיניים עם ישראל בדרג ממשלתי 1976 (Austria: Diplomatic Relations with Israel on a Governmental Level, 1976). 1.1.1976-31.12.1976. Israel State Archives (Item Reference: 000kcf1/Physical Reference: 8488/1-חצ). Jerusalem, Israel.

יחסים מדיניים עם אוסטריה בדרג ממשלתי 71–1970 (Austria: Diplomatic Relations with Austria on a Governmental Level, 1970–71). 1.1.1970-31.12.1971. Israel State Archives (Item Reference: 0002ysm/Physical Reference: 4556/30-חצ). Jerusalem, Israel.

לשכת ראש הממשלה יצחק רבין – אוסטריה 1974–77 (Austria: Office of Prime Minister Yitzhak Rabin, 1974–77). 20.4.1974-3.10.1977. Israel State Archives (Item Reference: 000wl1q/Physical Reference: 4212/9-א). Jerusalem, Israel.

פרוטוקול ב/שלד של הממשלה 3.10.1973 (Protocol of Government Meeting 3.10.1973). 3.10.1973. Israel State Archives (Item Reference: N/A as was sent by email directly by the director of the archive, Hagai Tsoref). Jerusalem, Israel.

משרד ראש הממשלה – לשכת ראש הממשלה גולדה מאיר 74–1973 (Prime Minister's Office: Office of Prime Minister Golda Meir 1973–74). 1.9.1973-30.6.1974. Israel State Archives (Item Reference: 1418909/Physical Reference: 7245/16-א). Jerusalem, Israel.

וינה. ספטמבר – דצמבר 1973 (Vienna: September–December 1973). 1.9.1973-31.12.1973. Israel State Archives (Item Reference: 000w3z1/Physical Reference: 7037/15-א). Jerusalem, Israel.

יחסים מדיניים עם אוסטריה בדרג ממשלתי 1981 (Austria: Diplomatic Relations with Israel on a Governmental Level, 1981). 16.4.1981-28.12.1981. Israel State Archives (Item Reference: 000bftp/Physical Reference: 8895/16-צח). Jerusalem, Israel.

ORAL HISTORIES

Personal Oral Histories

Avnery, Uri. Interview conducted in Tel Aviv. September 9, 2015.

Beck, Eldad. Interview conducted via Skype. November 26, 2019.

Beinisch, Yehezkel. Interview conducted in Jerusalem. July 29, 2015.

Ben-Ami, Naomi. Interview conducted via phone. January 19, 2020.

Ben-Yaacov, Yissakhar. Interview conducted in Ramat Gan. December 15, 2019.

Haber, Eitan. Interview conducted via phone. June 2, 2019.

Knapp, Ilan. Interview conducted via phone. August 11, 2019.

Lador-Fresher, Talya. Interview conducted in Jerusalem. December 9, 2019.

Lanc, Erwin. Interview conducted in Vienna. October 17, 2017.

Lazin, Fred. Interview conducted via phone. April 12, 2020.

Lennkh, Georg. Interview conducted in Vienna. February 22, 2015.

Liko, Hannah. Interview conducted in Jerusalem. December 3, 2019.

Muzicant, Ariel. Interview conducted via phone. December 11, 2018.

Nowotny, Thomas. Interview conducted via Skype. May 5, 2020.

Oberbaum, Menachem. Interview conducted via phone. January 1, 2020.

Petritsch, Wolfgang. Interview conducted in Vienna. August 18, 2014.

Rathkolb, Oliver. Interview conducted in Vienna. February 22, 2015.

Röhrlich, Elisabeth. Interview conducted via Skype. April 17, 2020.

Schmidt, Margit. Interview conducted in Vienna. February 21, 2014.

Segev, Tom. Interview conducted via phone. May 31, 2020.

Shay, Shaul. Interview conducted via phone. November 18, 2018.

Šmok, Martin. Interview conducted via Skype. November 11, 2018.

Taufar, Barbara. Interview conducted in Kibbutz Farod. July 21, 2015.

————. Interview conducted via phone. April 20, 2020.

Zoref, Hagai. Interview conducted in Jerusalem. September 24, 2019.

Bruno Kreisky Archives: Oral Histories

Bin Talal, Hassan. "Interview zum Projekt: Die Beziehungen Österreich—Israel in der Ära Kreisky 1970–1983." By Peter Jankowitsch. 1997.

Burg, Yosef. "Interview zum Projekt: Die Beziehungen Österreich—Israel in der Ära Kreisky 1970–1983." By Barbara Taufar. 1997.

Eliav, Lowa. "Interview zum Projekt: Die Beziehungen Österreich—Israel in der Ära Kreisky 1970–1983." By Barbara Taufar. June 11, 1997.

Granot, Elazar. "Interview zum Projekt: Die Beziehungen Österreich—Israel in der Ära Kreisky 1970–1983." By Barbara Taufar. 1997.

Harish, Micha. "Interview zum Projekt: Die Beziehungen Österreich—Israel in der Ära Kreisky 1970–1983." By Barbara Taufar. 1997.

Klimowitzky, Yona. "Interview zum Projekt: Die Beziehungen Österreich—Israel in der Ära Kreisky 1970–1983." By Barbara Taufar. June 1997.

Peres, Shimon. "Interview zum Projekt: Die Beziehungen Österreich—Israel in der Ära Kreisky 1970–1983." By Barbara Taufar. June 3, 1997.

Sarid, Yossi. "Interview zum Projekt: Die Beziehungen Österreich—Israel in der Ära Kreisky 1970–1983." By Barbara Taufar. May 22, 1997.

Zucker, Dedi. "Interview zum Projekt: Die Beziehungen Österreich—Israel in der Ära Kreisky 1970–1983." By Barbara Taufar. 1997.

WORKS CITED

Aarikka-Stenroos, Leena. "The Contribution and Challenges of Narrative Data in Interorganizational Research." Paper presented at the IMP2010 conference, Budapest, Hungary, 2010.

Aberbach, David. "The Patriotism of Gentlemen with Red Hair: European Jews and the Liberal State, 1789–1939." *International Journal of Politics, Culture, and Society* 30 (2017): 129–46.

Aschheim, Daniel. "Bruno Kreisky's Premature Role as a Peacemaker in the Middle East: The Paradoxes of Jewishness, Socialism and the Middle Eastern Conflict." MA thesis, Hebrew University in Jerusalem, 2015.

Aschheim, Steven E. *Brothers and Strangers: The East European Jew in German and German Jewish Consciousness, 1800–1923.* Madison: University of Wisconsin Press, 1982.

Avner, Yehuda. "The Schoenau Ultimatum." *Jerusalem Post*, September 3, 2009. https://www.jpost.com/magazine/features/the-schoenau-ultimatum.

Bachleitner, Kathrin. "Golda Meir and Bruno Kreisky—A Political and Personal Duel." *Israel Studies* 23, no. 1 (2018): 26–49.

Bauck, Sönke, and Thomas Maier. "Entangled History." *Inter-American Wiki: Terms—Concepts—Critical Perspectives* (2015). https://www.uni-bielefeld.de/cias/wiki/e_Entangled_History.html.

Beit Hatfutsot: The Museum of the Jewish People. "Jewish Population and Immigration." Accessed March 7, 2022. https://www.bh.org.il/jewish-spotlight/austria/vienna/population/.

Beller, Steven. *Vienna and the Jews, 1867–1938: A Cultural History.* Cambridge: Cambridge University Press, 1991.

Ben-Yaacov, Yissakhar. *A Lasting Reward: Memoirs of an Israeli Diplomat.* Jerusalem: Gefen, 2012.

Berg, Matthew Paul, ed. *The Struggle for a Democratic Austria: Bruno Kreisky on Peace and Social Justice.* New York: Berghahn, 2000.

Beyrl, Maria, Peter Filzmaier, and Flooh Perlot. "Waldheim Affair: Austrian Political Controversy." In Encyclopaedia Britannica. Article published June 14, 2018. https://www.britannica.com/event/Waldheim-Affair.

Bielka, Erich, Peter Jankowitsch, and Hans Thalberg. *Die Ära Kreisky: Schwerpunkte der österreichischen Außenpolitik.* Werder: Baulino, 1985.

Birnbaum, Pierre. *Léon Blum: Prime Minister, Socialist, Zionist.* New Haven: Yale University Press, 2015.

Bischof, Günter. *Austria in the First Cold War, 1945–55.* London: Palgrave Macmillan, 1999.

———. "Victims? Perpetrators? 'Punching Bags' of European Historical Memory? The Austrians and Their World War II Legacies." *German Studies Review* 27, no. 1 (February 2004): 17–32.

Black, Ian, and Benny Morris. *Israel's Secret Wars: A History of Israel's Intelligence Services.* New York: Grove Press, 1991.

Böhler, Ingrid. "'Wenn die Juden ein Volk sind, so ist es ein mieses Volk.' Die Kreisky-Peter-Wiesenthal-Affäre 1975." In *Politische Affären und Skandale in Österreich: Von Mayerling bis Waldheim*, edited by Michael Gehler and Hubert Sickinger, 502–31. Thaur: Kulturverlag, 1996.

Bohr, Felix, Gunther Latsch, and Klaus Wiegrefe. "Germany's Secret Contacts to Palestinian Terrorists." *Der Spiegel*, August 28, 2012. https://www.spiegel.de/international/world/germany-maintained-contacts-with-palestinians-after-munich-massacre-a-852322.html.

Bunzl, John. *Between Vienna and Jerusalem: Reflections and Polemics on Austria, Israel and Palestine.* New York: Peter Lang, 1997.

Bunzl, Matti. "On the Politics and Semantics of Austrian Memory: Vienna's Monument against War and Fascism." *History and Memory* 7, no. 2 (Fall/Winter 1995): 7–40.

Burg, Avraham. *Defeating Hitler*. Tel Aviv: Yedioth Ahronoth, 2007.

Chamberlin, Paul Thomas. "Schönau and the Eagles of the Palestinian Revolution: Refugees, Guerillas, and Human Rights in the Global 1970s." *ColdWar History* 12, no. 4 (November 2012): 595–614.

Chase, Susan E. "Narrative Inquiry: Multiple Lenses, Approaches, Voices." In *The SAGE Handbook of Qualitative Research*, 3rd ed., edited by Norman K. Denzin and Yvonna S. Lincoln, 651–80. Thousand Oaks: SAGE, 2005.

Clandinin, D. Jean, and F. Michael Connelly. *Narrative Inquiry: Experience and Story in Qualitative Research*. San Francisco: Jossey-Bass, 2000.

Creswell, John W. *Qualitative Inquiry and Research Design: Choosing Among Five Approaches*. Thousand Oaks: SAGE, 1998.

Cronqvist, Marie, and Christoph Hilgert. "Entangled Media Histories: The Value of Transnational and Transmedial Approaches in Media Historiography." *Media History* 23, no. 1 (January 2017): 130–41.

Dahlke, Matthias. *Demokratischer Staat und transnationaler Terrorismus: Drei Wege zur Unnachgiebigkeit in Westeuropa 1972–1975*. Munich: Oldenbourg, 2011.

Dank, A. H. "Israel's Surprise in 1973 (Should It Have Happened?)." *Global Security*, April 1, 1984. http://globalsecurity.org/military/library/report/1984/DAH.htm.

Der Spiegel. "So weit zurück." May 25, 1970. http://www.spiegel.de/spiegel/print/d-44906295.html.

———. "Wir Österreicher wählen, wen wir wollen." April 14, 1986. https://www.spiegel.de/spiegel/print/d-13517709.html.

Edel, Leon. *Writing Lives: Principia Biographica*. English Language ed. New York: W. W. Norton and Company, 1987.

Elliott, Jane. *Using Narrative in Social Research: Qualitative and Quantitative Approaches.* London: SAGE, 2005.

Embacher, Helga. *Neubeginn ohne Illusionen: Juden in Österreich nach 1945.* Vienna: Picus, 1995.

Embacher, Helga, and Margit Reiter. *Gratwanderungen: Die Beziehungen zwischen Österreich und Israel im Schatten der Vergangenheit.* Vienna: Picus, 1998.

The Events of September 28th and 29th, 1973: A Documentary Report. Vienna: Austria Federal Chancellery, 1973.

Fischer, Heinz. *Die Kreisky Jahre, 1967–1983.* Sozialistische Bibliothek. Vienna: Löcker, 1994.

Flick, Uwe. *An Introduction to Qualitative Research.* London: SAGE, 2002.

Foulkes, Imogen. "Switzerland 'Made Secret Deal with PLO' after Bomb Attacks." *BBC News,* January 26, 2016. https://www.bbc.com/news/world-europe-35384354.

Gay, Peter. *Freud, Jews and Other Germans: Masters and Victims in Modernist Culture.* New York: Oxford University Press, 1978.

Gehler, Michael. *Österreichs Außenpolitik der Zweiten Republik.* Innsbruck: Studien Verlag, 2005.

Geller, Jay Howard. *The Scholems: A Story of the German-Jewish Bourgeoisie from Emancipation to Destruction.* Ithaca: Cornell University Press, 2019.

Gilboa, Yehoshua. *The Black Years of Soviet Jewry.* New York: Little, Brown and Company, 1971.

Gilman, Sander L. *Jewish Self-Hatred: Anti-Semitism and the Hidden Language of the Jews.* Baltimore: Johns Hopkins University Press, 1986.

Ginsburg, Mitch. "Yom Kippur War Revelations Underline Gravity of Iran Dilemma Facing Israel Today." *Times of Israel,* September 21, 2012. https://www.timesofisrael.com/yom-kippur-war-revelations-underline-the-gravity-of-the-iran-dilemma-facing-israels-leaders-today/.

Gitelman, Zvi. "Exiting from the Soviet Union: Emigrés or Refugees?" *Michigan Journal of International Law* 3, no. 1 (1982): 43–61.

Gordon, Milton M. *Assimilation in American Life: The Role of Race, Religion, and National Origins*. New York: Oxford University Press, 1964.

Green, Abigail. "The Limits of Intervention: Coercive Diplomacy and the Jewish Question in the Nineteenth Century." *International History Review* 36, no. 3 (2014): 473–92.

Halevi, Yossi Klein. Review of *When They Come for Us We'll Be Gone: The Epic Struggle to Save Soviet Jewry*, by Gal Beckerman. *New Republic*, November 25, 2010. https://newrepublic.com/article/79086/soviet-union-jews-movement.

Herf, Jeffrey. *Divided Memory: The Nazi Past in the Two Germanys*. Boston: Harvard University Press, 1997.

Hof, Tobias. "From Extremism to Terrorism: The Radicalisation of the Far Right in Italy and West Germany." *Contemporary European History* 27, no. 3 (2018): 412–31. doi:10.1017/S096077731800019X.

Höll, Otmar. "The Foreign Policy of the Kreisky Era." In *The Kreisky Era in Austria*, edited by Günter Bischof and Anton Pelinka, 32–78. Contemporary Austrian Studies 2. New Brunswick: Transaction, 1994.

Insight Team of the *London Sunday Times*. *The Yom Kippur War*. New York: Doubleday, 1974.

Iriye, Akira, and Pierre-Yves Saunier, eds. *The Palgrave Dictionary of Transnational History*. Basingstoke: Palgrave Macmillan, 2009.

Karpel, Dalia. "Hunting Simon Wiesenthal." *Haaretz*, September 8, 2010. http://www.haaretz.com/weekend/magazine/hunting-simon-wiesenthal-1.312914.

Klein, Aaron. "Shock Admission: Italy Made Deal with Terrorists." *WND*, August 18, 2008. https://www.wnd.com/2008/08/72780/.

Kocka, Jürgen. "Comparison and Beyond." *History and Theory* 42, no. 1 (February 2003): 39–44. http://www.jstor.org/stable/3590801.

Koelbl, Herlinde. *Jüdische Portraits: Photographien und Interviews von Herlinde Koelbl*. Frankfurt: S. Fischer, 1989.

Krasikov, Sana. "Declassified KGB Study Illuminates Early Years of Soviet Jewish Emigration." *Forward,* December 12, 2007. https://forward.com/news/12254/declassified-kgb-study-illuminates-early-years-of-00966/.

Kreisky, Bruno. *Erinnerungen: Das Vermächtnis des Jahrhundertpolitikers.* Edited by Oliver Rathkolb. Graz: Styria Premium, 2007.

——. "Interview von James Dorsey für die Holländische Zeitung *Trouw*, in *Die Furche*, 15 September 1978 (Auszug)." By James Dorsey. *Trouw*, September 15, 1978.

——. "Press Conference to International Press." *Simon Wiesenthal Archives*, November 1970.

Kriechbaumer, Robert. *Die Ära Kreisky: Österreich 1970–1983 in der historischen Analyse, im Urteil der politischen Kontrahenten und in Karikaturen von Ironimus.* Vienna: Böhlau, 2004.

Kumamoto, Robert. *International Terrorism and American Foreign Relations: 1945–1976.* Boston: Northeastern University Press, 1999.

Levy, Alan. *Die Akte Wiesenthal.* Vienna: Ueberreuter, 1995.

——. *Nazi Hunter: The Wiesenthal File.* London: Robinson, 2002.

Levy, Richard S., ed. *Antisemitism: A Historical Encyclopedia of Prejudice and Persecution.* Santa Barbara: ABC-CLIO, 2005.

Maimann, Helene. *Über Kreisky: Gespräche aus Distanz und Nähe.* Vienna: Falter Verlag, 2011.

Malina, Peter. "'Imagination Is More than Knowledge.' Bruno Kreisky's Life as Biography." In *The Kreisky Era in Austria*, edited by Günter Bischof and Anton Pelinka, 205–22. Contemporary Austrian Studies 2. New Brunswick: Transaction Publishers, 1994.

McKenzie-Smith, Robert H. "Crisis Decisionmaking in Israel: The Case of the October 1973 Middle East War." *Naval War College Review* 29, no. 3 (1976): 39–52.

Meir, Golda. "Speech Made to the Assembly: Monday 1 October 1973." Published on the *Parliamentary Assembly* website, presented to the Parliamentary Assembly of the Council of Europe, Strasbourg, France, October 1973. http://www.assembly.coe.int/nw/xml/Speeches/Speech-XML2HTML-EN.asp?SpeechID=146.

Mitchell, Matthew Craig, and Margaret Egudo. "A Review of Narrative Methodology." Edinburgh: DSTO Systems Sciences Laboratory, 2003. https://www.webpages.uidaho.edu/css506/506%20readings/review%20of%20narritive%20methodology%20australian%20gov.pdf.

Moyn, Samuel. *The Last Utopia: Human Rights in History*. Cambridge: The Belknap Press, 2010.

Muravchik, Joshua. *Making David into Goliath: How the World Turned Against Israel*. New York: Encounter Books, 2014.

Patel, Klaus Kiran. "Transnational History." *European History Online*, December 3, 2010. http://ieg-ego.eu/en/threads/theories-and-methods/transnational-history.

Pelinka, Anton. "Austria's Attitude Toward Israel: Following the European Mainstream." *Jerusalem Center for Public Affairs*, September 26, 2006. http://jcpa.org/article/austria%E2%80%99s-attitude-toward-israel-following-the-european-mainstream/.

Peres, Shimon. SBKA, VII.4 Nahost 5. Statement presented at the Party Leaders Conference at Bommersvik, Sweden, July 20–21, 1979.

Petritsch, Wolfgang. *Bruno Kreisky: Die Biografie*. Vienna: Residenz, 2010.

Pick, Hella. *Guilty Victim: Austria from the Holocaust to Haider*. London: I. B. Tauris, 2000.

———. *Simon Wiesenthal: A Life in Search of Justice*. Boston: Northeastern University Press, 1996.

Pinnegar, Stefinee, and J. Gary Daynes. "Locating Narrative Inquiry Historically: Thematics in the Turn to Narrative." In *Handbook of Narrative Inquiry: Mapping a Methodology*, edited by D. Jean Clandinin, 3–34. Thousand Oaks: Sage Publications, 2007.

Pirker, Peter. "The Victim Myth Revisited: The Politics of History in Austria up until the Waldheim Affair." In *Myths in Austrian History: Construction and Deconstruction*, edited by Günter Bischof, Marc Landry, and Christian Karner, 153–74. Contemporary Austrian Studies 29. New Orleans: University of New Orleans Press, 2020.

Polkinghorne, Donald E. *Narrative Knowing and the Human Sciences*. Albany: State University of New York Press, 1988.

Rabinbach, Anson. *The Crisis of Austrian Socialism: From Red Vienna to Civil War, 1927–1934*. Chicago: University of Chicago Press, 1983.

————. "The Jewish Question in the German Question." Special issue on the Historikerstreit, *New German Critique*, no. 44 (Spring-Summer 1988): 159–92.

Rath, Ari. "ברונו קרייסקי שלא הכרנו" (Bruno Kreisky We Did Not Know) *Haaretz*. https://www.haaretz.co.il/opinions/1.1231102.

Rathkolb, Oliver. *Die paradoxe Republik: Österreich 1945 bis 2005*. 3rd ed. Vienna: Paul Zsolnay, 2005.

————. "Die Wiedererrichtung des Auswärtigen Dienstes nach 1945" (unpublished research report, Austrian Ministry of Science, 1988), quoted in Bischof, Günter. "Victims? Perpetrators? 'Punching Bags' of European Historical Memory? The Austrians and Their World War II Legacies." *German Studies Review* 27, no. 1 (2004): 17–32.

————. "A New Historiography of Bruno Kreisky." In *Austrian Studies Today*, edited by Günter Bischof and Ferdinand Karlhofer, 37–43. Contemporary Austrian Studies 25. New Orleans: University of New Orleans Press, 2016.

Reiter, Andrea. *Contemporary Jewish Writing: Austria after Waldheim*. Milton Park: Routledge, 2013.

Riegler, Thomas. *Im Fadenkreuz: Österreich und der Nahostterrorismus 1973 bis 1985*. Vienna: V&R unipress, 2011.

Röhrlich, Elisabeth. "A Century in a Lifetime: Biographical Approaches to Bruno Keisky (1911-1990)." In *Austrian Lives*, edited by Günter Bischof, Fritz Plasser, and Eva Maltschnig, 147–63. Contemporary Austrian Studies 21. New Orleans: University of New Orleans Press, 2012.

————. *Kreiskys Außenpolitik: Zwischen österreichischer Identität und internationalem Programm*. Vienna: V&R unipress, 2009.

Rosenbaum, Eli M. *Betrayal: The Untold Story of the Kurt Waldheim Investigation and Cover-Up*. With William Hoffer. New York: St. Martin's Press, 1993.

Said, Edward W. *Orientalism*. New York: Vintage Books, 1979.

Sartre, Jean-Paul. *Anti-Semite and Jew: An Exploration of the Etiology of Hate*. New York: Schocken Books, 1948.

Schmid, Gerhard, and Werner Gatty. *Die Ära Kreisky: Österreich im Wandel 1970–1983*. Innsbruck: StudienVerlag, 1997.

Schnitzler, Arthur. *Der Weg ins Freie*. Frankfurt: Fischer, 1908.

Schorske, Carl E. *Fin-de-siècle Vienna: Politics and Culture*. New York: Vintage Books, 1980.

Secher, Herbert Pierre. *Bruno Kreisky, Chancellor of Austria: A Political Biography*. Pittsburgh: Dorrance, 1994.

—————. "Kreisky and the Jews." In *The Kreisky Era in Austria*, edited by Günter Bischof and Anton Pelinka, 10–31. Contemporary Austrian Studies 2. New Brunswick: Transaction Publishers, 1994.

Segev, Tom. "Between Two Worlds." *Haaretz,* September 20, 2006. https://www.haaretz.com/1.4867032.

—————. "שיעור היסטוריה | קנצלר אוסטריה ברונו קרייסקי - יהודי מסובך". (History Lesson, Austrian Chancellor Bruno Kreisky – a Complicated Jew) *Haaretz,* October 21, 2010. https://www.haaretz.co.il/misc/1.1226539.

—————. *Simon Wiesenthal: The Life and Legends*. New York: Doubleday, 2010.

Shay, Shaul. "האם חטיפת רכבת היהודים באוסטריה הייתה פעולת הסחה לפני מלחמת יום הכיפורים?" (Was the Abduction of the Jewish Train in Austria a Diversionary Act before the Yom Kippur War?) *Israel Defense,* December 15, 2011. shorturl.at/cegkV.

Smith, Colin. *Carlos, Portrait of a Terrorist: In Pursuit of the Jackal 1975–2011*. London: Penguin, 2012.

Smith, Terence. "Mrs. Meir, in Strasbourg, Expects Austrian Reversal." *New York Times,* October 1, 1973. https://www.nytimes.com/1973/10/01/archives/mrs-meir-in-strasbourg-expects-austrian-reversal-speaks-in-hebrew.html.

Šmok, Martin. "Teroristé z internátu L'udovíta Štúra." (Terrorists from the L'udovít Štúr boarding school) *Studie a články*, February 2018. https://www.ustrcr.cz/wp-content/uploads/2018/07/PD_2_18_s15-24.pdf.

Sorkin, David. "Emancipation and Assimilation: Two Concepts and their Application to the Study of German Jewish History." *Leo Baeck Institute Yearbook* 35, no.1 (January 1990): 17–33.

Sporrer, Maria, and Herbert Steiner. *Simon Wiesenthal: Ein unbequemer Zeitgenosse.* Vienna: Orac, 1992.

Sterling, Claire. *The Terror Network: The Secret War of International Terrorism.* New York: Henry Holt and Company, 1981.

Stögner, Karin. "Bruno Kreisky: Antisemitismus und der österreichische Umgang mit dem Nationalsozialismus." In *Kreisky-Haider: Bruchlinien österreichischer Identitäten*, edited by Anton Pelinka, Hubert Sickinger, and Karin Stögner, 25–110. Vienna: Braumüller, 2008.

Stourzh, Gerald, and Wolfgang Mueller. *A Cold War over Austria: The Struggle for the State Treaty, Neutrality, and the End of East-West Occupation, 1945–1955.* Lanham: Lexington Books, 2018.

Streissguth, Thomas. *International Terrorists.* Profiles. Minneapolis: Oliver Press Inc., 1993.

Timm, Angelika. "The Middle East Policy of the German Democratic Republic." *Journal of Arab Affairs* 12, no. 2 (Fall 1993): 160–75.

Uhl, Heidemarie. "Das 'erste Opfer': der österreichische Opfermythos und seine Transformationen in der Zweiten Republik." *Österreichische Zeitschrift für Politikwissenschaft* 30, no. 1 (2001): 19–34.

———. "From Victim Myth to Co-Responsibility Thesis: Nazi Rule, World War II, and the Holocaust in Austrian Memory." In *The Politics of Memory in Postwar Europe*, edited by Richard Ned Lebow, Wulf Kansteiner, and Claudio Fogu, 40–72. Durham: Duke University Press, 2006.

Vansant, Jacqueline. "Challenging Austria's Victim Status: National Socialism and Austrian Personal Narratives." *The German Quarterly* 67, no. 1 (Winter 1994): 38–57.

Vivekanandan, B. *Global Visions of Olof Palme, Bruno Kreisky and Willy Brandt: International Peace and Security, Co-operation, and Development*. London: Palgrave Macmillan, 2016.

Volkov, Shulamit. *Walther Rathenau: Weimar's Fallen Statesman*. New Haven: Yale University Press, 2012.

Wall, Irwin M. Review of *Pierre Mendès France*, by Jean Lacouture, translated by George Holoch. *Journal of Modern History* 58, no. 3 (September 1986): 736–38.

Wiesenthal, Simon. *Justice Not Vengeance*. London: Weidenfeld and Nicholson, 1988.

Wilson, Richard J. Review of *The Breakthrough: Human Rights in the 1970s*, edited by Jan Eckel and Samuel Moyn. *Human Rights Quarterly* 36 (2014): 915–30.

Wistrich, Robert S. *Anti-Zionism and Antisemitism: The Case of Bruno Kreisky*. Jerusalem: Hebrew University of Jerusalem, 2007.

————. *From Ambivalence to Betrayal: The Left, the Jews, and Israel*. Lincoln: University of Nebraska Press, 2012.

————. *The Jews of Vienna in the Age of Franz Joseph*. Oxford: Oxford University Press, 1989.

————. "The Kreisky Phenomenon: A Reassessment." In *Austrians and Jews in the Twentieth Century: From Franz Joseph to Waldheim*, edited by Robert S. Wistrich, 234–51. London: Palgrave Macmillan, 1992.

————. *Socialism and the Jews: The Dilemmas of Assimilation in Germany and Austria-Hungary*. Rutherford: Fairleigh Dickinson University Press, 1982.

Wodak, Ruth. "Turning the Tables: Antisemitic Discourse in Post-War Austria." *Discourse and Society* 2, no. 1 (1991): 65–83.

Wodak, Ruth, Peter Nowak, Johanna Pelikan, Helmut Gruber, Rudolf de Cillia, and Richard Mitten. *Wir sind alle unschuldige Täter: Diskurshistorische Studien zum Nachkriegsantisemitismus*. Frankfurt: Suhrkamp, 1990.

Yallop, David. *Tracking the Jackal: The Search for Carlos, the World's Most Wanted Man*. New York: Random House, 1993.

Yedioth Ahronoth / AFP. "שליח קהיר – היום לווינה; נושא איגרת-תודה מסדאת." (Cairo Courier - Today to Vienna; Subject of a Thank-You Note from Sadat) October 3, 1973: 1. Yedioth Ahronoth Archive, National Library of Israel.

Yedioth Ahronoth / AP. "החוטפים מוינה ציטטו מבמסיבת עיתונאים בלוב את משה דיין." (The Kidnappers from Vienna Quoted Moshe Dayan from a Press Conference in Libya) October 1, 1973: 2. Yedioth Ahronoth Archive, National Library of Israel.

Zaretsky, Natasha. *No Direction Home: The American Family and the Fear of National Decline, 1968–1980*. Chapel Hill: University of North Carolina Press, 2007.

INDEX

A

B

N

O

P